SACRED SPACE

the prayer book
2014

from the website www.sacredspace.ie

GW00597228

VERITAS

Sacred Space the Prayer Book and www. sacredspace.ie

Sacred Space—The Prayer Book has been developed and produced by the Irish Jesuits since 1999 for its popular website www.sacred space.ie. The online site now attracts over 5 million visits each year from Christians of all denominations.

Updated on a daily basis with new insights and prayer offerings, the site is compatible with smartphones, tablets and other mobile devices. Registered users now have the opportunity to customise their prayer experience with music and visual options. The secret of Sacred Space's success is its simplicity. At its core is a simple daily prayer, based on scripture. But behind this apparently simple offering is a comprehensive daily spiritual guide and a translation service into nineteen languages, most recently Russian and Arabic, Italian and Filipino.

Registered users of the site can also receive regular newsletters, undertake online retreats, pray with the Pope and add their prayer requests into the chapel of intercession. The site has a small team of full and part-time staff, backed up by national and international volunteers including communities of contemplative nuns who pray for the intentions of the visitors.

Another area of the online offering is Living Space. Here you will find commentaries on the daily scripture readings.

www.sacredspace.ie is a registered charity of the Irish Province of the Jesuits.

How to use this book

We invite you to make a sacred space in your day and spend ten minutes praying here and now, wherever you are, with the help of a prayer guide and scripture chosen specially for each day. Every place is a sacred space so you may wish to have this book on your desk at work or available to be picked up and read at any time of the day, whilst travelling, sitting on a park bench, or on your bedside table . . . Remember that God is everywhere, all around us, constantly reaching out to us, even in the most unlikely situations. When we know this, and with a bit of practice, we can pray anywhere.

The structure is simple. At the beginning of each week you are offered a Prayer Advice—Something to Think and Pray About each day.

A set of prayer stages follow, which focus you on God:

The presence of God
Freedom
Consciousness
The Word—Daily Scripture and Inspiration Points
Conversation
Conclusion

It is important to come back to these stages each day as they are all integral to the prayer. The first three prepare our hearts to hear the Word of God in quietness.

The stages are *for doing*, not only for reading. Each stage is an exercise or meditation to help you to get in touch with God's presence in your life.

When you pray, you are not alone. We invite you to join the many people around the world who pray with us in sacred space.

Acknowledgements

The publisher would like to thank Brian Grogan SJ and the Sacred Space team for their kind assistance in making this book possible. Correspondence with the Sacred Space team can be directed to feedback@sacredspace.ie where comments or suggestions relating to the book or to www.sacredspace.ie will always be welcome.

We acknowledge with deep gratitude the writers who contributed to this volume:

Paul Andrews SJ; Jean Cleary; Michael Drennan SJ; Philip Fogarty SJ; Michael Paul Gallagher SJ; Helen Gallivan; Pat Gayer OSA; Brian Grogan SJ; Carmel Harkin; Finbarr Lynch SJ; Sr Anne Lyons, pbvm; Dermot Mansfield SJ; Aidan Mathews; Donal Neary SJ; Fergus O'Keefe SJ and Ann Schmitz. Several authors chose to remain anonymous. To all of them our sincere thanks.

Published in 2014 by
Veritas Publications
7–8 Lower Abbey Street
Dublin 1
Ireland
Email: publications@veritas.ie
Website: www.veritas.ie

ISBN 9781 84730 510 7

Copyright © Sacred Space 2014

A catalogue record for this book is available from the British Library.

Design and typesetting: Bernard Metcalfe, Biz Write Pty Ltd
Cover design: Luke Harris, Chameleon Print Design
Printed in Singapore by Toppan Security Printing Pte. Ltd.
International Standard Serial Number ISSN 1449-048X

Contents

december 1–7

Something to think and pray about each day this week:

A new beginning

He was a young man, caught in the web of drug addiction. She was the pharmacist who with genuine love and care dispensed to him the daily dose of methadone to help him to break free from the effects of drugs. He shared with her his desire to re-order his life, to become free of the paralysing effects of addiction. His spoke of his hope for a new beginning, and she supported him as best she could. Suddenly he stopped coming. She wondered about him. Where was he? She watched and waited but he never returned.

Years passed. One day her son invited a friend home for an evening meal. When she opened the door, standing before her was the young man of earlier years. Healthy and well, he now worked as a social worker with others caught in addiction. He shared how her words, like an arrow, had struck his heart, opening him to reform, freedom and hope.

John the Baptist, the arrow in God's quiver, waited in the wilderness. At the appointed time he was sprung forth from God's bow. John pointed a people who lived in dread and uncertainty to a greater power and a greater love revealed in the person of Jesus.

Can you find yourself among the many people who went out to hear John's message? What might he say to you?

Can you be a John the Baptist to others?

The Presence of God

Lord, help me to be fully alive to your holy presence.
Enfold me in your love.
Let my heart become one with yours.

Freedom

Many countries are at this moment suffering
the agonies of war.
I bow my head in thanksgiving for my freedom.
I pray for all prisoners and captives.

Consciousness

At this moment, Lord, I turn my thoughts to You.
I will leave aside my chores and preoccupations.
I will take rest and refreshment in your presence Lord.

The Word

The word of God comes to us through the scriptures.
May the Holy Spirit enlighten my mind and my heart to
respond to the gospel teachings. (Please turn to your scripture
on the following pages. Inspiration points are there should you
need them. When you are ready, return here to continue.)

Conversation

Sometimes I wonder what I might say
if I were to meet You in person, Lord.
I might say 'Thank You, Lord' for always being there for me.
I know with certainty there were times when you carried me,
when through your strength I got through the dark times in
my life.

Conclusion

Glory be to the Father, and to the Son, and to the Holy Spirit,
As it was in the beginning, is now and ever shall be,
World without end. Amen

Sunday 1st December,
First Sunday of Advent   **Matthew 24:42–44**

Jesus said, "Keep awake therefore, for you do not know on what day your Lord is coming. But understand this: if the owner of the house had known in what part of the night the thief was coming, he would have stayed awake and would not have let his house be broken into. Therefore you also must be ready, for the Son of Man is coming at an unexpected hour."

- Staying awake means noticing and being alert. As I take time to pray, I allow the things I have been too busy to see, to come to my notice.
- Looking ahead, I consider what might help me to remain alert.

Monday 2nd December   **Matthew 8:5–11**

When Jesus entered Capernaum, a centurion came to him, appealing to him and saying, "Lord, my servant is lying at home paralyzed, in terrible distress." And he said to him, "I will come and cure him." The centurion answered, "Lord, I am not worthy to have you come under my roof; but only speak the word, and my servant will be healed. For I also am a man under authority, with soldiers under me; and I say to one, 'Go,' and he goes, and to another, 'Come,' and he comes, and to my slave, 'Do this,' and the slave does it." When Jesus heard him, he was amazed and said to those who followed him, "Truly I tell you, in no one in Israel have I found such faith. I tell you, many will come from east and west and will eat with Abraham and Isaac and Jacob in the kingdom of heaven."

- It was not easy for an officer in the imperial army to come as a beggar to an itinerant Jewish rabbi. The centurion made an extraordinary leap out of his own culture and pride into a recognition of Jesus' power. Jesus was amazed at his faith.
- Have I the insight to perceive holiness and God's hand at work around me, or am I imprisoned in the stereotypes of my culture?

Tuesday 3rd December,
St Francis Xavier   Luke 10:21–24

At that same hour Jesus rejoiced in the Holy Spirit and said, "All things have been handed over to me by my Father; and no one knows who the Son is except the Father, or who the Father is except the Son and anyone to whom the Son chooses to reveal him." Then turning to the disciples, Jesus said to them privately, "Blessed are the eyes that see what you see! For I tell you that many prophets and kings desired to see what you see, but did not see it, and to hear what you hear, but did not hear it."

- Here I am brought in on a big secret—the love which the Father and Son have for each other. They share a common love for me too, and welcome me into their family life and joy.
- I may seem very ordinary, but I have high connections! So have others, so let me never rubbish them.

Wednesday 4th December   Matthew 15:32–37

Then Jesus called his disciples to him and said, "I have compassion for the crowd, because they have been with me now for three days and have nothing to eat; and I do not want to send them away hungry, for they might faint on the way." The disciples said to him, "Where are we to get enough bread in the desert to feed so great a crowd?" Jesus asked them, "How many loaves have you?" They said, "Seven, and a few small fish." Then ordering the crowd to sit down on the ground, he took the seven loaves and the fish; and after giving thanks he broke them and gave them to the disciples, and the disciples gave them to the crowds. And all of them ate and were filled; and they took up the broken pieces left over, seven baskets full.

- Here are details that touch me, Lord. You felt compassion, which carries a weight of meaning. It is more than a warm feeling; it meant that you did something about it. Save me from warm feelings that are a substitute for effective action.
- You did not play the magician but started with what the apostles already had to hand, seven loaves and a few small fish. Teach me, Lord, to use everything I am given.

Thursday 5th December Matthew 7:21, 24–27

Jesus said to the people, "Not everyone who says to me, 'Lord, Lord,' will enter the kingdom of heaven, but only one who does the will of my Father in heaven." "Everyone then who hears these words of mine and acts on them will be like a wise man who built his house on rock. The rain fell, the floods came, and the winds blew and beat on that house, but it did not fall, because it had been founded on rock. And everyone who hears these words of mine and does not act on them will be like a foolish man who built his house on sand. The rain fell, and the floods came, and the winds blew and beat against that house, and it fell—and great was its fall!"

- St Ignatius remarks that love is found in deeds rather than in words. Jesus praises good deeds over good intentions that are not carried out. I pray to be like a good servant who does the work assigned me by God.
- It is comforting in troubled situations to remember that God is rock solid. I ask for grace always to trust in God no matter what may fall apart.

Friday 6th December Matthew 9:27–31

As Jesus went on his way, two blind men followed him, crying loudly, "Have mercy on us, Son of David!" When he entered the house, the blind men came to him; and Jesus said to them, "Do you believe that I am able to do this?" They said to him, "Yes, Lord." Then he touched their eyes and said, "According to your faith let it be done to you." And their eyes were opened. Then Jesus sternly ordered them, "See that no one knows of this." But they went away and spread the news about him throughout that district.

- I am a cry for help; I am a longing and a yearning. I need God in every possible way, so I make the shout of the blind men my mantra.
- I stumble after the blind men into Jesus' house and let him touch my closed eyes. How does that feel? And how does it feel to open my eyes slowly and gaze for the first time on the face of Jesus?

Saturday 7th December　　　　**Matthew 9:35–10:1, 6–8**

Jesus went about all the cities and villages, teaching in their synagogues, and proclaiming the good news of the kingdom, and curing every disease and every sickness. When he saw the crowds, he had compassion for them, because they were harassed and helpless, like sheep without a shepherd. Then he said to his disciples, "The harvest is plentiful, but the laborers are few; therefore ask the Lord of the harvest to send out laborers into his harvest." Then Jesus summoned his twelve disciples and gave them authority over unclean spirits, to cast them out, and to cure every disease and every sickness. These twelve Jesus sent out with the following instructions: "Go rather to the lost sheep of the house of Israel. As you go, proclaim the good news, 'The kingdom of heaven has come near.' Cure the sick, raise the dead, cleanse the lepers, cast out demons. You received without payment; give without payment."

- Jesus has a mission for me. Who are the "lost sheep" today whom he may want me to help? Am I generous enough to do what he asks of me?
- "The kingdom of heaven has come near." This means that God's way of doing things is beginning to take over! How far has God's way of doing things taken over in me? Would people know?

Something to think and pray about each day this week:

Out of the wilderness

The documentary revealed the harrowed faces of victims of an over-inflated property bubble that had burst. Fear of loss of their homes was etched on every face. Then the scene changed to the Horn of Africa. I saw the hollowed faces and heard the unrelenting cries of this famine-stricken land. To clear my head of all this pain I went for a walk. Propped up against the wall of a great commercial building was a beggar. His voice of desperation and hunger tries to pierce my heart. Do I dare to stop and get involved, or do I keep my distance? Each victim voice challenges my carefully constructed defenses and my programs for personal happiness.

We are more than halfway through our Advent journey. Again the prophetic voice of John the Baptist calls for our attention. Those whom he disturbed challenged him: "Who are you?" His response was direct. "I am the voice of one crying out in the wilderness." John immersed himself in the flood of suffering of his day. He cried out against blatant injustice and corrupt systems. John was God's mouthpiece of love, compassion and hope.

John might ask you: "Who are you? For whom will your voice cry out this Advent time?" Perhaps you feel you are in a wilderness? The wilderness times in our lives are necessary. Until we see our world as starkly as God does, we will not stand rightly with those who suffer injustice, degradation and desperation.

The Presence of God

God is with me, but more,
God is within me, giving me existence.
Let me dwell for a moment on God's life-giving presence
in my body, my mind, my heart
and in the whole of my life.

Freedom

God is not foreign to my freedom.
Instead the Spirit breathes life into my most intimate desires,
gently nudging me towards all that is good.
I ask for the grace to let myself be enfolded by the Spirit.

Consciousness

Help me, Lord, to be more conscious of your presence.
Teach me to recognize your presence in others.
Fill my heart with gratitude for the times your love
has been shown to me through the care of others.

The Word

I read the Word of God slowly, a few times over, and I listen
to what God is saying to me. (Please turn to your scripture on
the following pages. Inspiration points are there should you
need them. When you are ready, return here to continue.)

Conversation

How has God's Word moved me? Has it left me cold?
Has it consoled me or moved me to act in a new way?
I imagine Jesus standing or sitting beside me,
I turn and share my feelings with him.

Conclusion

Glory be to the Father, and to the Son, and to the Holy Spirit,
As it was in the beginning, is now and ever shall be,
World without end. Amen

Sunday 8th December,
Second Sunday of Advent   Matthew 3:1–3

In those days John the Baptist appeared in the wilderness of Judea, proclaiming, "Repent, for the kingdom of heaven has come near." This is the one of whom the prophet Isaiah spoke when he said, "The voice of one crying out in the wilderness: 'Prepare the way of the Lord, make his paths straight.'"

- I may feel uncomfortable when confronted with John's call to repentance but I let myself listen, acknowledging that I am a sinner in need of God's mercy. If I cannot admit this, Advent is not for me.
- God does not want me to passively receive the Word. I work with God, preparing the way in my life, expectant and hopefully watching for God's approach.

Monday 9th December,
The Immaculate Conception
of the Blessed Virgin Mary   Luke 1:30–33

The angel said to her, "Do not be afraid, Mary, for you have found favor with God. And now, you will conceive in your womb and bear a son, and you will name him Jesus. He will be great, and will be called the Son of the Most High, and the Lord God will give to him the throne of his ancestor David. He will reign over the house of Jacob forever, and of his kingdom there will be no end."

- I imagine that I am visiting Mary when the angel comes. I watch and listen breathlessly to their conversation as if I had never heard it before. When the angel vanishes I sit with Mary. My heart is full of admiration for her as she takes on the task God is giving her.
- When I leave Mary and go home, I carry her words in my heart, and beg that I may say them when God asks something of me. "Let it be with me according to your word." I ask to be sensitive to the "angels" that may come my way today.

Tuesday 10th December   **Matthew 18:12–14**

What do you think? If a shepherd has a hundred sheep, and one of them has gone astray, does he not leave the ninety-nine on the mountains and go in search of the one that went astray? And if he finds it, truly I tell you, he rejoices over it more than over the ninety-nine that never went astray. So it is not the will of your Father in heaven that one of these little ones should be lost.

- Every gospel tells us something about God. Here I learn that God has a particular care for everyone, especially for those who have gone astray. This is a comfort to me because I often lose my way in life. God is watching out for me always.
- I ask the Lord that I too may care for the "little ones"—those who are vulnerable and cannot cope with life's demands.

Wednesday 11th December   **Matthew 11:28–30**

Jesus said, "Come to me, all you that are weary and are carrying heavy burdens, and I will give you rest. Take my yoke upon you, and learn from me; for I am gentle and humble in heart, and you will find rest for your souls. For my yoke is easy, and my burden is light."

- Most people would say that they are weary and weighed down with problems. Jesus offers himself as one who has his own burden, but is glad to shoulder my burden too.
- The yoke was originally a term for Roman oppression of the Jews. People felt crushed by Rome's demands. Jesus promises that if I join in with him, he will not be oppressive. I ask to feel the lightness and energy that he offers me.

Thursday 12th December   **Matthew 11:11–15**

Truly I tell you, among those born of women no one has arisen greater than John the Baptist; yet the least in the kingdom of heaven is greater than he. From the days of John the Baptist until now the kingdom of heaven has suffered violence, and the violent take it by force. For all the prophets and the law prophesied until John came; and if you are willing to accept it, he is Elijah who is to come. Let anyone with ears listen!

- I ponder on what Jesus said about the greatness of John. I think of what he had seen and heard so that I might profit from understanding what Jesus valued.
- John proclaimed the gospel, allowing his disciples to leave him to follow Jesus. I think of what it might mean to be less so that Jesus might be more.

Friday 13th December   Matthew 11:16–19

Jesus spoke to the crowds, "But to what will I compare this generation? It is like children sitting in the marketplaces and calling to one another, 'We played the flute for you, and you did not dance; we wailed, and you did not mourn.' For John came neither eating nor drinking, and they say, 'He has a demon'; the Son of Man came eating and drinking, and they say, 'Look, a glutton and a drunkard, a friend of tax collectors and sinners!' Yet wisdom is vindicated by her deeds."

- Both John and Jesus reveal what God is like, but they are misunderstood and cruelly rejected. I thank Jesus that he does not despair of humankind. He knows what we are like, yet he also sees what we can become. May I never despair of myself or others.
- How much am I willing to put myself out for others, as John and Jesus did? I pray not to be imprisoned in my comfort zones.

Saturday 14th December   Matthew 17:10–13

And the disciples asked him, "Why, then, do the scribes say that Elijah must come first?" He replied, "Elijah is indeed coming and will restore all things; but I tell you that Elijah has already come, and they did not recognize him, but they did to him whatever they pleased. So also the Son of Man is about to suffer at their hands." Then the disciples understood that he was speaking to them about John the Baptist.

- Jesus often uses the title "Son of Man" of himself. The title gathers together his passion and his return in glory. All human beings experience suffering and death, as he did. But because of him, we will then experience the glory of resurrection. I thank Jesus for achieving this for us.

- Like Elijah, John was austere, lived in the desert, and was a fearless prophet. Jesus admired him. John admired Jesus too, and referred to himself as the friend of the bridegroom. I too am a friend of the bridegroom, Jesus, and I rejoice in that.

december 15–21

Something to think and pray about each day this week:

Making room for God

We are entering the last week of Advent, a week commonly filled with frantic busyness before Christmas Day. St. Columcille can help us to find a quiet space amid all our busyness and to listen for God's annunciation to us. "Sometimes in a lonely cell, in the presence of my God, I stand and listen. In the silence of my heart, I can hear God's will when I listen. For I am but a servant, guided by my king when I listen."

Denise Levertov's poem *Annunciation* begins with the words "Hail, Space for the Uncontained God." Mary is asked to be just this—a space for God. Like us she had her dreams, but the Uncontained God draws her into a far greater dream for herself and all of us. She is caught in a dilemma. She must choose between her little personal dream and the expansive dream of God.

Despite her well-founded fears, Mary trusts that God will be ever present. The place of fear becomes the birthing place of Love. In Levertov's words: "Consent, courage unparallelled, opened her utterly."

Can I allow the unexpected God of surprises to cross my threshold space?

As I journey through this week, can I find room to receive and respond to the message of the Uncontained God? Someone wisely said: "Never be afraid to trust an unknown future to a known God."

The Presence of God
What is present to me is what has a hold on my becoming.
I reflect on the presence of God always there in love,
amidst the many things that have a hold on me.
I pause and pray that I may let God
affect my becoming in this precise moment.

Freedom
"There are very few people
who realize what God would make of them
if they abandoned themselves into his hands,
and let themselves be formed by his grace" (St Ignatius).
I ask for the grace to trust myself totally to God's love.

Consciousness
In the presence of my loving Creator,
I look honestly at my feelings over the last day,
the highs, the lows and the level ground.
Can I see where the Lord has been present?

The Word
God speaks to each one of us individually. I need to listen to
hear what he is saying to me. Read the text a few times, then
listen. (Please turn to your scripture on the following pages.
Inspiration points are there should you need them. When you
are ready, return here to continue.)

Conversation
What is stirring in me as I pray?
Am I consoled, troubled, left cold?
I imagine Jesus himself standing or sitting at my side,
and share my feelings with him.

Conclusion
Glory be to the Father, and to the Son, and to the Holy Spirit,
As it was in the beginning, is now and ever shall be,
World without end. Amen

Sunday 15th December,
Third Sunday of Advent   Matthew 11:2–6

When John heard in prison what the Messiah was doing, he sent word by his disciples and said to him, "Are you the one who is to come, or are we to wait for another?" Jesus answered them, "Go and tell John what you hear and see: the blind receive their sight, the lame walk, the lepers are cleansed, the deaf hear, the dead are raised, and the poor have good news brought to them. And blessed is anyone who takes no offense at me."

- Great as John was, we see that he did not live with pure certainty. He followed in faith even as he allowed good questions to be asked. I pray that I may ask the right questions and, like John the Baptist, always direct them to Jesus.
- Jesus does not answer with a statement of authority but points to his actions. I show who Jesus is to me by the way I live, by how I affirm and help the weak and poor.

Monday 16th December   Matthew 21:23–27

When Jesus entered the temple, the chief priests and the elders of the people came to him as he was teaching, and said, "By what authority are you doing these things, and who gave you this authority?" Jesus said to them, "I will also ask you one question; if you tell me the answer, then I will also tell you by what authority I do these things. Did the baptism of John come from heaven, or was it of human origin?" And they argued with one another, "If we say, 'From heaven,' he will say to us, 'Why then did you not believe him?' But if we say, 'Of human origin,' we are afraid of the crowd; for all regard John as a prophet." So they answered Jesus, "We do not know." And he said to them, "Neither will I tell you by what authority I am doing these things."

- God is busy in our world, trying to get people to see clearly. Like the priests and elders, do I sometimes evade the truth of what God is trying to tell me? I ask Jesus to help me to be a truthful person. Even small lies and deceptions should have no place in my speech.

- Among the people of God, authority can be misused. Jesus used his divine authority, not to dominate, but to serve. Whatever authority I have, let me use it in the loving service of others.

Tuesday 17th December   **Matthew 1:1–11**

An account of the genealogy of Jesus the Messiah, the son of David, the son of Abraham. Abraham was the father of Isaac, and Isaac the father of Jacob, and Jacob the father of Judah and his brothers, and Judah the father of Perez and Zerah by Tamar, and Perez the father of Hezron, and Hezron the father of Aram, and Aram the father of Aminadab, and Aminadab the father of Nahshon, and Nahshon the father of Salmon, and Salmon the father of Boaz by Rahab, and Boaz the father of Obed by Ruth, and Obed the father of Jesse, and Jesse the father of King David. And David was the father of Solomon by the wife of Uriah, and Solomon the father of Rehoboam, and Rehoboam the father of Abijah, and Abijah the father of Asaph, and Asaph the father of Jehoshaphat, and Jehoshaphat the father of Joram, and Joram the father of Uzziah, and Uzziah the father of Jotham, and Jotham the father of Ahaz, and Ahaz the father of Hezekiah, and Hezekiah the father of Manasseh, and Manasseh the father of Amos, and Amos the father of Josiah, and Josiah the father of Jechoniah and his brothers, at the time of the deportation to Babylon.

- Jesus' family tree is a colourful one. It includes a murderer and an adulterer, Jews and Gentiles, the famous and the nobodies. The powerful and the powerless find a place. So do females and males in odd relationships, as well as the upright and the good.
- All human life is here, to show that God includes everyone in divine planning. I marvel at this.

Wednesday 18th December   **Matthew 1:18–25**

Now the birth of Jesus the Messiah took place in this way. When his mother Mary had been engaged to Joseph, but before they lived together, she was found to be with child from the Holy Spirit. Her husband Joseph, being a righteous man and unwilling to expose her to public disgrace, planned to dismiss her quietly. But just when he had resolved to do this, an angel of the Lord appeared to him in a dream and said, "Joseph, son of David, do not be afraid to take Mary as your wife, for the child conceived in her is from the Holy Spirit. She will bear a son, and you are to name him Jesus, for he will save his people from their sins." All this took place to fulfill what had been spoken by the Lord through the prophet: "Look, the virgin shall conceive and bear a son, and they shall name him Emmanuel," which means, "God is with us." When Joseph awoke from sleep, he did as the angel of the Lord commanded him; he took her as his wife, but had no marital relations with her until she had borne a son; and he named him Jesus.

- The Spirit (or Breath) of God was seen as the source of all creation and of all human life. So, just as God created all that exists in the heavens and the earth, now, through the power of God's Spirit, Jesus is conceived in Mary's womb by a particular, concrete, and special case of God's creativity.
- The birth of any child brings with it a sense of awe and wonderment. Can I share a sense of awe and wonderment at the incredible fact that God becomes human in a baby boy?

Thursday 19th December   Luke 1:5–17

In the days of King Herod of Judea, there was a priest named Zechariah, who belonged to the priestly order of Abijah. His wife was a descendant of Aaron, and her name was Elizabeth. Both of them were righteous before God, living blamelessly according to all the commandments and regulations of the Lord. But they had no children, because Elizabeth was barren, and both were getting on in years. Once when he was serving as priest before God and his section was on duty, he was chosen by lot, according to the custom of the priesthood, to enter the sanctuary of the Lord and offer incense. Now at the time of the incense-offering, the whole assembly of the people was praying outside. Then there appeared to him an angel of the Lord, standing at the right side of the altar of incense. When Zechariah saw him, he was terrified; and fear overwhelmed him. But the angel said to him, "Do not be afraid, Zechariah, for your prayer has been heard. Your wife Elizabeth will bear you a son, and you will name him John. You will have joy and gladness, and many will rejoice at his birth, for he will be great in the sight of the Lord. He must never drink wine or strong drink; even before his birth he will be filled with the Holy Spirit. He will turn many of the people of Israel to the Lord their God. With the spirit and power of Elijah he will go before him, to turn the hearts of parents to their children, and the disobedient to the wisdom of the righteous, to make ready a people prepared for the Lord."

- "Both were getting on in years." Perhaps this is true of me also! But the message is that God can do great things in us when we feel we can do nothing. Even the daily prayer of the *Sacred Space* community affects the world for good in ways unknown to us.

- We may sometimes experience God in a way that leaves us speechless. It can bring a new awareness of the meaning of our lives before God, or something that God wants us to do.

Friday 20th December   Luke 1:26–33

In the sixth month the angel Gabriel was sent by God to a town in Galilee called Nazareth, to a virgin whose name was Mary. And he came to her and said, "Greetings, favored one! The Lord is with you." But she was much perplexed by his words and pondered what sort of greeting this might be. The angel said to her, "Do not be afraid, Mary, for you have found favor with God. And now, you will conceive in your womb and bear a son, and you will name him Jesus. He will be great, and will be called the Son of the Most High, and the Lord God will give to him the throne of his ancestor David. He will reign over the house of Jacob forever, and of his kingdom there will be no end."

- I allow the mystery of God's ways of working to overwhelm me. Nazareth is an unimportant town; Mary has no social standing. She is young in a world that values age, female in a world ruled by men, poor in a society where wealth matters so much.

- Yet this little girl from nowhere is chosen to be the Mother of God!

Saturday 21st December   Luke 1:39–45

In those days Mary set out and went with haste to a Judean town in the hill country, where she entered the house of Zechariah and greeted Elizabeth. When Elizabeth heard Mary's greeting, the child leapt in her womb. And Elizabeth was filled with the Holy Spirit and exclaimed with a loud cry, "Blessed are you among women, and blessed is the fruit of your womb. And why has this happened to me, that the mother of my Lord comes to me? For as soon as I heard the sound of your greeting, the child in my womb leapt for joy. And blessed is she who believed that there would be a fulfillment of what was spoken to her by the Lord."

- This scene belongs to two strong women who share the joy of bringing the good news of salvation into the world.
- I thank God for all women who play their part in serving the plans of God.

Sacred Space

Something to think and pray about each day this week:

The eternal birth

The New York marathon was on television. To the cheers of the whole stadium the runners were making a final sprint. As I watched, a young man requested permission to be allowed to stand at the finishing line. His beloved was one of the competitors, and he wanted to be there when she arrived. Finally the moment came. He fell on bended knees before her, and taking her hand, he publicly proclaimed his unending love for her, and asked her to marry him. A hushed expectancy descended as he waited with bated breath for her response. Her resounding "Yes!" was met with rapturous applause. It was a moment of good news and great joy!

Christmas proclaims the greatest love story ever told. God's public demonstration of unconditional love of us is revealed in a humble and unobtrusive manner—in the form of a baby. God has housed himself in human hearts and we can receive and welcome him, and live from his love. Meister Eckhart wrote: "What good is it to me if this eternal birth of the divine Son takes place unceasingly, but does not take place within myself? And what good is it to me if Mary is full of grace if I am not also full of grace? What good is it to me for the Creator to give birth to his Son, if I do not also give birth to him in my time and my culture?"

The Presence of God
God is with me, but more, God is within me.
Let me dwell for a moment on God's life-giving presence
in my body, in my mind, in my heart,
as I sit here, right now.

Freedom
'A thick and shapeless tree-trunk would never believe
that it could become a statue, admired as a miracle of
sculpture,
and would never submit itself to the chisel of the sculptor,
who sees by her genius what she can make of it' (St Ignatius).
I ask for the grace to let myself be shaped by my loving
Creator.

Consciousness
Knowing that God loves me unconditionally,
I can afford to be honest about how I am.
How has the last day been, and how do I feel now?
I share my feelings openly with the Lord.

The Word
I read the Word of God slowly, a few times over, and I listen
to what God is saying to me. (Please turn to your scripture on
the following pages. Inspiration points are there should you
need them. When you are ready, return here to continue.)

Conversation
Do I notice myself reacting as I pray with the Word of God?
Do I feel challenged, comforted, angry?
Imagining Jesus sitting or standing by me,
I speak out my feelings, as one trusted friend to another.

Conclusion
Glory be to the Father, and to the Son, and to the Holy Spirit,
As it was in the beginning, is now and ever shall be,
World without end. Amen

Sunday 22nd December,
Fourth Sunday of Advent   Matthew 1:24

When Joseph awoke from sleep, he did as the angel of the Lord commanded him; he took her as his wife.

- The humility of Joseph was not something weak or wilting. He followed the word of the Lord and became Mary's husband. I allow the richness of that word to show me how Joseph was a disciple and see what I might learn from him.
- Attending to his dreams, Joseph took care not to ignore how God was communicating with him. I look to God for a way forward in my problems.

Monday 23rd December   Luke 1:57–66

Now the time came for Elizabeth to give birth, and she bore a son. Her neighbors and relatives heard that the Lord had shown his great mercy to her, and they rejoiced with her. On the eighth day they came to circumcise the child, and they were going to name him Zechariah after his father. But his mother said, "No; he is to be called John." They said to her, "None of your relatives has this name." Then they began motioning to his father to find out what name he wanted to give him. He asked for a writing tablet and wrote, "His name is John." And all of them were amazed. Immediately his mouth was opened and his tongue freed, and he began to speak, praising God. Fear came over all their neighbors, and all these things were talked about throughout the entire hill country of Judea. All who heard them pondered them and said, "What then will this child become?" For, indeed, the hand of the Lord was with him.

- I join in the excitement around the birth of Elizabeth's baby. I become aware that God is fulfilling his plans through human beings who collaborate. So too God wants the child called John, and this is what happens. In Luke's understanding of salvation, what God decides will eventually be fulfilled.
- I ask for faith to believe this and to be free of anxiety.

Tuesday 24th December   **Luke 1:67–79**

Then his father Zechariah was filled with the Holy Spirit and spoke this prophecy: "Blessed be the Lord God of Israel, for he has looked favorably on his people and redeemed them. He has raised up a mighty savior for us in the house of his servant David, as he spoke through the mouth of his holy prophets from of old, that we would be saved from our enemies and from the hand of all who hate us. Thus he has shown the mercy promised to our ancestors, and has remembered his holy covenant, the oath that he swore to our ancestor Abraham, to grant us that we, being rescued from the hands of our enemies, might serve him without fear, in holiness and righteousness before him all our days. And you, child, will be called the prophet of the Most High; for you will go before the Lord to prepare his ways, to give knowledge of salvation to his people by the forgiveness of their sins. By the tender mercy of our God, the dawn from on high will break upon us, to give light to those who sit in darkness and in the shadow of death, to guide our feet into the way of peace."

- The Holy Spirit has a busy time in the infancy stories! Elizabeth, Mary and now Zechariah all experience themselves as filled with the Spirit of God. The Spirit is busy today in the *Sacred Space* community: it is the Holy Spirit who prays through us all. I ponder this in wonder and gratitude.
- Many people today sit in darkness and in the shadow of death. Zechariah has a message of hope for them. I ask that I may bring some light to such people, especially at this holy time.

Wednesday 25th December,
Feast of the Nativity of the Lord   **John 1:1–5**

In the beginning was the Word, and the Word was with God, and the Word was God. He was in the beginning with God. All things came into being through him, and without him not one thing came into being. What has come into being in him was life, and the life was the light of all people. The light shines in the darkness, and the darkness did not overcome it.

- We celebrate today the presence of God among us. Slowly and mysteriously Jesus brings light into the web of human history. Slowly his light overcomes our darkness, so that eventually everyone is enlightened.
- I imagine myself in a dark place: I see the light coming and it bathes me in its radiance. I give thanks for all of this.

Thursday 26th December,
St Stephen, the first Martyr   Matthew 10:17–22

Jesus said to his apostles, "Beware of them, for they will hand you over to councils and flog you in their synagogues; and you will be dragged before governors and kings because of me, as a testimony to them and the Gentiles. When they hand you over, do not worry about how you are to speak or what you are to say; for what you are to say will be given to you at that time; for it is not you who speak, but the Spirit of your Father speaking through you. Brother will betray brother to death, and a father his child, and children will rise against parents and have them put to death; and you will be hated by all because of my name. But the one who endures to the end will be saved."

- It is a shock to read this gospel immediately after Christmas. But this is the world into which Jesus comes. He does not retreat from it in fear or disgust. He will wrap it in his love, and that will be enough to save humankind. I ask for Jesus' courage and love.
- The three divine Persons are mentioned in this gospel. They are busy about this world which they love. They stand with us and empower us. I can rely on them as I try to live out my calling as a disciple.

Friday 27th December,
St John, Evangelist   John 20:1a, 2–8

Early on the first day of the week, while it was still dark, Mary Magdalene came to the tomb and saw that the stone had been removed from the tomb. So she ran and went to Simon Peter and the other disciple, the one whom Jesus loved, and said to them, "They have taken the Lord out of the tomb, and we do not know where they have laid him." Then Peter and the other disciple set out and went toward the tomb. The two were running together, but the other disciple outran Peter and reached the tomb first. He bent down to look in and saw the linen wrappings lying there, but he did not go in. Then Simon Peter came, following him, and went into the tomb. He saw the linen wrappings lying there, and the cloth that had been on Jesus' head, not lying with the linen wrappings but rolled up in a place by itself. Then the other disciple, who reached the tomb first, also went in, and he saw and believed.

- The resurrection is a divine initiative to save our world. God breaks through into human history and nothing will ever be the same again. We have new hope, not in ourselves but in what God is doing.
- We live in a world that is experiencing the birth pangs of resurrection. I ask that I may witness to this by my way of life.

Saturday 28th December,
The Holy Innocents   Matthew 2:16–18

When Herod saw that he had been tricked by the wise men, he was infuriated, and he sent and killed all the children in and around Bethlehem who were two years old or under, according to the time that he had learned from the wise men. Then was fulfilled what had been spoken through the prophet Jeremiah: "A voice was heard in Ramah, wailing and loud lamentation, Rachel weeping for her children; she refused to be consoled, because they are no more."

- Herod fears that the child will overthrow him. So he must kill him. But Jesus only wants to bring Herod abundant life and true freedom.
- I travel in imagination with the Holy Family as they flee to Egypt; I remember all the refugee families across the world today. I ask to be shown what I can do to help them.

december 29–january 4

Something to think and pray about each day this week:

Embracing the newness
The beginning of the year is a time for thinking afresh. Even if our body is ageing, our thinking can be evergreen. God always thinks freshly, because God is young, and always in the present. We see from the gospels that Jesus lived totally in the present. He was open to the emerging moment. We may think that being new is something for the future, that the next year will be new, even the next day. But nothing can be new except the now. It's exciting to be able to live like that.

Prayer always invites us into newness of life. Prayer never lets the Spirit sit still except in the stillness of love. The new year invites us to create something new each day—the newness of love, of joy and often of endurance. To live for the day is to live always new. Prayer plunges us into the places of the Spirit where energy is available, like a flower reviving after a drought, or a faulty computer finding its way again, or a patient getting therapy. Prayer is the space where we entrust into God's memory what hurts our memory. We allow God's forgiving and healing grace to make all things new in us.

It is good to give time to prayer—even a little a day—throughout the new year. And each of us might commend the riches of *Sacred Space* to at least one other person this week.

The Presence of God

As I sit here, the beating of my heart,
the ebb and flow of my breathing, the movements of my mind
are all signs of God's ongoing creation of me.
I pause for a moment, and become aware
of this presence of God within me.

Freedom

I ask for the grace
to let go of my own concerns
and be open to what God is asking of me,
to let myself be guided and formed by my loving Creator.

Consciousness

In the presence of my loving Creator,
I look honestly at my feelings over the last day,
the highs, the lows and the level ground.
Can I see where the Lord has been present?

The Word

I take my time to read the Word of God, slowly, a few times,
allowing myself to dwell on anything that strikes me. (Please
turn to your scripture on the following pages. Inspiration
points are there should you need them. When you are ready,
return here to continue.)

Conversation

Remembering that I am still in God's presence,
I imagine Jesus himself standing or sitting beside me,
and say whatever is on my mind, whatever is in my heart,
speaking as one friend to another.

Conclusion

Glory be to the Father, and to the Son, and to the Holy Spirit,
As it was in the beginning, is now and ever shall be,
World without end. Amen

Sunday 29th December,
The Holy Family   Matthew 2:13–15, 19–23

Now after they had left, an angel of the Lord appeared to Joseph in a dream and said, "Get up, take the child and his mother, and flee to Egypt, and remain there until I tell you; for Herod is about to search for the child, to destroy him." Then Joseph got up, took the child and his mother by night, and went to Egypt, and remained there until the death of Herod. This was to fulfill what had been spoken by the Lord through the prophet, "Out of Egypt I have called my son." When Herod died, an angel of the Lord suddenly appeared in a dream to Joseph in Egypt and said, "Get up, take the child and his mother, and go to the land of Israel, for those who were seeking the child's life are dead." Then Joseph got up, took the child and his mother, and went to the land of Israel. But when he heard that Archelaus was ruling over Judea in place of his father Herod, he was afraid to go there. And after being warned in a dream, he went away to the district of Galilee. There he made his home in a town called Nazareth, so that what had been spoken through the prophets might be fulfilled, "He will be called a Nazorean."

- Why choose this story to celebrate the Holy Family? It is not a story of peaceful routine, but rather of drama and hazards and difficult decisions. Jesus and his family are displaced persons seeking a place to live.
- Lord, you have tasted human uncertainties, and the difficulties of survival. Your mother, so blissfully happy when she prayed the *Magnificat*, had to adjust rapidly to homelessness and the life of asylum-seekers. Let me be equally adaptable when you ask me to taste uncertainties and plans going awry.

Monday 30th December   Luke 2:36–40

There was also a prophet, Anna the daughter of Phanuel, of the tribe of Asher. She was of a great age, having lived with her husband for seven years after her marriage, then as a widow to the age of eighty-four. She never left the temple but worshipped there with fasting and prayer night and day. At that moment she came, and began to praise God and to speak about the child to all who were looking for the redemption of Jerusalem. When they had finished everything required by the law of the Lord, they returned to Galilee, to their own town of Nazareth. The child grew and became strong, filled with wisdom; and the favor of God was upon him.

- The Christmas season celebrates the birth of a child but the gospels include many venerable figures like Simeon, Elizabeth, Zechariah and, today, Anna. These people remind me of the fullness of life and wisdom that enrich human experience.
- I pray that young and old people may benefit from each other's company.

Tuesday 31st December   John 1:6–14

There was a man sent from God, whose name was John. He came as a witness to testify to the light, so that all might believe through him. He himself was not the light, but he came to testify to the light. The true light, which enlightens everyone, was coming into the world. He was in the world, and the world came into being through him; yet the world did not know him. He came to what was his own, and his own people did not accept him. But to all who received him, who believed in his name, he gave power to become children of God, who were born, not of blood or of the will of the flesh or of the will of man, but of God. And the Word became flesh and lived among us, and we have seen his glory, the glory as of a father's only son, full of grace and truth.

- We often say that it is hard to pray because we cannot imagine God. But God has seen this problem, and has painted a perfect self-portrait in Jesus. Now we know what God thinks about us and how much God loves us.
- I make a New Year resolution: that in the year ahead I will give quality time to getting to know Jesus better.

Wednesday 1st January,
Solemnity of Mary, Mother of God   Luke 2:16–21

So they went with haste and found Mary and Joseph, and the child lying in the manger. When they saw this, they made known what had been told them about this child; and all who heard it were amazed at what the shepherds told them. But Mary treasured all these words and pondered them in her heart. The shepherds returned, glorifying and praising God for all they had heard and seen, as it had been told them. After eight days had passed, it was time to circumcise the child; and he was called Jesus, the name given by the angel before he was conceived in the womb.

- An outstanding characteristic of Luke's gospel is that all barriers are down. Shepherds who have no social status are the very ones whom the Lord holds in special regard. Those who have nothing open themselves to the angel's message. Their response is joy and praise for the mystery of love unwrapped before them, a vulnerable child and two inexperienced parents.

- Lord, like Mary may I find room in my cluttered life simply to rest and be quiet in your presence. Mary's heart was a sacred space, and mine is also. Fill it with the joy of your presence.

Thursday 2nd January   John 1:19–28

This is the testimony given by John when the Jews sent priests and Levites from Jerusalem to ask him, "Who are you?" He confessed and did not deny it, but confessed, "I am not the Messiah." And they asked him, "What then? Are you Elijah?" He said, "I am not." "Are you the prophet?" He answered, "No." Then they said to him, "Who are you? Let us have an answer for those who sent us. What do you say about yourself?" He said, "I am the voice of one crying out in the wilderness, 'Make straight the way of the Lord,'" as the prophet Isaiah said. Now they had been sent from the Pharisees. They asked him, "Why then are you baptizing if you are neither the Messiah, nor Elijah, nor the prophet?" John answered them, "I baptize with water. Among you stands one whom you do not know, the one who is coming after me; I am not worthy to untie the thong of his sandal." This took place in Bethany across the Jordan where John was baptizing.

- The identity question "Who are you?" leaps from this text. John knows who he is. He is clear about his call, his identity and mission. "I am a voice for the voiceless, a finger post pointing to the true Way—Jesus Christ."
- In prayer today I walk with John in the desert. I let him ask me: "Who are you?" Can I express my relationship with Jesus with John's conviction and integrity?

Friday 3rd January   John 1:29–34

The next day John saw Jesus coming toward him and declared, "Here is the Lamb of God who takes away the sin of the world! This is he of whom I said, 'After me comes a man who ranks ahead of me because he was before me.' I myself did not know him; but I came baptizing with water for this reason, that he might be revealed to Israel." And John testified, "I saw the Spirit descending from heaven like a dove, and it remained on him. I myself did not know him, but the one who sent me to baptize with water said to me, 'He on whom you see the Spirit descend and remain is the one who baptizes with the Holy Spirit.' And I myself have seen and have testified that this is the Son of God."

- John's mission has reached its completion. His function was to point people in the direction of Jesus, the Lamb of God. With these words John draws back the curtain and Jesus takes centre stage in our human story, inviting us to be with him.
- John knew "who" Jesus is, but "what" Jesus is was suddenly revealed. He sees the Spirit descend and remain on Jesus. The Spirit takes up permanent abode in him. As I move through today can I be aware that my life is pervaded with the Spirit of God?

Saturday 4th January   John 1:35–39

The next day John again was standing with two of his disciples, and as he watched Jesus walk by, he exclaimed,

"Look, here is the Lamb of God!" The two disciples heard him say this, and they followed Jesus. When Jesus turned and saw them following, he said to them, "What are you looking for?" They said to him, "Rabbi" (which translated means Teacher), "where are you staying?" He said to them, "Come and see." They came and saw where he was staying, and they remained with him that day.

- A life-changing moment unfolds before our eyes. The disciples are directed towards the wandering rabbi. In response, Jesus does something so characteristic of him. He asks the most fundamental question of life: "What are you looking for?"
- As I journey through my life, do I ask myself the question: "What am I looking for?"

Sacred Space

Something to think and pray about each day this week:

Within God's gaze
New resolutions seemed full of promise last week. But some have already got lost in the ordinariness which takes over as the year gets under way. Prayer can be somewhat the same. It is sometimes energizing, but often mundane, even boring. This should not upset us. The tones and colors of prayer are affected by life's ups and downs, and by the ordinary moods of everyday.

The Divine we meet in prayer knows all that. We are not persons of great prayer, but Jesus knows us through and through, and remains our friend for all time. Prayer is simple. It is about befriending the Mystery of God and ourselves. We allow God to befriend us in all that is our life. Prayer is as simple as that— just being with the divine as I am, here and now, and believing that the Divine is with me. Ignatius of Loyola invites us to start our prayer like that. He says: "I will consider how God looks at me." Teresa of Avila says: "Gaze at God gazing at you, lovingly and humbly." One of the French mystics wrote: "You gazed on me and you smiled!"

Connectedness is the key. Because I believe that I am loved, I can allow the Divine to look at me. Prayer then transforms the ordinary and the mundane. It makes the Now a moment of grace and joy. It can happen here and now as you read this reflection!

The Presence of God
I pause for a moment
and reflect on God's life-giving presence
in every part of my body, in everything around me,
in the whole of my life.

Freedom
Many countries are at this moment suffering
the agonies of war.
I bow my head in thanksgiving for my freedom.
I pray for all prisoners and captives.

Consciousness
Knowing that God loves me unconditionally,
I look honestly over the last day, its events and my feelings.
Do I have something to be grateful for? Then I give thanks.
Is there something I am sorry for? Then I ask forgiveness.

The Word
God speaks to each one of us individually. I need to listen to
hear what he is saying to me. Read the text a few times, then
listen. (Please turn to your scripture on the following pages.
Inspiration points are there should you need them. When you
are ready, return here to continue.)

Conversation
How has God's Word moved me? Has it left me cold?
Has it consoled me or moved me to act in a new way?
I imagine Jesus standing or sitting beside me,
I turn and share my feelings with him.

Conclusion
Glory be to the Father, and to the Son, and to the Holy Spirit,
As it was in the beginning, is now and ever shall be,
World without end. Amen

Sunday 5th January,
The Epiphany of the Lord Matthew 2:1–6

In the time of King Herod, after Jesus was born in Bethlehem of Judea, wise men from the East came to Jerusalem, asking, "Where is the child who has been born king of the Jews? For we observed his star at its rising, and have come to pay him homage." When King Herod heard this, he was frightened, and all Jerusalem with him; and calling together all the chief priests and scribes of the people, he inquired of them where the Messiah was to be born. They told him, "In Bethlehem of Judea; for so it has been written by the prophet: 'And you, Bethlehem, in the land of Judah, are by no means least among the rulers of Judah; for from you shall come a ruler who is to shepherd my people Israel.'"

- The Magi, three pilgrim astrologers of the East, follow a star in search of the divine. God chooses to reveal himself to outsiders, strangers, and foreigners. I learn that in the kingdom of God there are no outsiders, nor discrimination.
- What star am I being called to follow this year? What gifts from my treasure chest will I offer him in service of his mission? Lord, send me out each day to be a bearer of your love to all whom I encounter.

Monday 6th January Matthew 4:17, 23–25

From that time Jesus began to proclaim, "Repent, for the kingdom of heaven has come near." Jesus went throughout Galilee, teaching in their synagogues and proclaiming the good news of the kingdom and curing every disease and every sickness among the people. So his fame spread throughout all Syria, and they brought to him all the sick, those who were afflicted with various diseases and pains, demoniacs, epileptics, and paralytics, and he cured them. And great crowds followed him from Galilee, the Decapolis, Jerusalem, Judea, and from beyond the Jordan.

- This is Jesus' inaugural speech, with its message of good news, and it captivates his audience. In him, message and messenger are united. Jesus offers truth, healing, hope, compassion, and peace to the hopeless.

- Lord, you call on me to reform my life and place my faith in this good news. Deepen my belief. May I take you at your word and trust in the God of love you came to reveal.

Tuesday 7th January   Mark 6:34–44

As he went ashore, he saw a great crowd; and he had compassion for them, because they were like sheep without a shepherd; and he began to teach them many things. When it grew late, his disciples came to him and said, "This is a deserted place, and the hour is now very late; send them away so that they may go into the surrounding country and villages and buy something for themselves to eat." But he answered them, "You give them something to eat." They said to him, "Are we to go and buy two hundred denarii worth of bread, and give it to them to eat?" And he said to them, "How many loaves have you? Go and see." When they had found out, they said, "Five, and two fish." Then he ordered them to get all the people to sit down in groups on the green grass. So they sat down in groups of hundreds and of fifties. Taking the five loaves and the two fish, he looked up to heaven, and blessed and broke the loaves, and gave them to his disciples to set before the people; and he divided the two fish among them all. And all ate and were filled; and they took up twelve baskets full of broken pieces and of the fish. Those who had eaten the loaves numbered five thousand men.

- Mark's story has several levels. On one level the multiplication of the loaves simply represents Jesus' compassion as he puts his divine power at the service of a hungry multitude. On another level, the feeding looks forward to what Jesus will do at the Last Supper when he "looks up to heaven, blesses and breaks the loaves, and gives them to the disciples."
- What place does Eucharist play in my life?

Wednesday 8th January   Mark 6:45–52

Immediately he made his disciples get into the boat and go on ahead to the other side, to Bethsaida, while he dismissed the crowd. After saying farewell to them, he went up on the mountain to pray. When evening came, the boat was out on the sea, and he was alone on the land. When he saw that they were straining at the oars against an adverse wind, he came towards them early in the morning, walking on the sea. He intended to pass them by. But when they saw him walking on the sea, they thought it was a ghost and cried out; for they all saw him and were terrified. But immediately he spoke to them and said, "Take heart, it is I; do not be afraid." Then he got into the boat with them and the wind ceased. And they were utterly astounded, for they did not understand about the loaves, but their hearts were hardened.

- Most of Jesus' signs and miracles happen when someone or a group asks with the heart. He is no magician or easy gift giver. Jesus interacts with us in faith.
- What do you really want to ask him for in prayer? What storm in life needs calming? In your life or in another's? We know and believe that no prayer is unheard but that something good happens in our life when we speak to Jesus from the heart.

Thursday 9th January   Luke 4:14–22

Then Jesus, filled with the power of the Spirit, returned to Galilee, and a report about him spread through all the surrounding country. He began to teach in their synagogues and was praised by everyone. When he came to Nazareth, where he had been brought up, he went to the synagogue on the sabbath day, as was his custom. He stood up to read, and the scroll of the prophet Isaiah was given to him. He unrolled the scroll and found the place where it was written: "The Spirit of the Lord is upon me, because he has anointed me to bring good news to the poor. He has sent me to proclaim release to the captives and recovery of sight to the blind, to let the oppressed go free, to proclaim the year of the Lord's favor." And he rolled up the scroll, gave it back to the attendant, and sat down. The eyes of all in the synagogue were fixed on him. Then he began to say to them, "Today this scripture has been fulfilled in your hearing."

- The good news might be summed up like this: we are all children of God, we are all brothers and sisters, and evil does not finally prevail in the world. Imagine that on the newspaper banners around town!
- Can you recall moments and times when the gospel words lifted your heart, calmed fears, renewed hope and refreshed your whole life? Then it is good news and the good news is Jesus in your life. Give thanks for good news.

Friday 10th January   Luke 5:12–16

Once, when Jesus was in one of the cities, there was a man covered with leprosy. When he saw Jesus, he bowed with his face to the ground and begged him, "Lord, if you choose, you can make me clean." Then Jesus stretched out his hand, touched him, and said, "I do choose. Be made clean." Immediately the leprosy left him. And he ordered him to tell no one. "Go," he said, "and show yourself to the priest, and, as Moses commanded, make an offering for your cleansing, for a testimony to them." But now more than ever the word about Jesus spread abroad; many crowds would gather to hear him and to be cured of their diseases. But he would withdraw to deserted places and pray.

- Jesus touches the leper, though his disease may be contagious. Can I allow Jesus to touch and heal my blemishes? Lord, heal not only the surface, but the depths of my heart!
- Jesus often goes off to pray. Was his prayer very different from ours? At the heart of all real prayer is mutual love. "Dear God, you love me, and I love you too!" I think Jesus might have prayed like that.

Saturday 11th January   John 3:25–30

Now a discussion about purification arose between John's disciples and a Jew. They came to John and said to him,

"Rabbi, the one who was with you across the Jordan, to whom you testified, here he is baptizing, and all are going to him." John answered, "No one can receive anything except what has been given from heaven. You yourselves are my witnesses that I said, 'I am not the Messiah, but I have been sent ahead of him.' He who has the bride is the bridegroom. The friend of the bridegroom, who stands and hears him, rejoices greatly at the bridegroom's voice. For this reason my joy has been fulfilled. He must increase, but I must decrease."

- Jesus varies his modes of ministry, always trying to communicate the love of God to his insensitive audiences: baptising, miracles, parables, preaching and debating.
- Finally comes the most radical mode: his total self-donation in the Eucharist and on the Cross. Has he won me over yet?

Sacred Space

Something to think and pray about each day this week:

In God's good time

Tourists in Barcelona like to visit the unfinished cathedral, The Holy Family, now a World Heritage site. Antoni Gaudi began work on it in 1883, but at his death in 1926, less than a quarter of the project was complete. But Gaudi remarked shortly before his death: "My Client is not in a hurry." Other architects have played their part since then. Mid-point in construction of this extraordinary work was reached in 2010, and completion is planned for the centenary of the architect's death.

This remarkable undertaking has much to teach us. Firstly, Gaudi is right about God's leisurely style! God seems not to be in a hurry about a completion date for the epic that is world history. But like the cathedral, enough of the divine design is available to enable us to have some image of the final master-piece. Secondly, whereas only top class architects are allowed to work on the cathedral, each of us—every person on this planet, every member of the *Sacred Space* community—is invited to contribute to shaping God's project for us. Strangely, God trusts us not to make a total mess of it!

Thirdly, Christian belief can appear as a jumble of disconnected facts, rather like the rocks on the cathedral building. But the keyword to Christian faith is relationships! God is a relating God. This concept unifies every aspect of Christian life.

The Presence of God

'The world is charged with the grandeur of God' (Gerard Manley Hopkins).
I dwell for a moment on the presence of God
around me, in every part of my body,
and deep within my being.

Freedom

"In these days, God taught me
as a schoolteacher teaches a pupil" (St Ignatius).
I remind myself that there are things God has to teach me yet,
and ask for the grace to hear them and let them change me.

Consciousness

How do I find myself today?
Where am I with God? With others?
Do I have something to be grateful for? Then I give thanks.
Is there something I am sorry for? Then I ask forgiveness.

The Word

I read the Word of God slowly, a few times over, and I listen
to what God is saying to me. (Please turn to your scripture on
the following pages. Inspiration points are there should you
need them. When you are ready, return here to continue.)

Conversation

Sometimes I wonder what I might say
if I were to meet You in person, Lord.
I might say 'Thank You, Lord' for always being there for me.
I know with certainty there were times when you carried me,
when through your strength I got through the dark times in
my life.

Conclusion

Glory be to the Father, and to the Son, and to the Holy Spirit,
As it was in the beginning, is now and ever shall be,
World without end. Amen

Sunday 12th January,
The Baptism of the Lord   Matthew 3:13–17

Then Jesus came from Galilee to John at the Jordan, to be baptized by him. John would have prevented him, saying, "I need to be baptized by you, and do you come to me?" But Jesus answered him, "Let it be so now; for it is proper for us in this way to fulfill all righteousness." Then he consented. And when Jesus had been baptized, just as he came up from the water, suddenly the heavens were opened to him and he saw the Spirit of God descending like a dove and alighting on him. And a voice from heaven said, "This is my Son, the Beloved, with whom I am well pleased."

- The grace of my baptism is alive and evident whenever I am humble enough to yield to the Spirit of God. I pray for the humility that Jesus shows.
- I give thanks for my baptism; I am a child of God and set in the world to give glory to God, to serve those around me and to grow in the image of God.

Monday 13th January   Mark 1:14–20

Now after John was arrested, Jesus came to Galilee, proclaiming the good news of God, and saying, "The time is fulfilled, and the kingdom of God has come near; repent, and believe in the good news." As Jesus passed along the Sea of Galilee, he saw Simon and his brother Andrew casting a net into the sea—for they were fishermen. And Jesus said to them, "Follow me and I will make you fish for people." And immediately they left their nets and followed him. As he went a little farther, he saw James son of Zebedee and his brother John, who were in their boat mending the nets. Immediately he called them; and they left their father Zebedee in the boat with the hired men, and followed him.

- Jesus' arrival at Galilee ushers in a new era. Jesus' own person and ministry is the beginning of the kingdom of God. The kingdom is a dynamic and active reality. Jesus' words and deeds are always in service of this kingdom.

- Lord, you call the disciples to follow you and share in your mission. Their response is radical and immediate. May nothing hinder me from responding to your daily call to follow you.

Tuesday 14th January   Mark 1:21–28

Jesus entered the synagogue and taught. They were astounded at his teaching, for he taught them as one having authority, and not as the scribes. Just then there was in their synagogue a man with an unclean spirit, and he cried out, "What have you to do with us, Jesus of Nazareth? Have you come to destroy us? I know who you are, the Holy One of God." But Jesus rebuked him, saying, "Be silent, and come out of him!" And the unclean spirit, convulsing him and crying with a loud voice, came out of him. They were all amazed, and they kept on asking one another, "What is this? A new teaching—with authority! He commands even the unclean spirits, and they obey him." At once his fame began to spread throughout the surrounding region of Galilee.

- Demon possession was an accepted fact in New Testament times. Whether I believe in personal demons or not, I am sometimes conscious of being pulled away from God.
- Holy One of God, when the pull of darker forces disturbs and draws me away from you, be with me and draw me ever closer to you.

Wednesday 15th January   Mark 1:29–34

As soon as they left the synagogue, they entered the house of Simon and Andrew, with James and John. Now Simon's mother-in-law was in bed with a fever, and they told him about her at once. He came and took her by the hand and lifted her up. Then the fever left her, and she began to serve them. That evening, at sundown, they brought to him all who were sick or possessed with demons. And the whole city was gathered around the door. And he cured many who were sick with various diseases, and cast out many demons; and he would not permit the demons to speak, because they knew him.

- Despite their brief acquaintance with Jesus, the disciples grasped that Jesus is empowered by the Spirit. His first act of healing is in favour of a woman. Healed of her fever, Peter's mother-in-law embodies true discipleship—the service of others.

- Lord, deliver me from seeking your help only in times of difficulty. May I grow in grateful love for the ways you daily raise me up and call me to the service of the community.

Thursday 16th January   Mark 1:40–42

A leper came to Jesus begging him, and kneeling he said to him, "If you choose, you can make me clean." Moved with pity, Jesus stretched out his hand and touched him, and said to him, "I do choose. Be made clean!" Immediately the leprosy left him, and he was made clean.

- Jesus, the compassionate one, enters fully into the human mess of our lives. Leprosy was the most dreaded of diseases in his day. Jesus risks conflict and division for the sake of a nobody who was suffering exclusion and isolation from family and community.
- The leper approaches in confident trust and Jesus touches his sore, leprous body. Lord, how do I approach you in prayer? Begging, kneeling, and asking for what I want? Let me feel your touch.

Friday 17th January   Mark 2:1–12

When he returned to Capernaum after some days, it was reported that he was at home. So many gathered around that there was no longer room for them, not even in front of the door; and he was speaking the word to them. Then some people came, bringing to him a paralyzed man, carried by four of them. And when they could not bring him to Jesus because of the crowd, they removed the roof above him; and after having dug through it, they let down the mat on which the paralytic lay. When Jesus saw their faith, he said to the paralytic, "Son, your sins are forgiven." Now some of the scribes were sitting there, questioning in their hearts, "Why does this fellow speak in this way? It is blasphemy! Who can forgive sins but God alone?" At once Jesus perceived in his spirit that they were discussing these questions among themselves; and he said to them, "Why do you raise such questions in your hearts? Which is easier, to say to the paralytic, 'Your sins are forgiven,' or to say, 'Stand up and take your mat and walk'? But so that you may know that the Son of Man has authority on earth to forgive sins"—he said to the paralytic— "I say to you, stand up, take your mat and go to your home." And he stood up, and immediately took the mat and went out before all of them; so that they were all amazed and glorified God, saying, "We have never seen anything like this!"

- Jesus exudes a magnetic and powerful influence. From the religious authorities he evokes controversy and conflict. From those who carried the paralysed man, comes a response of faith. They see in Jesus God's agent of forgiveness. They see someone who breaks through legalism to liberate their friend in soul and body.
- The difficulties of life can lead me to a paralysis of faith and an inability to reach out to the Lord. I recall with gratitude the faith of those who carried me to God in dark times.

Saturday 18th January   Mark 2:13–17

Jesus went out again beside the sea; the whole crowd gathered around him, and he taught them. As he was walking along, he saw Levi son of Alphaeus sitting at the tax booth, and he said to him, "Follow me." And he got up and followed him. And as he sat at dinner in Levi's house, many tax collectors and sinners were also sitting with Jesus and his disciples—for there were many who followed him. When the scribes of the Pharisees saw that he was eating with sinners and tax collectors, they said to his disciples, "Why does he eat with tax collectors and sinners?" When Jesus heard this, he said to them, "Those who are well have no need of a physician, but those who are sick; I have come to call not the righteous but sinners."

- Jesus cuts through the carefully constructed assumptions of the Pharisees. What a shock that must have been! Levi, a most unlikely man, despised by the righteous, is the recipient of God's gracious mercy and forgiveness. Jesus sees his hidden potential and invites him into friendship.
- Lord, hypocrisy, arrogance and contempt have no place in your table fellowship. Heal my arrogant, despising, and judging heart so that I can sit at table with you.

Something to think and pray about each day this week:

Building true relationships

Christian life is all about relationships. We Christians believe that God is not one Person but three, and that these Three share infinitely happy relationships with one another. They desire to share their happiness with us. Everything of value in our life flows from this project of theirs.

Thus, each sacrament is a personal encounter with Christ. At every important moment in my life, Christ is there to deepen his relationship with me. He sets things up so that at birth, adolescence, marriage, sickness and dying, he can meet me and enrich me in special ways. In the Eucharist Christ is the welcoming host, fostering good relationships. The community he is forming listens to his Word and responds as best it can.

Sin is about spoiled relationships rather than about breaking a rule. When I wound the precious fabric of human and divine bondings, I hurt myself, others and God. The sacrament of reconciliation is not just a telling of my sins but a restoring of good relationships.

We are to tend our relationships carefully: they are the stuff of eternity. When human history is completed, there awaits us a cosmic and ever-flowing celebration of good relationships. We call this heaven: everyone, divine and human, will be a friend to me, and I to them. But the process is under way, here and now.

The Presence of God
As I sit here, God is present,
breathing life into me and into everything around me.
For a few moments, I sit silently,
and become aware of God's loving presence.

Freedom
If God were trying to tell me something, would I know?
If God were reassuring me or challenging me, would I notice?
I ask for the grace to be free of my own preoccupations
and open to what God may be saying to me.

Consciousness
In God's loving presence I unwind the past day,
starting from now and looking back, moment by moment.
I gather in all the goodness and light, in gratitude.
I attend to the shadows and what they say to me,
seeking healing, courage, forgiveness.

The Word
I take my time to read the Word of God, slowly, a few times,
allowing myself to dwell on anything that strikes me. (Please
turn to your scripture on the following pages. Inspiration
points are there should you need them. When you are ready,
return here to continue.)

Conversation
What is stirring in me as I pray?
Am I consoled, troubled, left cold?
I imagine Jesus himself standing or sitting at my side,
and share my feelings with him.

Conclusion
Glory be to the Father, and to the Son, and to the Holy Spirit,
As it was in the beginning, is now and ever shall be,
World without end. Amen

Sunday 19th January,
Second Sunday in Ordinary Time   John 1:29–34

The next day John saw Jesus coming toward him and declared, "Here is the Lamb of God who takes away the sin of the world! This is he of whom I said, 'After me comes a man who ranks ahead of me because he was before me.' I myself did not know him; but I came baptizing with water for this reason, that he might be revealed to Israel." And John testified, "I saw the Spirit descending from heaven like a dove, and it remained on him. I myself did not know him, but the one who sent me to baptize with water said to me, 'He on whom you see the Spirit descend and remain is the one who baptizes with the Holy Spirit.' And I myself have seen and have testified that this is the Son of God."

- Although he prepared the way for Jesus, John acknowledges that he did not know who to expect. As I do my best, in my way, to prepare the way for Jesus, I cannot always know just what to be ready for.
- John remained active and vigilant. I pray that I may find the balance between keeping occupied in God's service without letting my occupations overwhelm me.

Monday 20th January   Mark 2:18–22

Now John's disciples and the Pharisees were fasting; and people came and said to him, "Why do John's disciples and the disciples of the Pharisees fast, but your disciples do not fast?" Jesus said to them, "The wedding-guests cannot fast while the bridegroom is with them, can they? As long as they have the bridegroom with them, they cannot fast. The days will come when the bridegroom is taken away from them, and then they will fast on that day. "No one sews a piece of unshrunk cloth on an old cloak; otherwise, the patch pulls away from it, the new from the old, and a worse tear is made. And no one puts new wine into old wineskins; otherwise, the wine will burst the skins, and the wine is lost, and so are the skins; but one puts new wine into fresh wineskins."

- "New wine, new wineskins." Lord, you caution me from having a closed mind. You challenge me not to cling to old ways, and to be receptive to the new.
- Grant me openness of heart and mind. Let me trust in the depths of your creative Spirit who is making all things new.

Tuesday 21st January   Mark 2:23–28

One sabbath Jesus was going through the grainfields; and as they made their way his disciples began to pluck heads of grain. The Pharisees said to him, "Look, why are they doing what is not lawful on the sabbath?" And he said to them, "Have you never read what David did when he and his companions were hungry and in need of food? He entered the house of God, when Abiathar was high priest, and ate the bread of the Presence, which it is not lawful for any but the priests to eat, and he gave some to his companions." Then he said to them, "The sabbath was made for humankind, and not humankind for the sabbath; so the Son of Man is lord even of the sabbath."

- Controversy between Jesus and the Pharisees rustles through the pages of Mark's gospel. Jesus comes fearlessly and immediately to the defence of his hungry disciples. Human need supersedes the ritual demands of the Sabbath.
- Forgiveness, mercy, and compassion are at the heart of true religion. Without these all the rest is heartless and empty. Lord, would others see me as a truly religious person?

Wednesday 22nd January   Mark 3:1–6

Again he entered the synagogue, and a man was there who had a withered hand. They watched him to see whether he would cure him on the sabbath, so that they might accuse him. And he said to the man who had the withered hand, "Come forward." Then he said to them, "Is it lawful to do good or to do harm on the sabbath, to save life or to kill?" But they were silent. He looked around at them with anger; he was grieved at their hardness of heart and said to the man, "Stretch out your hand." He stretched it out, and his hand was restored.

The Pharisees went out and immediately conspired with the Herodians against him, how to destroy him.

- This controversy over a man with a withered hand seals Jesus' fate. For Jesus, religion meant service, doing good, restoring life. This shocks the Pharisees. For them religion meant observance of rules and ritual. In the face of Jesus' ways, their hearts are rigid and unbending.
- As I pray this gospel scene am I aware of my own reactions? How do I respond to the good that others do? Are there times when evil triumphs because of my rigid silence?

Thursday 23th January   Mark 3:7–12

Jesus departed with his disciples to the sea, and a great multitude from Galilee followed him; hearing all that he was doing, they came to him in great numbers from Judea, Jerusalem, Idumea, beyond the Jordan, and the region around Tyre and Sidon. He told his disciples to have a boat ready for him because of the crowd, so that they would not crush him; for he had cured many, so that all who had diseases pressed upon him to touch him. Whenever the unclean spirits saw him, they fell down before him and shouted, "You are the Son of God!" But he sternly ordered them not to make him known.

- The magnetism of Jesus is revealed here. Ordinary unimportant people offer him an enthusiastic reception. They approach him with one desire—to touch him and be healed. Loving energy flows out from Jesus.
- Am I easy about joining this enthusiastic crowd of poor people? Can I admit that I too need the healing touch of the Son of God? Do I radiate healing to others?

Friday 24th January   Mark 3:13–19

He went up the mountain and called to him those whom he wanted, and they came to him. And he appointed twelve, whom he also named apostles, to be with him, and to be sent out to proclaim the message, and to have authority to cast out demons. So he appointed the twelve: Simon (to whom he gave the name Peter); James son of Zebedee and John the brother of James (to whom he gave the name Boanerges, that is, Sons of Thunder); and Andrew, and Philip, and Bartholomew, and Matthew, and Thomas, and James son of Alphaeus, and Thaddaeus, and Simon the Cananaean, and Judas Iscariot, who betrayed him.

- Jesus did not choose people because of what they were. He chose them for what they could become under his direction and power.
- Lord, I am nothing remarkable, yet you call me to be with you. Give me courage to serve you with generous commitment.

Saturday 25th January,
Conversion of St Paul, Apostle   Mark 16:15

Jesus said to the disciples, "Go into all the world and proclaim the good news to the whole creation."

- The good news is not just for men and women, but is for the whole creation. I think of how I depend on God's complex creation and consider whether I am living in a way that is respectful of the world.
- Jesus says, "Go"; I extend my prayer beyond the limits of my concerns and pray for the wider world that I live in connection with.

Something to think and pray about each day this week:

My own story

Each of us is a book, telling the personalized story of grace. Yours is a unique story, a first edition. It is as yet incomplete. There are, you hope, plenty of blank pages still in your book. But you may consider that your tale is pretty ordinary and dull. Your image of yourself may be of someone who plods along quietly and alone, and that no intelligent publisher would dream that your manuscript could become a best-seller.

But when you catch on to the fact that your text is divinely co-authored, everything changes. You look back on the chapters written so far with a new interest. You begin to see what the ghost-writer—God!—has been up to. You discover that the story-line is incredibly rich, and that the plot got under way a long time ago, 13.7 billion years ago in fact, when our world began. Your autobiography will be no paperback but a blockbuster!

Maybe you begin to get into the habit of consulting with your ghost-writer on how to construct each chapter, first one then the next. As you look further ahead, you come to see that the final chapter will be written not by you but by God. Yet it won't be simply a conclusion followed by a full stop. Instead, there will be a semi-colon, which we call "death" and then the plot will open out into exciting scenarios you cannot now dream of.

The Presence of God
As I sit here with these words in front of me, God is here.
Around me, in my sensations, in my thoughts and deep
within me.
I pause for a moment, and become aware
of God's life-giving presence.

Freedom
I need to rise above the noise;
the noise that interrupts, that separates,
the noise that isolates.
I need to listen to God again.

Consciousness
I remind myself that I am in the presence of the Lord.
I will take refuge in His loving heart.
He is my strength in times of weakness.
He is my comforter in times of sorrow.

The Word
God speaks to each one of us individually. I need to listen to
what he is saying to me. (Please turn to your scripture on the
following pages. Inspiration points are there should you need
them. When you are ready, return here to continue.)

Conversation
Do I notice myself reacting as I pray with the Word of God?
Do I feel challenged, comforted, angry?
Imagining Jesus sitting or standing by me,
I speak out my feelings, as one trusted friend to another.

Conclusion
Glory be to the Father, and to the Son, and to the Holy Spirit,
As it was in the beginning, is now and ever shall be,
World without end. Amen

Sunday 26th January,
Third Sunday in Ordinary Time   Matthew 4:18–23

As Jesus walked by the Sea of Galilee, he saw two brothers, Simon, who is called Peter, and Andrew his brother, casting a net into the lake—for they were fishermen. And he said to them, "Follow me, and I will make you fish for people." Immediately they left their nets and followed him. As he went from there, he saw two other brothers, James son of Zebedee and his brother John, in the boat with their father Zebedee, mending their nets, and he called them. Immediately they left the boat and their father, and followed him. Jesus went throughout Galilee, teaching in their synagogues and proclaiming the good news of the kingdom and curing every disease and every sickness among the people.

- Jesus must have watched Simon and Andrew, noticing how they cast their nets. I take some time with this image, letting it speak to me about what Jesus valued in them.
- I might imagine Jesus watching me in my daily life, allowing him to value what I do and letting him call me to serve him in my particular way.

Monday 27th January   Mark 3:22–30

And the scribes who came down from Jerusalem said, "He has Beelzebul, and by the ruler of the demons he casts out demons." And he called them to him, and spoke to them in parables, "How can Satan cast out Satan? If a kingdom is divided against itself, that kingdom cannot stand. And if a house is divided against itself, that house will not be able to stand. And if Satan has risen up against himself and is divided, he cannot stand, but his end has come. But no one can enter a strong man's house and plunder his property without first tying up the strong man; then indeed the house can be plundered. "Truly I tell you, people will be forgiven for their sins and whatever blasphemies they utter; but whoever blasphemes against the Holy Spirit can never have forgiveness, but is guilty of an eternal sin"—for they had said, "He has an unclean spirit."

- Jesus is indeed the stronger one. He takes on the forces of evil; the powers of darkness cannot master him. But the scribes resist the power of the Spirit and spread malicious stories about him.
- Am I open to the Spirit of God? Lord, help me to distinguish the promptings of the good Spirit from those of the forces of evil.

Tuesday 28th January   Mark 3:31–35

Then the mother and brothers of Jesus came; and standing outside, they sent to him and called him. A crowd was sitting around him; and they said to him, "Your mother and your brothers and sisters are outside, asking for you." And he replied, "Who are my mother and my brothers?" And looking at those who sat around him, he said, "Here are my mother and my brothers! Whoever does the will of God is my brother and sister and mother."

- Is Jesus rejecting his own mother and family? Not at all, but he is reminding his disciples that there is a kinship that takes priority over blood relations. It is centred on a radical call to be like him. Relationship with him brings intimacy, like that of a mother, brother, or sister.
- Lord, through my daily encounter with you in *Sacred Space*, may our relationship deepen. Lead me to do only your will.

Wednesday 29th January   Mark 4:2–9

Jesus began to teach them many things in parables, and in his teaching he said to them: "Listen! A sower went out to sow. And as he sowed, some seed fell on the path, and the birds came and ate it up. Other seed fell on rocky ground, where it did not have much soil, and it sprang up quickly, since it had no depth of soil. And when the sun rose, it was scorched; and since it had no root, it withered away. Other seed fell among thorns, and the thorns grew up and choked it, and it yielded no grain. Other seed fell into good soil and brought forth grain, growing up and increasing and yielding thirty and sixty and a hundredfold." And he said, "Let anyone with ears to hear listen!"

- Jesus hints at four sowings in the story: with the first there is failure, then initial growth, more promising growth and in the last case, a huge harvest.
- Prayer introduces us to the word of God and in prayer we hope that this word may reach deep into our hearts. Prayer takes time. When it takes root it then bears fruit in life.

Thursday 30th January   Mark 4:21–25

He said to them, "Is a lamp brought in to be put under the bushel basket, or under the bed, and not on the lampstand? For there is nothing hidden, except to be disclosed; nor is anything secret, except to come to light. Let anyone with ears to hear listen!" And he said to them, "Pay attention to what you hear; the measure you give will be the measure you get, and still more will be given you. For to those who have, more will be given; and from those who have nothing, even what they have will be taken away."

- Jesus says to me: "You are a lamp alight with my love. Now start shining!"
- "Anyone who has will be given more." Life is a risk, says Plato, but a beautiful risk. Lord, let me open my heart fully to you, and then share your love with all those whom you send my way.

Friday 31st January   Mark 4:26–29

Jesus said to the crowd, "The kingdom of God is as if someone would scatter seed on the ground, and would sleep and rise night and day, and the seed would sprout and grow, he does not know how. The earth produces of itself, first the stalk, then the head, then the full grain in the head. But when the grain is ripe, at once he goes in with his sickle, because the harvest has come."

- Seeds grow when the conditions are right. They need light, heat and energy. God's kingdom of love grows slowly and demands patience and faith.
- Lord, our world is blighted by the destructive seeds of greed and oppression. But deep down there are also small seeds of justice, peace and reconciliation peeping out. May I help them to grow.

Saturday 1st February   **Mark 4:35–41**

On that day, when evening had come, he said to them, "Let us go across to the other side." And leaving the crowd behind, they took him with them in the boat, just as he was. Other boats were with him. A great windstorm arose, and the waves beat into the boat, so that the boat was already being swamped. But he was in the stern, asleep on the cushion; and they woke him up and said to him, "Teacher, do you not care that we are perishing?" He woke up and rebuked the wind, and said to the sea, "Peace! Be still!" Then the wind ceased, and there was a dead calm. He said to them, "Why are you afraid? Have you still no faith?" And they were filled with great awe and said to one another, "Who then is this, that even the wind and the sea obey him?"

- Pitched and tossed on the sea, the disciples fear shipwreck. In desperation, they wake Jesus up. He had been asleep. But they had been asleep also! They had been asleep as to who he really is.
- Life's storms hit unexpectedly and toss me into a sea of chaos, doubt and anxiety. Lord, when the waves threaten to swamp my little boat, make me aware that I have you with me. Let me hear your voice saying: "Peace! Be still!"

Something to think and pray about each day this week:

The challenge of growth

Is there not a certain springtime in all prayer? Maybe we breathe easier with the passing of winter and its coldness. The time we spend in prayer refreshes both our bodies and our spirits. While all times and seasons are God's and we can never limit God's working, yet springtime can enliven us with the youthfulness and newness of the Creator each day.

Spring does not always come easily. For the trees which prepare to blossom afresh, there is pain for the wood as the bud breaks through. Sometimes too there is a bud that doesn't make it.

Prayer engages us to deepen our welcome and our openness to God. That is its task. Sometimes this will be easy: at other times it will painfully challenge us. Does not all challenge in the name of love have its own special sweet bitterness? There is a letting go of something we treasure in order to make space for something better. Any openness to love is an openness to the immense blessing of the Creator God. Like the spring our prayer brings a certain gentleness and warmth to us, the gentleness and warmth of God. Those who pray are being secretly nourished from within. The sap of divine life runs freely through them. It enables them to cope more generously with the demands of loving.

The Presence of God
At any time of the day or night we can call on Jesus.
He is always waiting, listening for our call.
What a wonderful blessing.
No phone needed, no emails, just a whisper.

Freedom
I will ask God's help,
to be free from my own preoccupations,
to be open to God in this time of prayer,
to come to love and serve him more.

Consciousness
How am I feeling? Light-hearted? Heavy-hearted?
I may be very much at peace, happy to be here.
Equally, I may be frustrated, worried or angry.
I acknowledge how I really am. It is the real me that the
Lord loves.

The Word
I read the Word of God slowly, a few times over, and I listen
to what God is saying to me. (Please turn to your scripture on
the following pages. Inspiration points are there should you
need them. When you are ready, return here to continue.)

Conversation
Remembering that I am still in God's presence,
I imagine Jesus himself standing or sitting beside me,
and say whatever is on my mind, whatever is in my heart,
speaking as one friend to another.

Conclusion
Glory be to the Father, and to the Son, and to the Holy Spirit,
As it was in the beginning, is now and ever shall be,
World without end. Amen

Sunday 2nd February,
Presentation of the Lord   Luke 2:25–30

Now there was a man in Jerusalem whose name was Simeon; this man was righteous and devout, looking forward to the consolation of Israel, and the Holy Spirit rested on him. It had been revealed to him by the Holy Spirit that he would not see death before he had seen the Lord's Messiah. Guided by the Spirit, Simeon came into the temple; and when the parents brought in the child Jesus, to do for him what was customary under the law, Simeon took him in his arms and praised God, saying, "Master, now you are dismissing your servant in peace, according to your word; for my eyes have seen your salvation, which you have prepared in the presence of all peoples, a light for revelation to the Gentiles and for glory to your people Israel." And the child's father and mother were amazed at what was being said about him.

- The feast of the Presentation can happen every day if I wish it so. This is because when I pray, I am presenting myself before God. God and I meet directly. When Jesus tells us to pray always, he is inviting us to live out our lives with this awareness of God.
- Like Simeon, I can take the child in my arms. Perhaps the child wakes up and smiles at me. What goes on in my heart when this happens? Simeon praised God. I give thanks that God is presented to me in such a tangible and vulnerable form.

Monday 3rd February   Mark 5:1–8, 17–20

They came to the other side of the sea, to the country of the Gerasenes. And when he had stepped out of the boat, immediately a man out of the tombs with an unclean spirit met him. He lived among the tombs; and no one could restrain him any more, even with a chain; for he had often been restrained with shackles and chains, but the chains he wrenched apart, and the shackles he broke in pieces; and no one had the strength to subdue him. Night and day among the tombs and on the mountains he was always howling and bruising himself with stones. When he saw Jesus from a distance, he ran and bowed down before him; and he shouted at the top of his voice, "What have you to do with me, Jesus, Son of the Most High God? I adjure you by God, do not torment me." For he had said to him, "Come out of the man, you unclean spirit!"… Then the people who had seen what had happened began to beg Jesus to leave their neighborhood. As Jesus was getting into the boat, the man who had been possessed by demons begged him that he might be with him. But Jesus refused, and said to him, "Go home to your friends, and tell them how much the Lord has done for you, and what mercy he has shown you." And he went away and began to proclaim in the Decapolis how much Jesus had done for him; and everyone was amazed.

- Can I identify with the demoniac? Do I sometimes live in the tombs of self-destruction, negativity and self-criticism? What chains of addiction shackle me?
- I run to Jesus. I ask him to free me so that my true self may emerge. May I never forget I am the beloved of God!

Tuesday 4th February   **Mark 5:21, 25–34**

When Jesus had crossed again in the boat to the other side, a great crowd gathered around him; and he was by the sea. Now there was a woman who had been suffering from hemorrhages for twelve years. She had endured much under many physicians, and had spent all that she had; and she was no better, but rather grew worse. She had heard about Jesus, and came up behind him in the crowd and touched his cloak, for she said, "If I but touch his clothes, I will be made well." Immediately her hemorrhage stopped; and she felt in her body that she was healed of her disease. Immediately aware that power had gone forth from him, Jesus turned about in the crowd and said, "Who touched my clothes?" And his disciples said to him, "You see the crowd pressing in on you; how can you say, 'Who touched me?'" He looked all round to see who had done it. But the woman, knowing what had happened to her, came in fear and trembling, fell down before him, and told him the whole truth. He said to her, "Daughter, your faith has made you well; go in peace, and be healed of your disease."

- With daring and initiative the woman breaks through physical, social and religious boundaries to experience the power of Jesus' healing touch. Human suffering awakens Jesus' compassion. Crossing the barriers of his day, he talks to the woman.
- As I contemplate this scene, can I risk revealing to the Lord my deepest concerns for myself and others? Can I trust that he will intervene and act?

Wednesday 5th February   **Mark 6:1–6**

Jesus went on to his hometown, and his disciples followed him. On the sabbath he began to teach in the synagogue, and many who heard him were astounded. They said, "Where did this man get all this? What is this wisdom that has been given to him? What deeds of power are being done by his hands! Is not this the carpenter, the son of Mary and brother of James and Joses and Judas and Simon, and are not his sisters here with us?" And they took offence at him. Then Jesus said to them, "Prophets are not without honor, except in their hometown, and among their own kin, and in their own house." And he could do no deed of power there, except that he laid his hands on a few sick people and cured them. And he was amazed at their unbelief. Then he went about among the villages teaching.

- Small-minded folk are uncomfortable with greatness. They bring others down by latching onto the fact that they are different and therefore unwelcome. Do I ever diminish others, or am I open to their special gifts and talents?
- Notice that Jesus is puzzled and disappointed, as we would be. But he doesn't slam the door on his neighbors. He will try some other way to win their hearts.

Thursday 6th February   **1 Kings 2:1–4**

When David's time to die drew near, he charged his son Solomon, saying: "I am about to go the way of all the earth. Be strong, be courageous, and keep the charge of the

Lord your God, walking in his ways and keeping his statutes, his commandments, his ordinances, and his testimonies, as it is written in the law of Moses, so that you may prosper in all that you do and wherever you turn. Then the Lord will establish his word that he spoke concerning me: 'If your heirs take heed to their way, to walk before me in faithfulness with all their heart and with all their soul, there shall not fail you a successor on the throne of Israel.'"

- "Be strong, be courageous." Sooner or later we all face situations where we have to stand up for ourselves and what we believe in, without the help of parents, family or friends; where we are ready to be unloved, and to persevere in our beliefs.
- As Sam Johnson said: "Where courage is missing, no other virtue can survive except by accident."

Friday 7th February   Mark 6:22–27

When his daughter Herodias came in and danced, she pleased Herod and his guests; and the king said to the girl, "Ask me for whatever you wish, and I will give it." And he solemnly swore to her, "Whatever you ask me, I will give you, even half of my kingdom." She went out and said to her mother, "What should I ask for?" She replied, "The head of John the baptizer." Immediately she rushed back to the king and requested, "I want you to give me at once the head of John the Baptist on a platter." The king was deeply grieved; yet out of regard for his oaths and for the guests, he did not want to refuse her. Immediately the king sent a soldier of the guard with orders to bring John's head. He went and beheaded him in the prison.

- Herod was too concerned with the promise that he had made and his status in the eyes of his guests: he did not have the humility to back down. Sometimes I need to check that I am not simply being stubborn in persisting with what I have set my mind to.
- Herod was unable to listen to his heart: he let his heart be swayed by his pride. God speaks to me through my emotions, I take time to listen.

Saturday 8th February　　　　　　　　　　　**Mark 6:30–34**

The apostles gathered around Jesus, and told him all that they had done and taught. He said to them, "Come away to a deserted place all by yourselves and rest a while." For many were coming and going, and they had no leisure even to eat. And they went away in the boat to a deserted place by themselves. Now many saw them going and recognized them, and they hurried there on foot from all the towns and arrived ahead of them. As he went ashore, he saw a great crowd; and he had compassion for them, because they were like sheep without a shepherd; and he began to teach them many things.

- Jesus left the crowd behind him, although he was aware of their need. Despite all the demands on me, I allow myself to take this time with God, realising my need of peace and healing.
- Jesus asks me why I am afraid and shows me that there is nothing to fear if I have faith. I speak to Jesus, telling him of my life, asking him to draw me into his peace.

Sacred Space

Something to think and pray about each day this week:

Breaking through

Some years ago, a magic moment transformed the concourse of Antwerp Train Station. The travellers were all going their own way at the time, busy about their affairs. Suddenly a song from *The Sound of Music* fills the concourse. Actors in ordinary clothes begin to dance. The onlookers can't tell actors from spectators, so people stop what they're busy about and get in on the act themselves. Children start to dance, then adults too who have the hearts of children. People are drawn out of themselves by the fun of it all. Some hold their hands to their mouths in delighted awe, others begin to cry. Eventually the concourse is full of dancers. There's space for everyone, whether coordinated for dancing or not. Nobody's looking critically at how you perform your arthritic jig or that you wave your crutch. The outer circle is littered with bags and coats which people have shed in order to dance freely. Maybe the coat and the bag will be stolen, but who cares? Only a few onlookers hold back, but even they are intrigued, and others coax them in. Cameras flash so that this ecstatic moment can be recalled and passed on to friends. Laughter and tears of joy mingle with regret when the music ends.

Will God's springtime break in on our unsuspecting world somewhat like that, and happily last forever?

The Presence of God

I pause for a moment
and think of the love and the grace that God showers on me,
creating me in his image and likeness, making me his temple.

Freedom

Lord, grant me the grace to be free from the excesses of this
life.
Let me not get caught up with the desire for wealth.
Keep my heart and mind free to love and serve you.

Consciousness

In the presence of my loving Creator,
I look honestly at my feelings over the last day,
the highs, the lows and the level ground.
Can I see where the Lord has been present?

The Word

God speaks to each one of us individually. I need to listen to
what he is saying to me. (Please turn to your scripture on the
following pages. Inspiration points are there should you need
them. When you are ready, return here to continue.)

Conversation

Sometimes I wonder what I might say
if I were to meet You in person, Lord.
I might say 'Thank You, Lord' for always being there for me.
I know with certainty there were times when you carried me,
when through your strength I got through the dark times in
my life.

Conclusion

Glory be to the Father, and to the Son, and to the Holy Spirit,
As it was in the beginning, is now and ever shall be,
World without end. Amen

Sunday 9th February,
Fifth Sunday in Ordinary Time   Matthew 5:13–16

Jesus said to the crowds, "You are the salt of the earth; but if salt has lost its taste, how can its saltiness be restored? It is no longer good for anything, but is thrown out and trampled under foot. "You are the light of the world. A city built on a hill cannot be hidden. No one after lighting a lamp puts it under the bushel basket, but on the lampstand, and it gives light to all in the house. In the same way, let your light shine before others, so that they may see your good works and give glory to your Father in heaven."

- Jesus reminds me that faith is not a wet blanket on the joys of life but brings zest and spark. I ask Jesus to touch my imagination to show me how my faith can bring colour and life to me and to those around me.

- The salt under foot is wasted; the light under the tub puts itself out. I consider how I might better use my energies for the good of others and for the glory of God.

Monday 10th February   Mark 6:53–56

When Jesus and the disciples had crossed over, they came to land at Gennesaret and moored the boat. When they got out of the boat, people at once recognized him, and rushed about that whole region and began to bring the sick on mats to wherever they heard he was. And wherever he went, into villages or cities or farms, they laid the sick in the marketplaces, and begged him that they might touch even the fringe of his cloak; and all who touched it were healed.

- I imagine Jesus playing his part in rowing the boat, then mooring it. I watch as the word spreads that he has arrived. People rush about; they grab this chance to have their friends healed.

- Where am I in the scene? Am I helping others to reach him, or am I perhaps waiting for someone to bring me to Jesus? Can I let Jesus touch me?

Tuesday 11th February Mark 7:1–2, 5–8

Now when the Pharisees and some of the scribes who had come from Jerusalem gathered around him, they noticed that some of his disciples were eating with defiled hands, that is, without washing them. So the Pharisees and the scribes asked him, "Why do your disciples not live according to the tradition of the elders, but eat with defiled hands?" He said to them, "Isaiah prophesied rightly about you hypocrites, as it is written, 'This people honors me with their lips, but their hearts are far from me; in vain do they worship me, teaching human precepts as doctrines.' You abandon the commandment of God and hold to human tradition."

- It is good to have clean hands but what really matters is my heart. Is my heart far from God? Do I give more time to keeping a clean house than a clean heart?
- I pray for Church leaders. In these difficult times, they need a deep understanding of how God wants them to serve. May they not get lost in human traditions, but creatively reveal the compassionate face of God to the world.

Wednesday 12th February Mark 7:14–19a

Then Jesus called the crowd again and said to them, "Listen to me, all of you, and understand: there is nothing outside a person that by going in can defile, but the things that come out are what defile." When he had left the crowd and entered the house, his disciples asked him about the parable. He said to them, "Then do you also fail to understand? Do you not see that whatever goes into a person from outside cannot defile, since it enters, not the heart but the stomach, and goes out into the sewer?"

- I recognize that I am surrounded by so much that is good and I give thanks. I realize that good things sometimes distract me from the source of all goodness and I ask for forgiveness.
- I think of my words and actions and pray that what comes out of me brings goodness to others.

Thursday 13th February   Mark 7:24–30

From there Jesus set out and went away to the region of Tyre. He entered a house and did not want anyone to know he was there. Yet he could not escape notice, but a woman whose little daughter had an unclean spirit immediately heard about him, and she came and bowed down at his feet. Now the woman was a Gentile, of Syrophoenician origin. She begged him to cast the demon out of her daughter. He said to her, "Let the children be fed first, for it is not fair to take the children's food and throw it to the dogs." But she answered him, "Sir, even the dogs under the table eat the children's crumbs." Then he said to her, "For saying that, you may go—the demon has left your daughter." So she went home, found the child lying on the bed, and the demon gone.

- Jesus admired the woman's persistence in looking for a blessing for her daughter. I demonstrate my sincerity in prayer by my persistent trust in God.
- I pray for the humility I may need to change my mind when faced by another's need.

Friday 14th February   Mark 7:31–37

Then Jesus returned from the region of Tyre, and went by way of Sidon towards the Sea of Galilee, in the region of the Decapolis. They brought to him a deaf man who had an impediment in his speech; and they begged him to lay his hand on him. He took him aside in private, away from the crowd, and put his fingers into his ears, and he spat and touched his tongue. Then looking up to heaven, he sighed and said to him, "Ephphatha," that is, "Be opened." And immediately his ears were opened, his tongue was released, and he spoke plainly. Then Jesus ordered them to tell no one; but the more he ordered them, the more zealously they proclaimed it. They were astounded beyond measure, saying, "He has done everything well; he even makes the deaf to hear and the mute to speak."

- Jesus wants to take the man aside and asks him to keep his healing to himself. I pray for the wisdom that I may need to know when to speak and when to rest quietly with Jesus.

- The people around Jesus were able to recognize the good that he did. I ask God to strengthen me, to give me the courage to give good witness by how I live.

Saturday 15th February   Mark 8:1–10

In those days when there was again a great crowd without anything to eat, Jesus called his disciples and said to them, "I have compassion for the crowd, because they have been with me now for three days and have nothing to eat. If I send them away hungry to their homes, they will faint on the way—and some of them have come from a great distance." His disciples replied, "How can one feed these people with bread here in the desert?" He asked them, "How many loaves do you have?" They said, "Seven." Then he ordered the crowd to sit down on the ground; and he took the seven loaves, and after giving thanks he broke them and gave them to his disciples to distribute; and they distributed them to the crowd. They had also a few small fish; and after blessing them, he ordered that these too should be distributed. They ate and were filled; and they took up the broken pieces left over, seven baskets full.

- Lord, today let me see some of the miracles that surround me. So many good things happen to me that need not happen. I have food and drink, while others are "in the desert." Someone is good to me, someone smiles.
- I am also linked in with the *Sacred Space* community across the world. Others support me with their prayer, and I support them too. Thank you, Lord, for everything!

Something to think and pray about each day this week:

The pilgrim's way

Images of the life to come must be carefully presented. Older images of death, purgatory, hell and limbo, depicted God as a merciless judge who demands full payment for wrongdoing. How can we portray more accurately the truth of God's limitless love for us?

Newman reminds us that the human mind has to work with shadows and images until it finally emerges into the full light of truth. We now see only dimly as in a mirror. St Thomas Aquinas, who wrote a million words on things divine, said that we merely stammer in speaking of God. But while all images of God must fall short, they are all we have, so we must use them well.

Let us take heart from Vatican II's image of the pilgrim Church. Pilgrims use all available assistance to arrive at their destination. At crossroads they discuss the path that seems most promising. A French theologian uses the image of swimming: with each stroke you push a volume of water behind you as you move toward your objective. You move beyond it, but without that water you would never get there. Good images hint at the real thing: they orient us in the right direction. There is a Zen saying about a farmer pointing to the moon with a carrot. As we approach the world of divine mystery an amber light glows: it does not forbid entry but advises us to proceed with caution!

The Presence of God
'I stand at the door and knock,' says the Lord.
What a wonderful privilege
that the Lord of all creation desires to come to me.
I welcome His presence.

Freedom
Lord, grant me the grace to be free from the excesses of
this life.
Let me not get caught up with the desire for wealth.
Keep my heart and mind free to love and serve you.

Consciousness
'There is a time and place for everything,' as the saying goes.
Lord, grant that I may always desire
to spend time in your presence, to hear your call.

The Word
God speaks to each one of us individually. I need to listen to
what he is saying to me. (Please turn to your scripture on the
following pages. Inspiration points are there should you need
them. When you are ready, return here to continue.)

Conversation
The gift of speech is a wonderful gift.
May I use this gift with kindness.
May I be slow to utter harsh words,
hurtful words, and words spoken in anger.

Conclusion
Glory be to the Father, and to the Son, and to the Holy Spirit,
As it was in the beginning, is now and ever shall be,
World without end. Amen

Sunday 16th February,
Sixth Sunday in Ordinary Time   Matthew 5:17–20

Jesus said to the people, "Do not think that I have come to abolish the law or the prophets; I have come not to abolish but to fulfil. For truly I tell you, until heaven and earth pass away, not one letter, not one stroke of a letter, will pass from the law until all is accomplished. Therefore, whoever breaks one of the least of these commandments, and teaches others to do the same, will be called least in the kingdom of heaven; but whoever does them and teaches them will be called great in the kingdom of heaven."

- I think of all those who have taught me, calling to mind the people who have helped me to understand God's ways. I give thanks for them and ask God to bless them. I pray that I may be such a person for those around me.
- Jesus pointed to the continuity in God's work and action. I think of the traditions and teachings that have brought me to where I am and I ask God to continue to draw me to life.

Monday 17th February   Mark 8:11–13

The Pharisees came and began to argue with Jesus, asking him for a sign from heaven, to test him. And he sighed deeply in his spirit and said, "Why does this generation ask for a sign? Truly I tell you, no sign will be given to this generation." And he left them, and getting into the boat again, he went across to the other side.

- Prayer is a time of faith. Often we get no signs from God of the fruit of time spent with God. Feelings are not always high in prayer, but a grace of growth in faith and love is always given in prayer.
- Jesus is not always the man of big signs but is the one of constant and gentle love, given wholly in the sign of his death.

Tuesday 18th February   Mark 8:14–21

Now the disciples had forgotten to bring any bread; and they had only one loaf with them in the boat. And he cautioned them, saying, "Watch out—beware of the yeast of the Pharisees and the yeast of Herod." They said to one another, "It is because we have no bread." And becoming aware of it, Jesus said to them, "Why are you talking about having no bread? Do you still not perceive or understand?"

- They had no bread but what they forgot was that they had Jesus. Prayer is opening ourselves to the presence of Jesus in our time of prayer and in life.
- The centre of Christian life and Christian prayer is Jesus. The fruits of Christian prayer are to live like him. The basis of prayer is faith. Ask for an increase in faith, ask to live like him.

Wednesday 19th February   Mark 8:22–26

They came to Bethsaida. Some people brought a blind man to Jesus and begged him to touch him. He took the blind man by the hand and led him out of the village; and when he had put saliva on his eyes and laid his hands on him, he asked him, "Can you see anything?" And the man looked up and said, "I can see people, but they look like trees, walking." Then Jesus laid his hands on his eyes again; and he looked intently and his sight was restored, and he saw everything clearly. Then he sent him away to his home, saying, "Do not even go into the village."

- The man who had been blind came to healing gradually and with effort. I look to see how God works in me in this gradual way.
- Many people in the gospels are brought to Jesus by others. I bring those who are in need, looking out for the good of those around me.

Thursday 20th February   Mark 8:27–33

Jesus went on with his disciples to the villages of Caesarea Philippi; and on the way he asked his disciples, "Who do people say that I am?" And they answered him, "John the Baptist; and others, Elijah; and still others, one of the prophets." He asked them, "But who do you say that I am?" Peter answered him, "You are the Messiah." And he sternly ordered them not to tell anyone about him. Then he began to teach them that the Son of Man must undergo great suffering, and be rejected by the elders, the chief priests, and the scribes, and be killed, and after three days rise again. He said all this quite openly. And Peter took him aside and began to rebuke him. But turning and looking at his disciples, he rebuked Peter and said, "Get behind me, Satan! For you are setting your mind not on divine things but on human things."

- The disciples saw that Jesus was famous and could not see how that might end in suffering. Jesus quietly invites me to accompany him, to learn from him and to accept difficulties with him.
- Peter wanted to manage Jesus. Perhaps I, too, seek to limit Jesus in my life, preferring to direct him rather than follow him.

Friday 21st February   Mark 8:34–37

Jesus called the crowd with his disciples, and said to them, "If any want to become my followers, let them deny themselves and take up their cross and follow me. For those who want to save their life will lose it, and those who lose their life for my sake, and for the sake of the gospel, will save it. For what will it profit them to gain the whole world and forfeit their life? Indeed, what can they give in return for their life?"

- Following Jesus means making choices and choices mean that we leave some possibilities behind. As I deny myself, I ask Jesus to help me not to become regretful or nostalgic but to face the future confidently.
- Keeping all options open means choosing nothing. I cannot do that, but ask God's help to make good choices and to take the risks in faith that being a follower demands.

Saturday 22nd February,
Chair of St Peter, Apostle   Matthew 16:13–19

Now when Jesus came into the district of Caesarea Philippi, he asked his disciples, "Who do people say that the Son of Man is?" And they said, "Some say John the Baptist, but others Elijah, and still others Jeremiah or one of the prophets."

He said to them, "But who do you say that I am?" Simon Peter answered, "You are the Messiah, the Son of the living God." And Jesus answered him, "Blessed are you, Simon son of Jonah! For flesh and blood has not revealed this to you, but my Father in heaven. And I tell you, you are Peter, and on this rock I will build my church, and the gates of Hades will not prevail against it. I will give you the keys of the kingdom of heaven, and whatever you bind on earth will be bound in heaven, and whatever you loose on earth will be loosed in heaven."

- No longer would the law of the Jewish scriptures be the norm; the new community with its leader, Peter, could decide on what of the law could be retained and what could be loosened.
- The person of Jesus, not the law of the past, is to be the centre of the new community. The words of Jesus are important because they are the Word of God, Jesus Christ, present now in his new community.

Something to think and pray about each day this week:

Bound to God's community

In the days of the death squads in El Salvador and the Argentine, thousands of catechists disappeared. The Christians of these countries developed a dramatic way to celebrate their belief that their community was strong and survived death. During the liturgy, the list of the "disappeared" would be read out, and one by one someone would stand and say for the person named: "Presente!" Each "disappeared" had a unique name and dignity, and each had a voice still, through the mouths of their caring sisters and brothers. The congregation drew strength and courage from them to continue to build the kingdom of God despite the risk of torture and death.

Early Christians expressed their bondedness with Jesus and with one another in the word *koinonia*, which means fellowship and suggests respect, equality and inclusion. *Koinonia* describes the community established through the work of Jesus. Because the founding members are the Father, Son and Holy Spirit, this community will last eternally. Because it is open to every human being, it offers a vision of universal reconciliation. This community took visible form 2,000 years ago, in the shape of the Christian Church. It has had an extraordinary history, sometimes glorious, sometimes disgraceful. However imperfect it is, it is the divine solution, operative now in our world, to the hatreds that fragment human community when left to itself.

The Presence of God

'I stand at the door and knock,' says the Lord.
What a wonderful privilege
that the Lord of all creation desires to come to me.
I welcome His presence.

Freedom

Lord, grant me the grace to be free from the excesses
of this life.
Let me not get caught up with the desire for wealth.
Keep my heart and mind free to love and serve you.

Consciousness

'There is a time and place for everything,' as the saying goes.
Lord, grant that I may always desire
to spend time in your presence, to hear your call.

The Word

God speaks to each one of us individually. I need to listen to
what he is saying to me. (Please turn to your scripture on the
following pages. Inspiration points are there should you need
them. When you are ready, return here to continue.)

Conversation

The gift of speech is a wonderful gift.
May I use this gift with kindness.
May I be slow to utter harsh words,
hurtful words, and words spoken in anger.

Conclusion

Glory be to the Father, and to the Son, and to the Holy Spirit,
As it was in the beginning, is now and ever shall be,
World without end. Amen

Sunday 23rd February,
Seventh Sunday in Ordinary Time   Matthew 5:38–42

Jesus said, "You have heard that it was said, 'An eye for an eye and a tooth for a tooth.' But I say to you, Do not resist an evildoer. But if anyone strikes you on the right cheek, turn the other also; and if anyone wants to sue you and take your coat, give your cloak as well; and if anyone forces you to go one mile, go also the second mile. Give to everyone who begs from you, and do not refuse anyone who wants to borrow from you."

- Jesus calls us to look beyond the limit of the law. We need to be generous and imaginative if we are to rise beyond the restrictions that life presents.
- I think of how I might be free from the constraints I find by acting from a generous spirit. I ask God to inspire and help me.

Monday 24th February   Mark 9:17–24

Someone from the crowd answered Jesus, "Teacher, I brought you my son; he has a spirit that makes him unable to speak; and whenever it seizes him, it dashes him down; and he foams and grinds his teeth and becomes rigid; and I asked your disciples to cast it out, but they could not do so." Jesus said: "Bring him to me." And they brought the boy to him. When the spirit saw him, immediately it convulsed the boy, and he fell on the ground and rolled about, foaming at the mouth. Jesus asked the father, "How long has this been happening to him?" And he said, "From childhood. It has often cast him into the fire and into the water, to destroy him; but if you are able to do anything, have pity on us and help us." Jesus said to him, "If you are able! All things can be done for the one who believes." Immediately the father of the child cried out, "I believe; help my unbelief!"

- I may resist Jesus in small ways, preferring to allow comforts and habits to keep my world arranged as I like it.
- With the father in the gospel I say, "I believe; help my unbelief!"

Tuesday 25th February **Mark 9:30–37**

They went on from there and passed through Galilee. He did not want anyone to know it; for he was teaching his disciples, saying to them, "The Son of Man is to be betrayed into human hands, and they will kill him, and three days after being killed, he will rise again." But they did not understand what he was saying and were afraid to ask him. Then they came to Capernaum; and when he was in the house he asked them, "What were you arguing about on the way?" But they were silent, for on the way they had argued with one another who was the greatest. He sat down, called the twelve, and said to them, "Whoever wants to be first must be last of all and servant of all." Then he took a little child and put it among them; and taking it in his arms, he said to them, "Whoever welcomes one such child in my name welcomes me, and whoever welcomes me welcomes not me but the one who sent me."

- Maybe the disciples were afraid to ask Jesus because they didn't want to know anything more about a future which would involve death and resurrection. The trusting nature of a child may have been an invitation to them to trust in Jesus even though the future was unknown.
- In prayer we can ask for the gift of this sort of trust for our own future.

Wednesday 26th February **Mark 9:38–40**

John said to Jesus, "Teacher, we saw someone casting out demons in your name, and we tried to stop him, because he was not following us." But Jesus said, "Do not stop him; for no one who does a deed of power in my name will be able soon afterwards to speak evil of me. Whoever is not against us is for us."

- The disciples thought of distinction and difference; Jesus did not tolerate their narrow vision. I pray that I may recognize good in a generous and appreciative way.
- Jesus sees all who act in his name as having much in common. I join in prayer with all who invoke Jesus' name today.

Thursday 27th February   **Mark 9:41**

Jesus said to his disciples, "For truly I tell you, whoever gives you a cup of water to drink because you bear the name of Christ will by no means lose the reward."

- The simplest action done for Christ's sake contains great meaning. I offer God my actions of this day, praying that they establish God's reign among those I meet.
- I thank God for all who have welcomed me and shown me hospitality or care. I pray that I may be gracious enough to let people serve me.

Friday 28th February   **Mark 10:1–9**

Jesus left that place and went to the region of Judea and beyond the Jordan. And crowds again gathered around him; and, as was his custom, he again taught them. Some Pharisees came, and to test him they asked, "Is it lawful for a man to divorce his wife?" He answered them, "What did Moses command you?" They said, "Moses allowed a man to write a certificate of dismissal and to divorce her." But Jesus said to them, "Because of your hardness of heart he wrote this commandment for you. But from the beginning of creation, 'God made them male and female.' 'For this reason a man shall leave his father and mother and be joined to his wife, and the two shall become one flesh.' So they are no longer two, but one flesh. Therefore what God has joined together, let no one separate."

- The contentious questions in Jesus' time remain difficult questions today. My prayer may be a time to pray with gratitude for those who witness to love and to have deep compassion for all whose relationships and commitments have brought suffering.
- Jesus calls us back to the original vision that God has for creation. I hear God calling me to life and holding me in love.

Saturday 1st March   **Mark 10:13–16**

People were bringing little children to Jesus in order that he might touch them; and the disciples spoke sternly to them. But when Jesus saw this, he was indignant and said to them,

"Let the little children come to me; do not stop them; for it is to such as these that the kingdom of God belongs. Truly I tell you, whoever does not receive the kingdom of God as a little child will never enter it." And he took them up in his arms, laid his hands on them, and blessed them.

- The children were interrupting adult talk, and Jesus welcomed that. He saw what they needed: time and touch. In today's world, a man may be under suspicion if he takes children up in his arms, lays his hands on them, and blesses them.
- Lord, guide us gently towards your own tenderness, your sense of what children need.

Something to think and pray about each day this week:

The wonders of creation
I have a daughter who works with poor children after school. She is a teacher herself and is wise enough to know that there are many kinds of education.

She asked me if, together, we could show the children how to bake cookies and simple cakes. We set to work. The children rolled up their sleeves, washed their hands carefully and formed a queue to weigh flour, butter and sugar. Breaking eggs was such a serious business! Mathematics came alive as they added the correct amounts to the mixture. Aromas were discovered; vanilla was a revelation. The boys wanted to know how fast the mixer could go if really pushed to its limit. The mixture was carefully spooned into the baking tins and then placed in the ovens.

While cleaning up the children began to notice the sweet smell from the oven. They looked through the glass door and one child gasped in wonder: "Gawd! A messy mixture went in and cakes are coming out."

Next the decoration of the cakes! Coloured icing, silver balls and chocolate buttons were heaped on each cookie and cake. The children were so proud of their work as they headed home.

I ask: Is God a master chef who enjoys sharing the work of creation with us, so that no matter what messy mixture "goes in," something wonderful and unique "comes out"?

The Presence of God
What is present to me is what has a hold on my becoming.
I reflect on the presence of God always there in love,
amidst the many things that have a hold on me.
I pause and pray that I may let God
affect my becoming in this precise moment.

Freedom
'There are very few people
who realize what God would make of them
if they abandoned themselves into his hands,
and let themselves be formed by his grace' (St Ignatius).
I ask for the grace to trust myself totally to God's love.

Consciousness
In the presence of my loving Creator,
I look honestly at my feelings over the last day,
the highs, the lows and the level ground.
Can I see where the Lord has been present?

The Word
God speaks to each one of us individually. I need to listen to
what he is saying to me. (Please turn to your scripture on the
following pages. Inspiration points are there should you need
them. When you are ready, return here to continue.)

Conversation
What is stirring in me as I pray?
Am I consoled, troubled, left cold?
I imagine Jesus himself standing or sitting at my side,
and share my feelings with him.

Conclusion
Glory be to the Father, and to the Son, and to the Holy Spirit,
As it was in the beginning, is now and ever shall be,
World without end. Amen

88

Sunday 2nd March,
Eighth Sunday in Ordinary Time   Matthew 6:25, 28–34

Jesus said to his disciples, "I tell you, do not worry about your life, what you will eat or what you will drink, or about your body, what you will wear. Is not life more than food, and the body more than clothing? "Consider the lilies of the field, how they grow; they neither toil nor spin, yet I tell you, even Solomon in all his glory was not clothed like one of these. But if God so clothes the grass of the field, which is alive today and tomorrow is thrown into the oven, will he not much more clothe you—you of little faith? Therefore do not worry, saying, 'What will we eat?' or 'What will we drink?' or 'What will we wear?' For it is the Gentiles who strive for all these things; and indeed your heavenly Father knows that you need all these things. But strive first for the kingdom of God and his right-eousness, and all these things will be given to you as well. So do not worry about tomorrow, for tomorrow will bring worries of its own. Today's trouble is enough for today.

- Jesus shows us that worry undermines faith. I bring my worries before God. I ask for help to bring them into a truer perspective.
- As a consumer, I may allow my values to be set by others. I review my wants and desires and ask God's help to be happy with the good things that I enjoy, to resist being wistful about what I am told I lack.

Monday 3rd March   Mark 10:17–21

As he was setting out on a journey, a man ran up and knelt before him, and asked him, "Good Teacher, what must I do to inherit eternal life?" Jesus said to him, "Why do you call me good? No one is good but God alone. You know the commandments: 'You shall not murder; You shall not commit adultery; You shall not steal; You shall not bear false witness; You shall not defraud; Honor your father and mother.'" He said to him, "Teacher, I have kept all these since my youth." Jesus, looking at him, loved him and said, "You lack one thing; go, sell what you own, and give the money to the poor, and you will have treasure in heaven; then come, follow me."

- I consider this scene and wonder what it was that Jesus loved about the young man. I allow myself time to think about what he loves about me—and I don't move on until I do!
- Jesus may show me the one thing that is holding me back from freedom. I can walk away or I can ask for help to deal with it.

Tuesday 4th March   Mark 10:28–30

Peter began to say to him, "Look, we have left everything and followed you." Jesus said, "Truly I tell you, there is no one who has left house or brothers or sisters or mother or father or children or fields, for my sake and for the sake of the good news, who will not receive a hundredfold now in this age— houses, brothers and sisters, mothers and children, and fields, with persecutions—and in the age to come eternal life."

- Peter often reminds us of our human inclinations; here he is concerned about himself.
- Jesus reminds Peter that there is a reward for discipleship but there is also a cost. I ask God to help me to recognize both, to be strengthened by God's gifts to meet the challenges I face.

Wednesday 5th March,
Ash Wednesday   Matthew 6:1–6

"Beware of practising your piety before others in order to be seen by them; for then you have no reward from your Father in heaven. So whenever you give alms, do not sound a trumpet before you, as the hypocrites do in the synagogues and in the streets, so that they may be praised by others. Truly I tell you, they have received their reward. But when you give alms, do not let your left hand know what your right hand is doing, so that your alms may be done in secret; and your Father who sees in secret will reward you. And whenever you pray, do not be like the hypocrites; for they love to stand and pray in the synagogues and at the street corners, so that they may be seen by others. Truly I tell you, they have received their reward. But whenever you pray, go into your room and shut the door and pray to your Father who is in secret; and your Father who sees in secret will reward you."

- "Hypocrites" refers to actors who only play various roles. They may play at being compassionate but have no genuine concern. This form of behavior really angers you, Jesus.
- Father, you see into the secret chambers of my heart. May my Lenten practices of prayer, fasting and almsgiving be performed not for public display but cheerfully and discreetly. Purify my wayward motivations so that I can become more like you.

Thursday 6th March   Luke 9:22–25

Jesus said to his disciples, "The Son of Man must undergo great suffering, and be rejected by the elders, chief priests, and scribes, and be killed, and on the third day be raised." Then he said to them all, "If any want to become my followers, let them deny themselves and take up their cross daily and follow me. For those who want to save their life will lose it, and those who lose their life for my sake will save it. What does it profit them if they gain the whole world, but lose or forfeit themselves?"

- The gospel is unambiguous—suffering and self-displacement are the hallmarks of a disciple. Jesus goes the way of the cross. He does not hoard his life, even though living must have had a special quality for him.
- I am called not to hoard my life, but to live generously. Lord, help me to let go of self-seeking. May I learn to accept life in a loving spirit as you did. Only so will I be a source of good to others.

Friday 7th March   Matthew 9:14–15

Then the disciples of John came to him, saying, "Why do we and the Pharisees fast often, but your disciples do not fast?" And Jesus said to them, "The wedding guests cannot mourn as long as the bridegroom is with them, can they? The days will come when the bridegroom is taken away from them, and then they will fast."

- Jesus uses the notion of fasting to reveal that the God whom the Jews hunger for has arrived. Rejoicing, not mourning, should be our response to the presence of divine mercy revealed in Jesus.

- Lord, this Lent let me feast with gratitude for your merciful love, and let me fast from oppressive behavior towards those around me. May my prayer and my fasting reveal my hunger for you.

Saturday 8th March   Luke 5:27–32

After this he went out and saw a tax collector named Levi, sitting at the tax booth; and he said to him, "Follow me." And he got up, left everything, and followed him. Then Levi gave a great banquet for him in his house; and there was a large crowd of tax collectors and others sitting at the table with them. The Pharisees and their scribes were complaining to his disciples, saying, "Why do you eat and drink with tax collectors and sinners?" Jesus answered, "Those who are well have no need of a physician, but those who are sick; I have come to call not the righteous but sinners to repentance."

- Tax-collectors were the most despised of people. But Jesus challenges the prejudices of his day. He calls Levi (St Matthew) and awakens him to his human potential and dignity.
- Matthew leaves the money-table to sit with Jesus at the banqueting table of forgiveness. Mercy is at the heart of Jesus' mission.

Something to think and pray about each day this week:

The blessed ones

My son is almost forty. At fourteen he started to question his faith. He later read and travelled extensively, searching for answers.

Being kind and gentle, he finds it difficult to accept the existence of God in our painful world. He loves people, and I thank God that he accepts me as I am. He loves animals too: his favourite animal has always been the wolf.

Recently he asked me to send him a medal of St Francis. I asked no questions but assumed an animal was in trouble. When I went to buy the medal, the lady in the shop first directed me to the medals of the wrong St Francis, St Francis Xavier! We finally found the one I needed, and to my surprise it showed St Francis befriending a wolf!

The assistant suggested that I bring my purchase into the nearby church where a priest was hearing confessions. He would, she said, bless the medal for me. But I had not been in a confessional for a very long time and I hesitated. Would the medal be enough to justify my visit?

I entered the confessional and told my story to the priest. Patient and polite, he listened intently and respectfully. He did not look at me as if I were strange. Older person that I am, he was even older, and, as a kindly if slightly surprised father, he blessed me, my son and the medal.

The Presence of God

Jesus waits silent and unseen to come into my heart.
I will respond to His call.
He comes with His infinite power and love
May I be filled with joy in His presence.

Freedom

I ask for the grace
to let go of my own concerns
and be open to what God is asking of me,
to let myself be guided and formed by my loving Creator.

Consciousness

Knowing that God loves me unconditionally,
I can afford to be honest about how I am.
How has the last day been, and how do I feel now?
I share my feelings openly with the Lord.

The Word

I read the Word of God slowly, a few times over, and I listen
to what God is saying to me. (Please turn to your scripture on
the following pages. Inspiration points are there should you
need them. When you are ready, return here to continue.)

Conversation

Remembering that I am still in God's presence,
I imagine Jesus himself standing or sitting beside me,
and say whatever is on my mind, whatever is in my heart,
speaking as one friend to another.

Conclusion

Glory be to the Father, and to the Son, and to the Holy Spirit,
As it was in the beginning, is now and ever shall be,
World without end. Amen

Sunday 9th March,
First Sunday of Lent   Matthew 4:1–11

Then Jesus was led up by the Spirit into the wilderness to be tempted by the devil. He fasted forty days and forty nights, and afterwards he was famished. The tempter came and said to him, "If you are the Son of God, command these stones to become loaves of bread." But he answered, "It is written, 'One does not live by bread alone, but by every word that comes from the mouth of God.'" Then the devil took him to the holy city and placed him on the pinnacle of the temple, saying to him, "If you are the Son of God, throw yourself down; for it is written, 'He will command his angels concerning you,' and 'On their hands they will bear you up, so that you will not dash your foot against a stone.'" Jesus said to him, "Again it is written, 'Do not put the Lord your God to the test.'" Again, the devil took him to a very high mountain and showed him all the kingdoms of the world and their splendor; and he said to him, "All these I will give you, if you will fall down and worship me." Jesus said to him, "Away with you, Satan! for it is written, 'Worship the Lord your God, and serve only him.'"

- Being human, just as I am, Jesus was tempted by fame, honor and power. Living fully in God's presence, he resisted the temptations and drew life from the Word of God.
- I think of how I, in resisting temptations, can bring the Word of God to life and allow God's angels to wait on me.

Monday 10th March   Matthew 25:37–40

"The righteous will answer him, 'Lord, when was it that we saw you hungry and gave you food, or thirsty and gave you something to drink? And when was it that we saw you a stranger and welcomed you, or naked and gave you clothing? And when was it that we saw you sick or in prison and visited you?' And the king will answer them, 'Truly I tell you, just as you did it to one of the least of these who are members of my family, you did it to me.'"

- Lord, you call me to recognize you in all those who are in need. May my response be one of concrete and loving service.

- St Ignatius says: "Love manifests itself in deeds more than words." St John of the Cross tells us: "In the evening of life, we will be examined in love."

Tuesday 11th March   Matthew 6:7–15

Jesus said, "When you are praying, do not heap up empty phrases as the Gentiles do; for they think that they will be heard because of their many words. Do not be like them, for your Father knows what you need before you ask him. Pray then in this way: 'Our Father in heaven, hallowed be your name. Your kingdom come. Your will be done, on earth as it is in heaven. Give us this day our daily bread. And forgive us our debts, as we also have forgiven our debtors. And do not bring us to the time of trial, but rescue us from the evil one. For if you forgive others their trespasses, your heavenly Father will also forgive you; but if you do not forgive others, neither will your Father forgive your trespasses.'"

- Jesus calls his disciples to pray and teaches them how. Prayer, he says, is not a magic formula but a trusting relationship between God and myself.
- The Our Father invites me to simplicity and sincerity of heart. It has an attitude of complete dependency on God. Jesus says: "Your father knows what you need before you ask."

Wednesday 12th March   Luke 11:29–32

When the crowds were increasing, he began to say, "This generation is an evil generation; it asks for a sign, but no sign will be given to it except the sign of Jonah. For just as Jonah became a sign to the people of Nineveh, so the Son of Man will be to this generation. The queen of the South will rise at the judgment with the people of this generation and condemn them, because she came from the ends of the earth to listen to the wisdom of Solomon, and see, something greater than Solomon is here! The people of Nineveh will rise up at the judgment with this generation and condemn it, because they repented at the proclamation of Jonah, and see, something greater than Jonah is here!"

- "Something greater than Solomon." This is how the Son of God humbly describes himself to people who resist belief. He, the wisdom and compassion of God, is in their midst, but they are blinded by their own concerns and do not see him.
- Would I travel great distances to meet him, as the Queen of Sheba did to meet Solomon? Do I often travel the short distance from my busy life into the world of prayer?

Thursday 13th March — Matthew 7:7–12

Jesus said to the disciples, "Ask, and it will be given you; search, and you will find; knock, and the door will be opened for you. For everyone who asks receives, and everyone who searches finds, and for everyone who knocks, the door will be opened. Is there anyone among you who, if your child asks for bread, will give a stone? Or if the child asks for a fish, will give a snake? If you then, who are evil, know how to give good gifts to your children, how much more will your Father in heaven give good things to those who ask him! In everything do to others as you would have them do to you; for this is the law and the prophets."

- "Do to others as you would have them do to you." This is the Golden Rule. However, do we tend to follow another rule, the rule of tit for tat?
- As Christians we must instead try to take our cue from Jesus. His goodwill toward us is not conditioned by the way people respond to him. I must try to be like God in this.

Friday 14th March — Matthew 5:20–24

Jesus said to his disciples, "For I tell you, unless your righteousness exceeds that of the scribes and Pharisees, you will never enter the kingdom of heaven. You have heard that it was said to those of ancient times, 'You shall not murder'; and 'whoever murders shall be liable to judgment.' But I say to you that if you are angry with a brother or sister, you will be liable to judgment; and if you insult a brother or sister, you will be liable to the council; and if you say, 'You fool,' you will be liable to the hell of fire. So when you are offering your gift at the altar, if you remember that your brother or sister has something against you, leave your gift there before the altar and go; first be reconciled to your brother or sister, and then come and offer your gift."

- Jesus is suspicious of attitudes creating division or superiority. When I see people who are looked down on, I pray with compassion as I realize my own sinfulness; when I see division in the world, I consider that I am not always an instrument of harmony.
- Any distance I imagine between me and God arises from my hesitation. God waits for me to put any impediments aside, dreaming of closeness with me.

Saturday 15th March   Matthew 5:43–48

Jesus said to the disciples, "You have heard that it was said, 'You shall love your neighbor and hate your enemy.' But I say to you, Love your enemies and pray for those who persecute you, so that you may be children of your Father in heaven; for he makes his sun rise on the evil and on the good, and sends rain on the righteous and on the unrighteous. For if you love those who love you, what reward do you have? Do not even the tax collectors do the same? And if you greet only your brothers and sisters, what more are you doing than others? Do not even the Gentiles do the same? Be perfect, therefore, as your heavenly Father is perfect."

- Love of enemies is special to Christianity. It is the most difficult thing in the world, and only the example of Jesus in the Passion makes it possible for us. If we don't love our enemies we are not yet inside the Kingdom of God.
- God, your love is love of another kind to ours. You simply love everyone, good and bad. You love me that way too! Nothing I do would make you love me less. If I could believe that, I would have some hope of loving others in the same way.

Something to think and pray about each day this week:

The presence of God
Where do I see and recognize God's presence? Where do I see the imprint of God's hand?

God is present in the Oncology ward where I work. Patients arrive for treatment, tired and apprehensive. They are newly vulnerable, and their expensively acquired market skills are gone for now. Yet their eyes fill with tentative hope of the beginning of healing. This is a different place to any they have known.

With the help of a caring staff, they learn to relax in the presence of their fellow patients. They remove wigs, hairpieces and jewellery, and expose poor hurting bodies. For the time they are here, they allow themselves simply to be who they are. As the medicine enters their bodies, the feelings of trust, hope and love are tangible all around. No market place here—simply pure and humble dependence on God, on science, on the loving kindness of others.

The trappings of the commercial world are no help when people are at their most vulnerable. The patients need not camouflage their poverty in the ways of the world. But they can trust, simply trust that in the Oncology ward they are in our Father's house. There they are welcomed simply as they are. There they are in the hands of good people, escorts of healing and grace, whom God has sent to them. It is all right to be poor here.

The Presence of God
For a few moments, I think of God's veiled presence in things:
in the elements, giving them existence;
in plants, giving them life; in animals, giving them sensation;
and finally, in me, giving me all this and more,
making me a temple, a dwelling-place of the Spirit.

Freedom
God is not foreign to my freedom.
Instead the Spirit breathes life into my most intimate desires,
gently nudging me towards all that is good.
I ask for the grace to let myself be enfolded by the Spirit.

Consciousness
Knowing that God loves me unconditionally,
I can afford to be honest about how I am.
How has the last day been, and how do I feel now?
I share my feelings openly with the Lord.

The Word
The word of God comes to us through the scriptures.
May the Holy Spirit enlighten my mind and my heart to
respond to the gospel teachings. (Please turn to your scripture
on the following pages. Inspiration points are there should you
need them. When you are ready, return here to continue.)

Conversation
How has God's Word moved me? Has it left me cold?
Has it consoled me or moved me to act in a new way?
I imagine Jesus standing or sitting beside me,
I turn and share my feelings with him.

Conclusion
Glory be to the Father, and to the Son, and to the Holy Spirit,
As it was in the beginning, is now and ever shall be,
World without end. Amen

Sunday 16th March,
Second Sunday of Lent   Matthew 17:1–9

Six days later, Jesus took with him Peter and James and his brother John and led them up a high mountain, by themselves. And he was transfigured before them, and his face shone like the sun, and his clothes became dazzling white. Suddenly there appeared to them Moses and Elijah, talking with him. Then Peter said to Jesus, "Lord, it is good for us to be here; if you wish, I will make three dwellings here, one for you, one for Moses, and one for Elijah." While he was still speaking, suddenly a bright cloud overshadowed them, and from the cloud a voice said, "This is my Son, the Beloved; with him I am well pleased; listen to him!" When the disciples heard this, they fell to the ground and were overcome by fear. But Jesus came and touched them, saying, "Get up and do not be afraid." And when they looked up, they saw no one except Jesus himself alone. As they were coming down the mountain, Jesus ordered them, "Tell no one about the vision until after the Son of Man has been raised from the dead."

- Jesus did not want fear to cause the disciples to miss the meaning of God's message. The voice from the cloud had a simple message for Jesus and for us.

- Jesus saw that there was a time for silence and a time to speak. I ask God to help me to know which is appropriate, and when. I may draw strength from considering how I have been able to show restraint in the past.

Monday 17th March,
St Patrick   Luke 10:1–7

After this the Lord appointed seventy others and sent them on ahead of him in pairs to every town and place where he himself intended to go. He said to them, 'The harvest is plentiful, but the labourers are few; therefore ask the Lord of the harvest to send out labourers into his harvest. Go on your way. See, I am sending you out like lambs into the midst of wolves. Carry no purse, no bag, no sandals; and greet no one on the road. Whatever house you enter, first say, "Peace to this house!" And if anyone is there who shares in peace, your peace will rest on that person; but if not, it will return to you. Remain in the same house, eating and drinking whatever they provide, for the labourer deserves to be paid. Do not move about from house to house.'

- The disciples are sent, not to announce their own messages, to proclaim their insights or to tell how they see things; they go with a simple message of peace that is never lost.

- Jesus cautioned the seventy-two against being too selective and choosy; they should announce God's ways wherever they find themselves. I need not wait for a better time or more suitable conditions but think of how I might announce the gospel where I am.

Tuesday 18th March   Matthew 23:1–12

Then Jesus said to the crowds and to his disciples, "The scribes and the Pharisees sit on Moses' seat; therefore, do whatever they teach you and follow it; but do not do as they do, for they do not practice what they teach. They tie up heavy burdens, hard to bear, and lay them on the shoulders of others; but they themselves are unwilling to lift a finger to move them. They do all their deeds to be seen by others; for they make their phylacteries broad and their fringes long. They love to have the place of honor at banquets and the best seats in the synagogues, and to be greeted with respect in the marketplaces, and to have people call them rabbi. But you are not to be called rabbi, for you have one teacher, and you are all students. And call no one your father on earth, for you have one Father—the one in heaven. Nor are you to be called instructors, for you have one instructor, the Messiah. The greatest among you will be your servant. All who exalt themselves will be humbled, and all who humble themselves will be exalted."

- Jesus, you gave the religious leaders of your day a hard time. But how do you find me? Do I play games to make people think that I am important? How much do I value my public image? Do I misuse my authority?

- Help me instead to be a humble servant to the needy, just like you.

Wednesday 19th March,
St Joseph   Matthew 1:18–25

Now the birth of Jesus the Messiah took place in this way. When his mother Mary had been engaged to Joseph, but before they lived together, she was found to be with child from the Holy Spirit. Her husband Joseph, being a righteous man and unwilling to expose her to public disgrace, planned to dismiss her quietly. But just when he had resolved to do this, an angel of the Lord appeared to him in a dream and said, "Joseph, son of David, do not be afraid to take Mary as your wife, for the child conceived in her is from the Holy Spirit. She will bear a son, and you are to name him Jesus, for he will save his people from their sins." All this took place to fulfill what had been spoken by the Lord through the prophet: "Look, the virgin shall conceive and bear a son, and they shall name him Emmanuel," which means, "God is with us." When Joseph awoke from sleep, he did as the angel of the Lord commanded him; he took her as his wife, but had no marital relations with her until she had borne a son; and he named him Jesus.

- Saint Luke tells the story of Jesus from Mary's point of view. Saint Matthew tells it from Joseph's. He is shown as an ordinary good Jew, obedient to the Law. God intervenes and shatters his life-expectations. Joseph is called to a new level of obedience.
- Lord, am I open to letting you break in on my life? Do I listen to your dreams for me, which may help to change the world?

Thursday 20th March   Luke 16:19–31

Jesus said to the Pharisees, "There was a rich man who was dressed in purple and fine linen and who feasted sumptuously every day. And at his gate lay a poor man named Lazarus, covered with sores, who longed to satisfy his hunger with what fell from the rich man's table; even the dogs would come and lick his sores. The poor man died and was carried away by the angels to be with Abraham. The rich man also died and was buried. In Hades, where he was being tormented, he looked up and saw Abraham far away with Lazarus by his side. He called out, 'Father Abraham, have mercy on me, and send Lazarus to dip the tip of his finger in water and cool my tongue; for I am in agony in these flames.' But Abraham said, 'Child, remember that during your lifetime you received your good things, and Lazarus in like manner evil things; but now he is comforted here, and you are in agony. Besides all this, between you and us a great chasm has been fixed, so that those who might want to pass from here to you cannot do so, and no one can cross from there to us.' He said, 'Then, father, I beg you to send him to my father's house—for I have five brothers—that he may warn them, so that they will not also come into this place of torment.' Abraham replied, 'They have Moses and the prophets; they should listen to them.' He said, 'No, father Abraham; but if someone goes to them from the dead, they will repent.' He said to him, 'If they do not listen to Moses and the prophets, neither will they be convinced even if someone rises from the dead.'"

- Some people can enjoy the height of fashion. For them, life is a daily feast in well-defended mansions. In contrast the poor are clothed in running sores and lie among dogs. They are famished and weak, and are excluded from the good things of life.
- Both rich and poor die, but then their fortunes are reversed. Because God is pure compassion, the poor are brought straight into the kingdom of God, while the rich have to endure the pain of conversion. I ponder the mystery of God's providence.

Friday 21st March   Matthew 21:33–43

Jesus said, "Listen to another parable. There was a landowner who planted a vineyard, put a fence around it, dug a wine press in it, and built a watch-tower. Then he leased it to tenants and went to another country. When the harvest time had come, he sent his slaves to the tenants to collect his produce. But the tenants seized his slaves and beat one, killed another, and stoned another. Again he sent other slaves, more than the first; and they treated them in the same way. Finally he sent his son to them, saying, 'They will respect my son.' But when the tenants saw the son, they said to themselves, 'This is the heir; come, let us kill him and get his inheritance.' So they seized him, threw him out of the vineyard, and killed him. Now when the owner of the vineyard comes, what will he do to those tenants?" They said to him, "He will put those wretches to a miserable death, and lease the vineyard to other tenants who will give him the produce at the harvest time. Jesus said to them, "Have you never read in the scriptures: 'The stone that the builders rejected has become the cornerstone; this was the Lord's doing, and it is amazing in our eyes.' Therefore I tell you, the kingdom of God will be taken away from you and given to a people that produces the fruits of the kingdom."

- One of the saddest statements in the gospels is this innocent comment of the father: "They will respect my son."
- I am frightened to think what would happen if Jesus came into our world today. His message about the Kingdom of God would put him in direct opposition to so many other kingdoms. He would become an enemy to be got rid of.

Saturday 22nd March   Luke 15:25–32

Now his elder son was in the field; and when he came and approached the house, he heard music and dancing. He called one of the slaves and asked what was going on. He replied, "Your brother has come, and your father has killed the fatted calf, because he has got him back safe and sound." Then he became angry and refused to go in. His father came out and began to plead with him. But he answered his father, "Listen! For all these years I have been working like a slave for you, and I have never disobeyed your command; yet you have never given me even a young goat so that I might celebrate with my friends. But when this son of yours came back, who has devoured your property with prostitutes, you killed the fatted calf for him!" Then the father said to him, "Son, you are always with me, and all that is mine is yours. But we had to celebrate and rejoice, because this brother of yours was dead and has come to life; he was lost and has been found."

- The father loves both sons, the bad and also the angry one. He keeps calling them sons, even though they both make fools of him. Jesus is revealing in this story what his own father is like.
- May I believe that God's hand is always stretched out toward sinners, including myself. God never stops wishing me well. May I act a bit like the father toward those who cause me hurt and humiliation.

Something to think and pray about each day this week:

To follow Jesus

Jesus says: "Whoever serves me must follow me." What does that mean, "to follow"?

To follow someone, I must know them well and admire them. And I suppose I would need to believe that I would be welcome company for them. We might not always agree, but we would have standards in common. But the choice "to follow" is mine, and it arises every day. Sometimes I remember that I am meant to be following Jesus, and other times I forget. My dog and I have something in common. When we go out for a walk, he gets preoccupied with all sorts of things, and so do I. I can walk for miles with ideas in my head, but with no thought of "following Jesus." I can also stray from the path he takes.

Then there are times when I do want to follow him, but don't know what best to do. I see injustice in the organisation where I work. I wonder if I should say nothing lest I make things worse, or should I try to change things? Or should I simply walk away? In a dysfunctional relationship, should I stay on and fight, even if there seems to be no hope that it will mend?

I make my own the Serenity Prayer:

God grant me the serenity
to accept the things I cannot change;
courage to change the things I can;
and wisdom to know the difference.

The Presence of God
Dear Jesus, today I call on you in a special way.
Mostly I come asking for favors.
Today I'd like just to be in Your presence.
Let my heart respond to Your Love.

Freedom
'I am free.'
When I look at these words in writing
They seem to create in me a feeling of awe.
Yes, a wonderful feeling of freedom.
Thank You, God.

Consciousness
Lord, You gave me the night to rest in sleep.
In my waking hours may I not forget your goodness to me.
Guide me to share your blessings with others.

The Word
I read the Word of God slowly, a few times over, and I listen
to what God is saying to me. (Please turn to your scripture on
the following pages. Inspiration points are there should you
need them. When you are ready, return here to continue.)

Conversation
Dear Jesus, I can open up my heart to you.
I can tell you everything that troubles me.
I know You care about all the concerns in my life.
Teach me to live in the knowledge
that You who care for me today,
will care for me tomorrow and all the days of my life.

Conclusion
Glory be to the Father, and to the Son, and to the Holy Spirit,
As it was in the beginning, is now and ever shall be,
World without end. Amen

Sunday 23rd March,
Third Sunday of Lent

John 4:5–10

Jesus came to a Samaritan city called Sychar, near the plot of ground that Jacob had given to his son Joseph. Jacob's well was there, and Jesus, tired out by his journey, was sitting by the well. It was about noon. A Samaritan woman came to draw water, and Jesus said to her, "Give me a drink." (His disciples had gone to the city to buy food.) The Samaritan woman said to him, "How is it that you, a Jew, ask a drink of me, a woman of Samaria?" (Jews do not share things in common with Samaritans.) Jesus answered her, "If you knew the gift of God, and who it is that is saying to you, 'Give me a drink', you would have asked him, and he would have given you living water."

- Several times, the Samaritan woman seems to resist; perhaps she has developed a defensive self-protecting habit. I ask God to help me to be open to receive good news from any source through which God may send it to me.
- "If only you knew what God is offering." Jesus yearns for me to be aware of the goodness of God's generosity towards me. I pray that I may open my heart to express my need and humbly receive the blessings of God.

Monday 24th March

Luke 4:24–30

And he said, "Truly I tell you, no prophet is accepted in the prophet's hometown. But the truth is, there were many widows in Israel in the time of Elijah, when the heaven was shut up three years and six months, and there was a severe famine over all the land; yet Elijah was sent to none of them except to a widow at Zarephath in Sidon. There were also many lepers in Israel in the time of the prophet Elisha, and none of them was cleansed except Naaman the Syrian." When they heard this, all in the synagogue were filled with rage. They got up, drove him out of the town, and led him to the brow of the hill on which their town was built, so that they might hurl him off the cliff. But he passed through the midst of them and went on his way.

- Jesus, you experienced rejection from those close to you whom you were trying to help. Did you feel shocked, angry, unsure, depressed? How do I feel when others reject me? What did you do with your feelings?
- You went off to serve others, with the same risk of rejection again. Help me not to give in to despair when a relationship is difficult.

Tuesday 25th March,
Annunciation of the Lord   Luke 1:26–33

In the sixth month the angel Gabriel was sent by God to a town in Galilee called Nazareth, to a virgin whose name was Mary. And he came to her and said, "Greetings, favored one! The Lord is with you." But she was much perplexed by his words and pondered what sort of greeting this might be. The angel said to her, "Do not be afraid, Mary, for you have found favour with God. And now, you will conceive in your womb and bear a son, and you will name him Jesus. He will be great, and will be called the Son of the Most High, and the Lord God will give to him the throne of his ancestor David. He will reign over the house of Jacob forever, and of his kingdom there will be no end."

- The vast project of God for all of humankind is first revealed to a girl, in a small flimsy house, in an unknown town, on an uncertain date and hour. God has a sense of humour and smiles at what we think important. Let me savour this homely scene. Let me see things more and more as God sees them.
- God seems to like small things. We are surrounded by divine mystery everywhere. The dawn breaks, a bird sings, a baby cries; nature provides food and drink for us. Everything is strange and full of wonder. Lord, give me again the mind of a child to notice your presence and your action.

Wednesday 26th March   Matthew 5:17–19

Jesus said to his disciples, "Do not think that I have come to abolish the law or the prophets; I have come not to abolish but to fulfill. For truly I tell you, until heaven and earth pass away, not one letter, not one stroke of a letter, will pass from the law until all is accomplished. Therefore, whoever breaks one of the least of these commandments, and teaches others to do the same, will be called least in the kingdom of heaven; but whoever does them and teaches them will be called great in the kingdom of heaven."

- Jesus loves his Jewish religion. Also he understands the heart of it. He wants to fulfil it by loving his Father perfectly, and by loving all God's people, even as far as dying for them. I pray to be a good disciple by living like that.
- Have I grasped the heart of my religion? Do I concentrate on loving God and my neighbour? Is there more love in the world because of my being around? In the evening of life I will be examined in love, not in the outer aspects of religion!

Thursday 27th March   Luke 11:14–20

Jesus was casting out a demon that was mute; when the demon had gone out, the one who had been mute spoke, and the crowds were amazed. But some of them said, "He casts out demons by Beelzebul, the ruler of the demons." Others, to test him, kept demanding from him a sign from heaven. But he knew what they were thinking and said to them, "Every kingdom divided against itself becomes a desert, and house falls on house. If Satan also is divided against himself, how will his kingdom stand? —for you say that I cast out the demons by Beelzebul. Now if I cast out the demons by Beelzebul, by whom do your exorcists cast them out? Therefore they will be your judges. But if it is by the finger of God that I cast out the demons, then the kingdom of God has come to you.

- Satan means "adversary" and refers to all that stands against the goodness of God. I may live under a corrupt government, where bad legislation oppresses the innocent, and unfair taxes enrich the powerful.
- Single-handed I cannot change an institution but I may be called by God to protest against wrong-doing. I can also pray! And I can get the *Sacred Space* community to pray with me.

Friday 28th March   **Mark 12:28–34**

One of the scribes came near and heard them disputing with one another, and seeing that he answered them well, he asked him, "Which commandment is the first of all?" Jesus answered, "The first is, 'Hear, O Israel: the Lord our God, the Lord is one; you shall love the Lord your God with all your heart, and with all your soul, and with all your mind, and with all your strength.' The second is this, 'You shall love your neighbor as yourself.' There is no other commandment greater than these." Then the scribe said to him, "You are right, Teacher; you have truly said that 'he is one, and besides him there is no other'; and 'to love him with all the heart, and with all the understanding, and with all the strength,' and 'to love one's neighbor as oneself,'—this is much more important than all whole burnt offerings and sacrifices." When Jesus saw that he answered wisely, he said to him, "You are not far from the kingdom of God." After that no one dared to ask him any question.

- Lord, why should I love you with all my heart? Because if a group of good people set up a beautiful house and gardens for me to live in, I would love them. If they worked against all that might hurt me, I would love them. If one of them were to die a horrible death to save me from disaster, I would love them. If they promised me eternal joy, I would love them.

Saturday 29th March   **Luke 18:9–14**

He also told this parable to some who trusted in themselves that they were righteous and regarded others with contempt: "Two men went up to the temple to pray, one a Pharisee and the other a tax collector. The Pharisee, standing by himself, was praying thus, 'God, I thank you that I am not like other people: thieves, rogues, adulterers, or even like this tax collector. I fast twice a week; I give a tenth of all my income.' But the tax collector, standing far off, would not even look up to heaven, but was beating his breast and saying, 'God, be merciful to me, a sinner!' I tell you, this man went down to his home justified rather than the other; for all who exalt themselves will be humbled, but all who humble themselves will be exalted."

- The Pharisee and the tax collector spoke about themselves to God. Their attitudes to others were starkly in contrast. As I come to pray I must speak to God humbly about myself and reverently about my neighbours.
- We may find ourselves saying: "Thank God I am not like the Pharisee!" This is to miss the point completely. God in fact justifies the ungodly, and I am "ungodly" until God justifies me.

Sacred Space

Something to think and pray about each day this week:

Glimpsing God

My son suffers from an ongoing auto-immune disease. For the past year he has also suffered severe chronic pain, the result of a traffic accident. Suffering and pain are very much part of his life. This means that he cannot work much of the time. With a young family, one of whom is a disabled little girl, there are huge worries—finance, future health, the ability to keep his job. Yet somehow he is blessed with the ability to see the glass as half full, mostly.

His little girl goes to a mainstream school. Yesterday I got a text from him saying that a child in her class had invited her on a play date. The text said he was sitting, crying with joy, because she was being treated as a "normal" friend. He finished his message by saying "This is a good day!" The message left me in tears at his ability to see the good in small things, instead of bemoaning so much else. He searches for these glimmers of joy and hope—and he finds them. Thank God for this son of mine who teaches me so much.

I now thank God for small glimmers of hope and joy. God is always busy, trying to bring good out of what is not good. That's what the Passion and Resurrection must mean. Lord, open our eyes so that we can see this Kindly Mystery at work, right before our eyes.

The Presence of God

I pause for a moment
and think of the love and the grace that God showers on me,
creating me in his image and likeness, making me his temple.

Freedom

Everything has the potential to draw forth from me a fuller
love and life.
Yet my desires are often fixed, caught, on illusions of
fulfillment.
I ask that God, through my freedom, may orchestrate
my desires in a vibrant loving melody rich in harmony.

Consciousness

In the presence of my loving Creator,
I look honestly at my feelings over the last day,
the highs, the lows and the level ground.
Can I see where the Lord has been present?

The Word

God speaks to each one of us individually. I need to listen to
what he is saying to me. (Please turn to your scripture on the
following pages. Inspiration points are there should you need
them. When you are ready, return here to continue.)

Conversation

What feelings are rising in me
as I pray and reflect on God's Word?
I imagine Jesus himself sitting or standing beside me,
and open my heart to him.

Conclusion

Glory be to the Father, and to the Son, and to the Holy Spirit,
As it was in the beginning, is now and ever shall be,
World without end. Amen

Sunday 30th March,
Fourth Sunday of Lent   John 9:1, 6–9, 13–17, 34–38

As Jesus walked along, he saw a man blind from birth. His disciples asked him, "Rabbi, who sinned, this man or his parents, that he was born blind?" Jesus answered, "Neither this man nor his parents sinned; he was born blind so that God's works might be revealed in him. We must work the works of him who sent me while it is day; night is coming when no one can work. As long as I am in the world, I am the light of the world."

- The man's blindness is cured, but the blindness of those who won't believe in Jesus remains. I think of how I grope, stumble and am unsure of my direction unless I can rely on Jesus, the light of the world.

- The opening question of the disciples was, "Who is to blame?" Jesus reminds us that sometimes no one is to blame; he tells us to that even difficult situations present an opportunity for us to be drawn into God's presence.

Monday 31st March   John 4:47–50

Now there was a royal official whose son lay ill in Capernaum. When he heard that Jesus had come from Judea to Galilee, he went and begged him to come down and heal his son, for he was at the point of death. Then Jesus said to him, "Unless you see signs and wonders you will not believe." The official said to him, "Sir, come down before my little boy dies." Jesus said to him, "Go; your son will live." The man believed the word that Jesus spoke to him and started on his way.

- The royal official was familiar with courtly procedures; he was able to name his need and recognize the one who might grant it. I pray for the presence of mind to be able to identify my petitions and ask for the humility I need to be able to ask for help.

- Is there some part of my heart that is at the point of death? If so, Lord, show me what it is.

Tuesday 1st April   **John 5:2–9**

Now in Jerusalem by the Sheep Gate there is a pool, called in Hebrew Beth-zatha, which has five porticoes. In these lay many invalids—blind, lame, and paralyzed. One man was there who had been ill for thirty-eight years. When Jesus saw him lying there and knew that he had been there a long time, he said to him, "Do you want to be made well?" The sick man answered him, "Sir, I have no one to put me into the pool when the water is stirred up; and while I am making my way, someone else steps down ahead of me." Jesus said to him, "Stand up, take your mat and walk." At once the man was made well, and he took up his mat and began to walk.

- Many people reject God because the god they have learnt about is a tyrant who interferes with their freedom. But the good news is all about setting us free.
- This story illustrates that dramatically. When God touches our hearts, we become truly free. Then we can live by love and enjoy the fullness of life.

Wednesday 2nd April   **John 5:17–23**

Jesus said to the Jews, "My Father is still working, and I also am working." For this reason the Jews were seeking all the more to kill him, because he was not only breaking the sabbath, but was also calling God his own Father, thereby making himself equal to God. Jesus said to them, "Very truly, I tell you, the Son can do nothing on his own, but only what he sees the Father doing; for whatever the Father does, the Son does likewise. The Father loves the Son and shows him all that he himself is doing; and he will show him greater works than these, so that you will be astonished. Indeed, just as the Father raises the dead and gives them life, so also the Son gives life to whomsoever he wishes. The Father judges no one but has given all judgment to the Son, so that all may honor the Son just as they honor the Father. Anyone who does not honor the Son does not honor the Father who sent him."

- We tend to imagine that God has nothing to do all day! But here we are shown that the Father is working, and the Son is working in harmony with him. They are busy about the saving of the world. They know my particular needs and they work "to bring me from death to life."
- I take time to thank them.

Thursday 3rd April   John 5:39–47

Jesus said to the Jews "You search the scriptures because you think that in them you have eternal life; and it is they that testify on my behalf. Yet you refuse to come to me to have life. I do not accept glory from human beings. But I know that you do not have the love of God in you. I have come in my Father's name, and you do not accept me; if another comes in his own name, you will accept him. How can you believe when you accept glory from one another and do not seek the glory that comes from the one who alone is God? Do not think that I will accuse you before the Father; your accuser is Moses, on whom you have set your hope. If you believed Moses, you would believe me, for he wrote about me. But if you do not believe what he wrote, how will you believe what I say?"

- Jesus knows us through and through. He focuses on the potential in each of us. But that potential comes to fulfilment only when we get to know him.
- This is why our *Sacred Space* prayer time is so important. Jesus, help me to know you better, day by day.

Friday 4th April   John 7:1–2, 10, 25–30

Jesus went about in Galilee. He did not wish to go about in Judea because the Jews were looking for an opportunity to kill him. Now the Jewish festival of Booths was near. But after his brothers had gone to the festival, then he also went, not publicly but as it were in secret. Now some of the people of Jerusalem were saying, "Is not this the man whom they are trying to kill? And here he is, speaking openly, but they say nothing to him! Can it be that the authorities really know that this is the Messiah? Yet we know where this man is from; but when the Messiah comes, no one will know where he is from." Then Jesus cried out as he was teaching in the temple, "You know me, and you know where I am from. I have not come on my own. But the one who sent me is true, and you do not know him. I know him, because I am from him, and he sent me." Then they tried to arrest him, but no one laid hands on him, because his hour had not yet come.

- Jesus, you were a hunted man. Your enemies tried to catch sight of you to arrest you. May I seek to find you in prayer and life with as much energy as your enemies had.
- Jesus is always aware of his Father. He wants nothing else in life or death than to please God. I reflect on myself: do I consult God before making important decisions?

Saturday 5th April John 7:40–49

When they heard these words, some in the crowd said, "This is really the prophet." Others said, "This is the Messiah." But some asked, "Surely the Messiah does not come from Galilee, does he? Has not the scripture said that the Messiah is descended from David and comes from Bethlehem, the village where David lived?" So there was a division in the crowd because of him. Some of them wanted to arrest him, but no one laid hands on him. Then the temple police went back to the chief priests and Pharisees, who asked them, "Why did you not arrest him?" The police answered, "Never has anyone spoken like this!" Then the Pharisees replied, "Surely you have not been deceived too, have you? Has any one of the authorities or of the Pharisees believed in him? But this crowd, which does not know the law—they are accursed."

- "Never has anyone spoken like this!" Have I the same simple openness to Jesus as had the temple police and the crowd? Help me, Jesus, to treasure every word that you have spoken.
- When I end my time of prayer let me always carry away a word or phrase from you. It will nourish me for the rest of the day.

Something to think and pray about each day this week:

Our link with God

A physicist once gave me the beginner's version of electrons. He emphasized that reality as we know it is marvelously inter-connected. Electrons at either end of the universe vibrate in synchronicity with one another. "So true is this," he said, "that we can't understand anything by itself, but only in its connect-edness. Everything is somehow in touch with everything else. And everyone is linked with everyone else, past, present and future. This means that only when the last of us has been gathered in will we know the full story of the human race. So think of history as being a bit like a cosmic joke: while you're telling a joke, people are puzzled. They wonder how the story is going to work out. Only with the punch line do they get the point and laugh."

So with the human story: we must be patient. God indeed exists, but so also does dreadful evil. God works within what is bad to bring good out of it. We see this in the Passion with the eyes of faith. What was the worst of Fridays becomes "Good" Friday only because of the love involved. At the end we will see how love has transformed all the sorrow and pain and tragedy of our story. Only then will the laughter begin, laughter of the purest and most liberating kind. "Blessed are you who weep now, for you will laugh" (Luke 6:21).

The Presence of God
I reflect for a moment on God's presence around me and in me.
Creator of the universe, the sun and the moon, the earth,
every molecule, every atom, everything that is:
God is in every beat of my heart. God is with me, now.

Freedom
'A thick and shapeless tree-trunk would never believe
that it could become a statue, admired as a miracle of sculpture,
and would never submit itself to the chisel of the sculptor,
who sees by her genius what she can make of it' (St Ignatius).
I ask for the grace to let myself be shaped by my loving Creator.

Consciousness
Knowing that God loves me unconditionally,
I look honestly over the last day, its events and my feelings.
Do I have something to be grateful for? Then I give thanks.
Is there something I am sorry for? Then I ask forgiveness.

The Word
I read the Word of God slowly, a few times over, and I listen
to what God is saying to me. (Please turn to your scripture on
the following pages. Inspiration points are there should you
need them. When you are ready, return here to continue.)

Conversation
What is stirring in me as I pray?
Am I consoled, troubled, left cold?
I imagine Jesus himself standing or sitting at my side,
and share my feelings with him.

Conclusion
Glory be to the Father, and to the Son, and to the Holy Spirit,
As it was in the beginning, is now and ever shall be,
World without end. Amen

Sunday 6th April,
Fifth Sunday of Lent   John 11:38–44

Jesus, again greatly disturbed, came to the tomb. It was a cave, and a stone was lying against it. Jesus said, "Take away the stone." Martha, the sister of the dead man, said to him, "Lord, already there is a stench because he has been dead for four days." Jesus said to her, "Did I not tell you that if you believed, you would see the glory of God?" So they took away the stone. And Jesus looked upwards and said, "Father, I thank you for having heard me. I knew that you always hear me, but I have said this for the sake of the crowd standing here, so that they may believe that you sent me." When he had said this, he cried with a loud voice, "Lazarus, come out!" The dead man came out, his hands and feet bound with strips of cloth, and his face wrapped in a cloth. Jesus said to them, "Unbind him, and let him go."

• My habits and hesitations bind me up; premature conclusions and judgements seem to be the immovable stone that shuts me in. Jesus does not accept them as final, but wants me to be free, calling me to light and life.

• I am reminded of Jesus' humanity as John tells me that Jesus was greatly disturbed at Martha's distress. I pray with compassion for all who are bereaved and think of what I might do through my presence or prayer.

Monday 7th April   John 8:7–11

When they kept on questioning him, he straightened up and said to them, "Let anyone among you who is without sin be the first to throw a stone at her." And once again he bent down and wrote on the ground. When they heard it, they went away, one by one, beginning with the elders; and Jesus was left alone with the woman standing before him. Jesus straightened up and said to her, "Woman, where are they? Has no one condemned you?" She said, "No one, sir." And Jesus said, "Neither do I condemn you. Go your way, and from now on do not sin again."

• As the people reflected on their lives and realized their need for forgiveness, they turned and went away. As I reflect on my life and consider my need for forgiveness I realize that I need to draw closer to Jesus, who loves me.

- I hear the words of Jesus speaking to me—not condemning me, but giving me a new mission and a new vision of myself.

Tuesday 8th April   **John 8:21–27**

Again Jesus said to them, "I am going away, and you will search for me, but you will die in your sin. Where I am going, you cannot come." Then the Jews said, "Is he going to kill himself? Is that what he means by saying, 'Where I am going, you cannot come'?" He said to them, "You are from below, I am from above; you are of this world, I am not of this world. I told you that you would die in your sins, for you will die in your sins unless you believe that I am he." They said to him, "Who are you?" Jesus said to them, "Why do I speak to you at all? I have much to say about you and much to condemn; but the one who sent me is true, and I declare to the world what I have heard from him." They did not understand that he was speaking to them about the Father.

- The evangelist wants the early Christians to realize that Jesus is totally unique: he belongs to the world of the divine. He reveals the mystery of what God is like.
- When I knock on God's door, Jesus opens it and invites me in to meet his Father!

Wednesday 9th April   **John 8:31–42**

Then Jesus said to the Jews who had believed in him, "If you continue in my word, you are truly my disciples; and you will know the truth, and the truth will make you free." They answered him, "We are descendants of Abraham and have never been slaves to anyone. What do you mean by saying, 'You will be made free'?" Jesus answered them, "Very truly, I tell you, everyone who commits sin is a slave to sin. The slave does not have a permanent place in the household; the son has a place there forever. So if the Son makes you free, you will be free indeed. I know that you are descendants of Abraham; yet you look for an opportunity to kill me, because there is no place in you for my word. I declare what I have seen in the Father's presence; as for you, you should do what you have heard from the Father." They answered him, "Abraham is our father." Jesus said to them, "If you were Abraham's children, you would be doing what Abraham did, but now you are trying to kill me, a man who has told you the truth that I heard from God. This is not what Abraham did. You are indeed doing what your father does." They said to him, "We are not illegitimate children; we have one father, God himself." Jesus said to them, "If God were your Father, you would love me, for I came from God and now I am here. I did not come on my own, but he sent me."

- The truth will make me free! Lord, may I be faithful to my time of prayer. By meeting you there and pondering your word, may I become a freer person.
- Happy children feel at home in their parents' house. They can run around and play and make noise. Do I feel at home in God's house? Or am I rather like a servant or a visitor? Lord, may I remember that I have a place in your house, forever.

Thursday 10th April   John 8:51–56

Jesus said, "Very truly, I tell you, whoever keeps my word will never see death." The Jews said to him, "Now we know that you have a demon. Abraham died, and so did the prophets; yet you say, 'Whoever keeps my word will never taste death.' Are you greater than our father Abraham, who died? The prophets also died. Who do you claim to be?" Jesus answered, "If I glorify myself, my glory is nothing. It is my Father who glorifies me, he of whom you say, 'He is our God,' though you do not know him. But I know him; if I were to say that I do not know him, I would be a liar like you. But I do know him and I keep his word. Your ancestor Abraham rejoiced that he would see my day; he saw it and was glad."

- Again the evangelist portrays Jesus as belonging to a higher world than his hearers. Death is the human condition, but Jesus lives beyond the borders of death. He is simply different.
- In my prayer I need not try to puzzle these things out. Instead I simply accept in faith the wonderful mystery of Jesus.

Friday 11th April   **John 10:31–38**

The Jews took up stones again to stone him. Jesus replied, "I have shown you many good works from the Father. For which of these are you going to stone me?" The Jews answered, "It is not for a good work that we are going to stone you, but for blasphemy, because you, though only a human being, are making yourself God." Jesus answered, "Is it not written in your law, 'I said, you are gods'? If those to whom the word of God came were called 'gods'—and the scripture cannot be annulled—can you say that the one whom the Father has sanctified and sent into the world is blaspheming because I said, 'I am God's Son'? If I am not doing the works of my Father, then do not believe me. But if I do them, even though you do not believe me, believe the works, so that you may know and understand that the Father is in me and I am in the Father."

- Jesus, you try yet again to convince the Jews that you are God's Son. You appeal to the good works you have done, then to Scripture. But nothing helps.
- Do you sometimes have a hard time trying to break open my heart too? Help me!

Saturday 12th April   **John 11:45–48**

Many of the Jews therefore, who had come with Mary and had seen what Jesus did, believed in him. But some of them went to the Pharisees and told them what he had done. So the chief priests and the Pharisees called a meeting of the council, and said, "What are we to do? This man is performing many signs. If we let him go on like this, everyone will believe in him, and the Romans will come and destroy both our holy place and our nation."

- God's project is awesome. It is "to gather into one the dispersed children of God." I am only a small disciple of Jesus. But I have a particular role to play in God's project. I am to build up human community and healthy relationships. This is my task at home, in school, in the workplace, the parish, and the neighbourhood
- God will always be helping me to do this. When I meet God face to face at the end of my life, I will be thanked for what I tried to do to advance the Kingdom of God.

Something to think and pray about each day this week:

Giving thanks

I awoke to brilliant sunshine. Our resident robin was singing his heart out close to my window. I wandered into the front garden and spotted a large purple crocus, just ready to open. My attention was drawn to it. I got a little stool and sat down to watch . . . and watch . . . and watch. Slowly, ever so slowly, the top of the tightly closed petals started to open. Then, over a period of some hours it opened, displaying a glorious yellow center and stamen. The bright golden yellow glowed in the sunshine, against the deep shining purple of the petals.

In the late afternoon I sat again to watch the closing ceremony. Almost imperceptibly, the petals drew closer and closer until the golden center was wrapped in its purple cocoon once more. As I left I had an irresistible impulse to tiptoe away. I went inside and said to my Mother, "Do you know what I spent the day doing, Mum? I was watching a crocus opening and closing!" She looked at me, threw her eyes up to heaven, smiled indulgently and said nothing.

Although they happened many years ago, I still remember those hours and the peace that I experienced that day I say, once again, "Thank You, God!"

As I pray the Passion this week, may I realize that all this was done for me, in great love. In return, may I say, "Thank you, Jesus!"

The Presence of God
In the silence of my innermost being,
in the fragments of my yearned-for wholeness,
can I hear the whispers of God's presence?
Can I remember when I felt God's nearness?
Recall when we walked together and I let myself be embraced
by God's love.

Freedom
There are very few people
who realize what God would make of them
if they abandoned themselves into his hands,
and let themselves be formed by his grace. (St Ignatius)
I ask for the grace to trust myself totally to God's love.

Consciousness
How do I find myself today?
Where am I with God? With others?
Do I have something to be grateful for? Then I give thanks.
Is there something I am sorry for? Then I ask forgiveness.

The Word
I take my time to read the Word of God, slowly, a few times,
allowing myself to dwell on anything that strikes me. (Please
turn to your scripture on the following pages. Inspiration
points are there should you need them. When you are ready,
return here to continue.)

Conversation
Do I notice myself reacting as I pray with the Word of God?
Do I feel challenged, comforted, angry?
Imagining Jesus sitting or standing by me,
I speak out my feelings, as one trusted friend to another.

Conclusion
Glory be to the Father, and to the Son, and to the Holy Spirit,
As it was in the beginning, is now and ever shall be,
World without end. Amen

Sunday 13th April,
Palm Sunday of the Lord's Passion   Matthew 26:14–18

Then one of the twelve, who was called Judas Iscariot, went to the chief priests and said, "What will you give me if I betray him to you?" They paid him thirty pieces of silver. And from that moment he began to look for an opportunity to betray him. On the first day of Unleavened Bread the disciples came to Jesus, saying, "Where do you want us to make the preparations for you to eat the Passover?" He said, "Go into the city to a certain man, and say to him, 'The Teacher says, My time is near; I will keep the Passover at your house with my disciples.'"

- The disciples had come a long journey to bring them to this point. Now, the depth of their discipleship would be challenged. I consider the journey I have travelled to arrive, with Jesus at my side, at this Palm Sunday. I receive strength as Jesus shares himself with me, especially in the difficult moments.
- I think of the characters in the gospel story and see where I can recognize myself among them: some profess their faith; some do as they are asked; some do simply what others do; some disappear in the moment of crisis.

Monday 14th April   John 12:1–6

Six days before the Passover Jesus came to Bethany, the home of Lazarus, whom he had raised from the dead. There they gave a dinner for him. Martha served, and Lazarus was one of those at the table with him. Mary took a pound of costly perfume made of pure nard, anointed Jesus' feet, and wiped them with her hair. The house was filled with the fragrance of the perfume. But Judas Iscariot, one of his disciples (the one who was about to betray him), said, "Why was this perfume not sold for three hundred denarii and the money given to the poor?" (He said this not because he cared about the poor, but because he was a thief; he kept the common purse and used to steal what was put into it.)

- On a previous occasion when Jesus had dined with Lazarus, Martha had complained that Mary wasn't helping her. Jesus commended Mary for listening. The situation hasn't changed here. Martha is still serving while Mary makes a dramatic gesture of love. Jesus again commends her for loving.

- In my life there should be a time for activity and a time for silence. Achieving the balance isn't easy. But it is in the silence that we gain the wisdom and strength for the activity.

Tuesday 15th April   John 13:31–33, 36–38

When Judas had gone out, Jesus said, "Now the Son of Man has been glorified, and God has been glorified in him. If God has been glorified in him, God will also glorify him in himself and will glorify him at once. Little children, I am with you only a little longer. You will look for me; and as I said to the Jews so now I say to you, 'Where I am going, you cannot come.'" Simon Peter said to him, "Lord, where are you going?" Jesus answered, "Where I am going, you cannot follow me now; but you will follow afterwards." Peter said to him, "Lord, why can I not follow you now? I will lay down my life for you." Jesus answered, "Will you lay down your life for me? Very truly, I tell you, before the cock crows, you will have denied me three times."

- Jesus calls the adults around him "little children." Even though he knew that all except John would desert him, they were still his "little children."
- What does it mean to be a "little child" of Jesus?

Wednesday 16th April   Matthew 26:14–19

Then one of the twelve, who was called Judas Iscariot, went to the chief priests and said, "What will you give me if I betray him to you?" They paid him thirty pieces of silver. And from that moment he began to look for an opportunity to betray him. On the first day of Unleavened Bread the disciples came to Jesus, saying, "Where do you want us to make the preparations for you to eat the Passover?" He said, "Go into the city to a certain man, and say to him, 'The Teacher says, My time is near; I will keep the Passover at your house with my disciples.'" So the disciples did as Jesus had directed them, and they prepared the Passover meal.

- We tend to think of Jesus' friends as only those who are named in the gospels or who travel with him. But he had many other friends, like the unnamed man who made him so welcome for the Passover Feast.
- The same is true today. Jesus has many unlikely friends in many unlikely places. We in the *Sacred Space* community are among them.

Thursday 17th April,
Holy Thursday   John 13:2–15

During supper Jesus, knowing that the Father had given all things into his hands, and that he had come from God and was going to God, got up from the table, took off his outer robe, and tied a towel around himself. Then he poured water into a basin and began to wash the disciples' feet and to wipe them with the towel that was tied around him. He came to Simon Peter, who said to him, "Lord, are you going to wash my feet?" Jesus answered, "You do not know now what I am doing, but later you will understand." Peter said to him, "You will never wash my feet." Jesus answered, "Unless I wash you, you have no share with me." Simon Peter said to him, "Lord, not my feet only but also my hands and my head!" Jesus said to him, "One who has bathed does not need to wash, except for the feet, but is entirely clean. And you are clean, though not all of you." For he knew who was to betray him; for this reason he said, "Not all of you are clean." After Jesus had washed their feet, had put on his robe, and had returned to the table, he said to them, "Do you know what I have done to you? You call me Teacher and Lord—and you are right, for that is what I am. So if I, your Lord and Teacher, have washed your feet, you also ought to wash one another's feet. For I have set you an example, that you also should do as I have done to you."

- The evangelist is awestruck at what Jesus did in washing the disciples' feet. It was the job of a slave.
- Jesus washes Judas' feet. Knowing that Judas is shortly going to betray him, Jesus still washes his feet. After that, is there anyone whom I can justifiably not love, or serve?

Friday 18th April,
Good Friday   John 19:16–24

So they took Jesus; and carrying the cross by himself, he went out to what is called The Place of the Skull, which in Hebrew is called Golgotha. There they crucified him, and with him two others, one on either side, with Jesus between them. Pilate also had an inscription written and put on the cross. It read, "Jesus of Nazareth, the King of the Jews." Many of the Jews read this inscription, because the place where Jesus was crucified was near the city; and it was written in Hebrew, in Latin, and in Greek. Then the chief priests of the Jews said to Pilate, "Do not write, 'The King of the Jews', but, 'This man said, I am King of the Jews.'" Pilate answered, "What I have written I have written." When the soldiers had crucified Jesus, they took his clothes and divided them into four parts, one for each soldier. They also took his tunic; now the tunic was seamless, woven in one piece from the top. So they said to one another, "Let us not tear it, but cast lots for it to see who will get it." This was to fulfil what the scripture says, "They divided my clothes among themselves, and for my clothing they cast lots." And that is what the soldiers did.

- They took Jesus. He carried his own cross. They crucified him. Such sparse language to tell a horrendous story. The pain and suffering behind these words is unimaginable. So is the love which makes him do it.
- He has given all. He is dying on the cross naked, bereft of his beauty and his dignity. He has one beloved gift left, and he gives that also. His mother. And John "took her into his own home." Let me do that.

Saturday 19th April,
Holy Saturday   Matthew 27:57–66

When it was evening, there came a rich man from Arimathea, named Joseph, who was also a disciple of Jesus. He went to Pilate and asked for the body of Jesus; then Pilate ordered it to be given to him. So Joseph took the body and wrapped it in a clean linen cloth and laid it in his own new tomb, which he had hewn in the rock. He then rolled a great stone to the door of the tomb and went away. Mary Magdalene and the other Mary were there, sitting opposite the tomb. The next day, that is, after the day of Preparation, the chief priests and the Pharisees gathered before Pilate and said, "Sir, we remember what that impostor said while he was still alive, 'After three days I will rise again.' Therefore command that the tomb be made secure until the third day; otherwise his disciples may go and steal him away, and tell the people, 'He has been raised from the dead', and the last deception would be worse than the first." Pilate said to them, "You have a guard of soldiers; go, make it as secure as you can." So they went with the guard and made the tomb secure by sealing the stone.

- The women did not leave the dead body to itself. They waited to see what would happen to it. It must have been a huge relief to them when Joseph came and laid the body of Jesus in his own tomb. Now they could go home—they knew where to come in the morning to anoint it.
- The religious leaders knew Jesus' prophecy about himself—that he would rise again on the third day. They also knew what it meant. But they were not prepared to accept it. Am I?

Sacred Space

Something to think and pray about each day this week:

Jesus lives

"On the third day he rose again." Such is the bald statement in the Creeds. But why does this give hope that you and I and all of us will, like Jesus, be brought after death into eternal life?

Let us admit that we are totally out of our depth in talking about the resurrection of Jesus, because it was a divine initiative. The best place to start is from God's viewpoint. God's question was: "How can we get across to the disciples that divine love conquers even death, and that Jesus will bring people through death into eternal life and joy?"

The disciples had seen that Jesus had brought several people back to life—the widow's son, Jairus' daughter and Lazarus. This gave them some hope about death. But now Jesus himself was dead. Death seemed to have conquered him. To be brought to believe that in his dying Jesus had overcome our death, the disciples would need a great deal of convincing.

So the divine Persons decide that the risen Jesus—the same, yet different—will encounter the shocked and hopeless disciples. He will meet them in their ordinary lives and gently draw the veil. Slowly they will recognize him. They will realize that he is alive, that he has come back to them, to bring them—and you and me—into the divine dimension of reality where he himself is.

The Presence of God
God is with me, but more,
God is within me, giving me existence.
Let me dwell for a moment on God's life-giving presence
in my body, my mind, my heart
and in the whole of my life.

Freedom
Many countries are at this moment suffering
the agonies of war.
I bow my head in thanksgiving for my freedom.
I pray for all prisoners and captives.

Consciousness
I remind myself that I am in the presence of the Lord.
I will take refuge in His loving heart.
He is my strength in times of weakness.
He is my comforter in times of sorrow.

The Word
I read the Word of God slowly, a few times over, and I listen
to what God is saying to me. (Please turn to your scripture on
the following pages. Inspiration points are there should you
need them. When you are ready, return here to continue.)

Conversation
How has God's Word moved me? Has it left me cold?
Has it consoled me or moved me to act in a new way?
I imagine Jesus standing or sitting beside me,
I turn and share my feelings with him.

Conclusion
Glory be to the Father, and to the Son, and to the Holy Spirit,
As it was in the beginning, is now and ever shall be,
World without end. Amen

Sunday 20th April,
Easter Sunday John 20:1–9

Early on the first day of the week, while it was still dark, Mary Magdalene came to the tomb and saw that the stone had been removed from the tomb. So she ran and went to Simon Peter and the other disciple, the one whom Jesus loved, and said to them, "They have taken the Lord out of the tomb, and we do not know where they have laid him." Then Peter and the other disciple set out and went toward the tomb. The two were running together, but the other disciple outran Peter and reached the tomb first. He bent down to look in and saw the linen wrappings lying there, but he did not go in. Then Simon Peter came, following him, and went into the tomb. He saw the linen wrappings lying there, and the cloth that had been on Jesus' head, not lying with the linen wrappings but rolled up in a place by itself. Then the other disciple, who reached the tomb first, also went in, and he saw and believed; for as yet they did not understand the scripture, that he must rise from the dead.

- Mary was first to announce the resurrection, the first to receive the encouragement and hope that the risen Jesus offers. I take some time with Mary asking her to guide me. I pray that I may notice and take heart as I see signs of resurrection in my life.
- Even at this marvellous moment, those who had been closest to Jesus did not understand the scriptures. I ask God to help me this Easter; that I may recognize the call to new life in myself.

Monday 21st April Matthew 28:8–10

So the women left the tomb quickly with fear and great joy, and ran to tell his disciples. Suddenly Jesus met them and said, "Greetings!" And they came to him, took hold of his feet, and worshiped him. Then Jesus said to them, "Do not be afraid; go and tell my brothers to go to Galilee; there they will see me."

- The women ran "with fear and great joy." They had just seen an angel who told them that Jesus was alive. What a jumble of emotions filled them: fear at being deceived and joy in belief. Have I ever felt like that?

- Jesus' words are reassuring: "Do not be afraid." They would have heard him say those words many times during his ministry. "Here I am. It is true. Go tell!"

Tuesday 22nd April   John 20:11–18

But Mary stood weeping outside the tomb. As she wept, she bent over to look into the tomb; and she saw two angels in white, sitting where the body of Jesus had been lying, one at the head and the other at the feet. They said to her, "Woman, why are you weeping?" She said to them, "They have taken away my Lord, and I do not know where they have laid him." When she had said this, she turned around and saw Jesus standing there, but she did not know that it was Jesus. Jesus said to her, "Woman, why are you weeping? Whom are you looking for?" Supposing him to be the gardener, she said to him, "Sir, if you have carried him away, tell me where you have laid him, and I will take him away." Jesus said to her, "Mary!" She turned and said to him in Hebrew, "Rabbouni!" (which means Teacher). Jesus said to her, "Do not hold on to me, because I have not yet ascended to the Father. But go to my brothers and say to them, 'I am ascending to my Father and your Father, to my God and your God.'" Mary Magdalene went and announced to the disciples, "I have seen the Lord"; and she told them that he had said these things to her.

- Mary is crying so much that she cannot see who the man is. She is not listening, so she does not recognize his voice. It is only when he says her name that she finally hears, sees, and believes. What in me can block out Jesus' voice?
- Jesus is anxious to send word to those disciples who had deserted him. He wants them to know that they are still his brothers and sisters, that his Father is still their Father, that they are forgiven.

Wednesday 23rd April   Luke 24:25–35

Then Jesus said to the two disciples, "Oh, how foolish you are, and how slow of heart to believe all that the prophets have declared! Was it not necessary that the Messiah should suffer these things and then enter into his glory?" Then beginning with Moses and all the prophets, he interpreted to them the things about himself in all the scriptures. As they came near the village to which they were going, he walked ahead as if he were going on. But they urged him strongly, saying, "Stay with us, because it is almost evening and the day is now nearly over." So he went in to stay with them. When he was at the table with the disciples, he took bread, blessed and broke it, and gave it to them. Then their eyes were opened, and they recognized him; and he vanished from their sight. They said to each other, "Were not our hearts burning within us while he was talking to us on the road, while he was opening the scriptures to us?" That same hour they got up and returned to Jerusalem; and they found the eleven and their companions gathered together. They were saying, "The Lord has risen indeed, and he has appeared to Simon!" Then they told what had happened on the road, and how he had been made known to them in the breaking of the bread.

- The Emmaus scene throws light on what goes on in the Eucharist. After feasting on the Word, we celebrate a sacred meal with God. Jesus gives us, not simply ordinary bread, but his very self.
- Deep down in that mysterious place we call the heart, we are nourished, given food for the journey of life. Our God is a self-giving God! All we need is to be empty and hungry enough to receive God.

Thursday 24th April   **Luke 24:35–40**

Then the disciples told what had happened on the road, and how he had been made known to them in the breaking of the bread. While they were talking about this, Jesus himself stood among them and said to them, "Peace be with you." They were startled and terrified, and thought that they were seeing a ghost. He said to them, "Why are you frightened, and why do doubts arise in your hearts? Look at my hands and my feet; see that it is I myself. Touch me and see; for a ghost does not have flesh and bones as you see that I have." And when he had said this, he showed them his hands and his feet.

- Some early Christians were tempted to think that the first disciples had only seen a ghost.
- I too can doubt the reality of the risen Jesus. Do I only believe in the Jesus whom I see on the Cross? I ask for faith to believe that Jesus is truly risen and that now he is always present.

Friday 25th April   John 21:1–7

After these things Jesus showed himself again to the disciples by the Sea of Tiberias; and he showed himself in this way. Gathered there together were Simon Peter, Thomas called the Twin, Nathanael of Cana in Galilee, the sons of Zebedee, and two others of his disciples. Simon Peter said to them, "I am going fishing." They said to him, "We will go with you." They went out and got into the boat, but that night they caught nothing. Just after daybreak, Jesus stood on the beach; but the disciples did not know that it was Jesus. Jesus said to them, "Children, you have no fish, have you?" They answered him, "No." He said to them, "Cast the net to the right side of the boat, and you will find some." So they cast it, and now they were not able to haul it in because there were so many fish. That disciple whom Jesus loved said to Peter, "It is the Lord!"

- Am I like the disciples? They had seen the risen Lord, spoken with him, been missioned by him. They should be energetic about their new task. Yet here they are, going fishing!
- Do I live out my days as if life were just ordinary and humdrum? As if the resurrection had not occurred? But the Holy Spirit is commissioning me too to spread the Good News! Nothing can be "ordinary" any more.

Saturday 26th April   Mark 16:9–15

Now after he rose early on the first day of the week, he appeared first to Mary Magdalene, from whom he had cast out seven demons. She went out and told those who had been with him, while they were mourning and weeping. But when they heard that he was alive and had been seen by her, they would not believe it. After this he appeared in another form to two of them, as they were walking into the country. And they went back and told the rest, but they did not believe them. Later he appeared to the eleven themselves as they were sitting at the table; and he upbraided them for their lack of faith and stubbornness, because they had not believed those who saw him after he had risen. And he said to them, "Go into all the world and proclaim the good news to the whole creation."

- A woman is the first witness to Jesus' resurrection. This was no accident! Yet in our world women are still often relegated to second place.
- But God intends otherwise, as Jesus shows. Lord, what can I do to advance the full participation of women in the Christian assembly?

Sacred Space

Something to think and pray about each day this week:

Meeting the risen Jesus

The evidence for Jesus' resurrection can neither be proved nor disproved scientifically, but the disciples were so transformed by it that they gave their lives to share the good news of it with an incredulous world.

The change in the disciples from cowardice to commitment is impossible to discredit from a historical standpoint. While they did not fully understand their own message—it was too profound for them—they believed, because they had met him, that their Master was indeed risen, and risen for them and for all of us. Conviction grew as they preached. Read the *Acts of the Apostles* from this point of view. Amazing things happened. People listened and were converted. True community got under way. The sick were healed; prison doors opened. Their worst enemy, Saul, was won over. Joy, hope and energy flowed wherever people believed the good news.

The history of Christianity is sometimes wonderful, and at other times appalling. The graced side shows that for those who truly accept that Jesus is risen, everything is changed and made new. Life takes on vivid colors, and everything becomes important, especially persons. Why are we important? Because the good news is that all of us are children of the resurrection, and must treat each other as such. Our DNA is divine!

The Presence of God

To be present is to arrive as one is and open up to the other.
At this instant, as I arrive here, God is present waiting for me.
God always arrives before me, desiring to connect with me
even more than my most intimate friend.
I take a moment and greet my loving God.

Freedom

"In these days, God taught me
as a schoolteacher teaches a pupil" (St Ignatius).
I remind myself that there are things God has to teach me yet,
and ask for the grace to hear them and let them change me.

Consciousness

How am I really feeling? Light-hearted? Heavy-hearted?
I may be very much at peace, happy to be here.
Equally, I may be frustrated, worried or angry.
I acknowledge how I really am. It is the real me that the
Lord loves.

The Word

I take my time to read the Word of God, slowly, a few times,
allowing myself to dwell on anything that strikes me. (Please
turn to your scripture on the following pages. Inspiration
points are there should you need them. When you are ready,
return here to continue.)

Conversation

What feelings are rising in me
as I pray and reflect on God's Word?
I imagine Jesus himself sitting or standing beside me,
and open my heart to him.

Conclusion

Glory be to the Father, and to the Son, and to the Holy Spirit,
As it was in the beginning, is now and ever shall be,
World without end. Amen

Sunday 27th April,
Second Sunday of Easter   **John 20:19–21**

When it was evening on that day, the first day of the week, and the doors of the house where the disciples had met were locked for fear of the Jews, Jesus came and stood among them and said, "Peace be with you." After he said this, he showed them his hands and his side. Then the disciples rejoiced when they saw the Lord. Jesus said to them again, "Peace be with you. As the Father has sent me, so I send you."

- Jesus repeats his greeting, "Peace be with you." As Jesus wishes the same blessing for me I consider what might come between me and the blessing Jesus offers.
- Fear caused the disciples to lock the doors. This security did not, however, bring them peace. Closing people out leads them to be seen as a threat and seems at odds with Jesus' way.

Monday 28th April   **John 3:1–8**

Now there was a Pharisee named Nicodemus, a leader of the Jews. He came to Jesus by night and said to him, "Rabbi, we know that you are a teacher who has come from God; for no one can do these signs that you do apart from the presence of God." Jesus answered him, "Very truly, I tell you, no one can see the kingdom of God without being born from above." Nicodemus said to him, "How can anyone be born after having grown old? Can one enter a second time into the mother's womb and be born?" Jesus answered, "Very truly, I tell you, no one can enter the kingdom of God without being born of water and Spirit. What is born of the flesh is flesh, and what is born of the Spirit is spirit. Do not be astonished that I said to you, 'You must be born from above.' The wind blows where it chooses, and you hear the sound of it, but you do not know where it comes from or where it goes. So it is with everyone who is born of the Spirit."

- Night-time can be a good time to pray. The busy world is quieter then and I am less likely to be disturbed. The night carries its own rich mystery too, which helps me to compose myself within the mystery of God.

- Monks pray in the night all their lives: can I do so for at least a few minutes before retiring?

Tuesday 29th April   John 3:7–15

Jesus said to Nicodemus, "Do not be astonished that I said to you, 'You must be born from above.' The wind blows where it chooses, and you hear the sound of it, but you do not know where it comes from or where it goes. So it is with everyone who is born of the Spirit." Nicodemus said to him, "How can these things be?" Jesus answered him, "Are you a teacher of Israel, and yet you do not understand these things? Very truly, I tell you, we speak of what we know and testify to what we have seen; yet you do not receive our testimony. If I have told you about earthly things and you do not believe, how can you believe if I tell you about heavenly things? No one has ascended into heaven except the one who descended from heaven, the Son of Man. And just as Moses lifted up the serpent in the wilderness, so must the Son of Man be lifted up, that whoever believes in him may have eternal life."

- Jesus talks about "heavenly things" but we spend most of our lives talking about "earthly things." Lord, keep me faithful to my daily prayer time so that you and I may chat about the divine dimension which pervades all earthly things.
- There is a divine dimension to each person. There is a depth in our hearts where God dwells. It is our most sacred space. God works there, deeper down than psychology can reach.

Wednesday 30th April   John 3:16–21

Jesus said, "For God so loved the world that he gave his only Son, so that everyone who believes in him may not perish but may have eternal life. Indeed, God did not send the Son into the world to condemn the world, but in order that the world might be saved through him. Those who believe in him are not condemned; but those who do not believe are condemned already, because they have not believed in the name of the only Son of God. And this is the judgment, that the light has come into the world, and people loved darkness rather than light because their deeds were evil. For all who do evil hate the light and do not come to the light, so that their deeds may not be exposed. But those who do what is true come to the light, so that it may be clearly seen that their deeds have been done in God."

- It has been said that if all the Gospels were lost except the first verse in this passage, we would have enough to survive. "God so loved the world that he gave his only Son!" This is the heart of the good news, and I must be eternally grateful for it.

Thursday 1st May   John 3:31–36

John the Baptist said to his disciples, "The one who comes from above is above all; the one who is of the earth belongs to the earth and speaks about earthly things. The one who comes from heaven is above all. He testifies to what he has seen and heard, yet no one accepts his testimony. Whoever has accepted his testimony has certified this, that God is true. He whom God has sent speaks the words of God, for he gives the Spirit without measure. The Father loves the Son and has placed all things in his hands. Whoever believes in the Son has eternal life; whoever disobeys the Son will not see life, but must endure God's wrath."

- Some people spend most of their lives trying to trace a relative. Why? Because we live by our relationships. They determine our quality of life. Deeper than all human relations is our relationship with God. It is right to give it as much time as we can.
- The time we give to prayer always bears fruit, even when it is dry and distracted. In prayer we are exposed to God, who heals and strengthens us.

Friday 2nd May   John 6:1–14

After this Jesus went to the other side of the Sea of Galilee, also called the Sea of Tiberias. A large crowd kept following him, because they saw the signs that he was doing for the sick. Jesus went up the mountain and sat down there with his disciples. Now the Passover, the festival of the Jews, was near. When he looked up and saw a large crowd coming toward him, Jesus said to Philip, "Where are we to buy bread for these people to eat?" He said this to test him, for he himself knew what he was going to do. Philip answered him, "Six months' wages would not buy enough bread for each of them to get a little." One of his disciples, Andrew, Simon Peter's brother, said to him, "There is a boy here who has five barley loaves and two fish. But what are they among so many people?" Jesus said, "Make the people sit down." Now there was a great deal of grass in the place; so they sat down, about five thousand in all. Then Jesus took the loaves, and when he had given thanks, he distributed them to those who were seated; so also the fish, as much as they wanted. When they were satisfied, he told his disciples, "Gather up the fragments left over, so that nothing may be lost." So they gathered them up, and from the fragments of the five barley loaves, left by those who had eaten, they filled twelve baskets. When the people saw the sign that he had done, they began to say, "This is indeed the prophet who is to come into the world."

- Where do I place myself in this wonderful scene? In the crowd? With Philip and Andrew? With the boy who risks letting his lunch go? Do I offer what little I have? Do I hold out empty hands for bread and fish?
- Do I help tidy up? Do I catch on to what has happened? Do I go with Jesus as he escapes "into the mountain"?

Saturday 3rd May,
Ss Philip and James, Apostles   John 14:8–14

Philip said to Jesus, "Lord, show us the Father, and we will be satisfied." Jesus said to him, "Have I been with you all this time, Philip, and you still do not know me? Whoever has seen me has seen the Father. How can you say, 'Show us the Father'? Do you not believe that I am in the Father and the Father is in me? The words that I say to you I do not speak on my own; but the Father who dwells in me does his works. Believe me that

I am in the Father and the Father is in me; but if you do not, then believe me because of the works themselves. Very truly, I tell you, the one who believes in me will also do the works that I do and, in fact, will do greater works than these, because I am going to the Father. I will do whatever you ask in my name, so that the Father may be glorified in the Son. If in my name you ask me for anything, I will do it."

- Philip is captivated by Jesus. But now he starts to wonder what the Father is like. We too can think that the Father must be very different from the Son. But in fact the Son is the presence of the Father in visible form.
- People say, "Nobody knows what God is like." This was true before Jesus came, but now we can know! God is like Jesus, totally on our side. God, like Jesus, loves us limitlessly. We need not fear God, because God is purest love towards us.

Sacred Space

Something to think and pray about each day this week:

Love in full flower

Gardens grow beautifully in summer! The closed buds of autumn and the wilderness of the winter give way to nourishment and flowering. The beauty about a summer garden may remind us, perhaps, of other gardens—Eden, the place of peace, where God walked in the evening with friends, and where humans and animals dwelt in harmony. All was well there, for a while. But in that garden, somehow, man and woman said "No!" to the invitation to be in truth the images of God.

Another garden was the place of conflict, where Jesus struggled while his friends slept. In the Gethsemane garden was love, love given in suffering for others, given in doing what was right in the name of God. And in the faint full moon was the shout of Jesus, "Let this cup pass from me. But if not, all is well." All will indeed be well when we try to live in love for God. And all manner of things shall be well. It is to this that the mystery of prayer leads.

The Easter garden follows. There all is complete, and the mature roots of love come to full flower.

The Presence of God

What is present to me is what has a hold on my becoming.
I reflect on the presence of God always there in love,
amidst the many things that have a hold on me.
I pause and pray that I may let God
affect my becoming in this precise moment.

Freedom

If God were trying to tell me something, would I know?
If God were reassuring me or challenging me, would I notice?
I ask for the grace to be free of my own preoccupations
and open to what God may be saying to me.

Consciousness

Knowing that God loves me unconditionally,
I can afford to be honest about how I am.
How has the last day been, and how do I feel now?
I share my feelings openly with the Lord.

The Word

God speaks to each one of us individually. I need to listen to
what he is saying to me. (Please turn to your scripture on the
following pages. Inspiration points are there should you need
them. When you are ready, return here to continue.)

Conversation

What is stirring in me as I pray?
Am I consoled, troubled, left cold?
I imagine Jesus himself standing or sitting at my side,
and share my feelings with him.

Conclusion

Glory be to the Father, and to the Son, and to the Holy Spirit,
As it was in the beginning, is now and ever shall be,
World without end. Amen

Sunday 4th May,
Third Sunday of Easter   Luke 24:13–27

Now on that same day two of them were going to a village called Emmaus, about seven miles from Jerusalem, and talking with each other about all these things that had happened. While they were talking and discussing, Jesus himself came near and went with them, but their eyes were kept from recognizing him. And he said to them, "What are you discussing with each other while you walk along?" They stood still, looking sad. Then one of them, whose name was Cleopas, answered him, "Are you the only stranger in Jerusalem who does not know the things that have taken place there in these days?" He asked them, "What things?" They replied, "The things about Jesus of Nazareth, who was a prophet mighty in deed and word before God and all the people, and how our chief priests and leaders handed him over to be condemned to death and crucified him. But we had hoped that he was the one to redeem Israel. Yes, and besides all this, it is now the third day since these things took place. Moreover, some women of our group astounded us. They were at the tomb early this morning, and when they did not find his body there, they came back and told us that they had indeed seen a vision of angels who said that he was alive. Some of those who were with us went to the tomb and found it just as the women had said; but they did not see him." Then he said to them, "Oh, how foolish you are, and how slow of heart to believe all that the prophets have declared! Was it not necessary that the Messiah should suffer these things and then enter into his glory?" Then beginning with Moses and all the prophets, he interpreted to them the things about himself in all the scriptures.

- The disciples on the road were talking about what had happened yet were without insight. They were downbeat, dejected, walking away. When they fell in step with Jesus they found they had a listener who brought them to hear their narrative differently.
- Jesus helped the disciples to see the pattern of his life. How has my life been conformed to the shape of Jesus life?

Monday 5th May   **John 6:22–27**

The next day the crowd that had stayed on the other side of the lake saw that there had been only one boat there. They also saw that Jesus had not got into the boat with his disciples, but that his disciples had gone away alone. Then some boats from Tiberias came near the place where they had eaten the bread after the Lord had given thanks. So when the crowd saw that neither Jesus nor his disciples were there, they themselves got into the boats and went to Capernaum looking for Jesus. When they found him on the other side of the lake, they said to him, "Rabbi, when did you come here?" Jesus answered them, "Very truly, I tell you, you are looking for me, not because you saw signs, but because you ate your fill of the loaves. Do not work for the food that perishes, but for the food that endures for eternal life, which the Son of Man will give you."

- The crowds search energetically for Jesus, rowing right across the lake in search of him. At last they find him and are content.
- Jesus, inflame my heart with a strong desire to keep in touch with you. In searching for you I find happiness.

Tuesday 6th May   **John 6:30–35**

So they said to him, "What sign are you going to give us then, so that we may see it and believe you? What work are you performing? Our ancestors ate the manna in the wilderness; as it is written, 'He gave them bread from heaven to eat.'" Then Jesus said to them, "Very truly, I tell you, it was not Moses who gave you the bread from heaven, but it is my Father who gives you the true bread from heaven. For the bread of God is that which comes down from heaven and gives life to the world." They said to him, "Sir, give us this bread always." Jesus said to them, "I am the bread of life. Whoever comes to me will never be hungry, and whoever believes in me will never be thirsty."

- Many people today are searching for God. They need signs to know where God is. Am I such a sign in any way?
- When Jesus explains the Scriptures he opens up a new horizon to us. Jesus himself is the sign we need, and he is close. He feeds me with his own life. Do I nourish others?

Wednesday 7th May   John 6:35–40

J esus said to them, "I am the bread of life. Whoever comes to me will never be hungry, and whoever believes in me will never be thirsty. But I said to you that you have seen me and yet do not believe. Everything that the Father gives me will come to me, and anyone who comes to me I will never drive away; for I have come down from heaven, not to do my own will, but the will of him who sent me. And this is the will of him who sent me, that I should lose nothing of all that he has given me, but raise it up on the last day. This is indeed the will of my Father, that all who see the Son and believe in him may have eternal life; and I will raise them up on the last day."

- I ask Jesus to help me to be as he was: not self-serving on some personal project, but doing the will of God.
- It may be that in my prayer I recognize what is enduring, what is at the heart of life. I may glimpse what it means to live in eternal life, seeing my experience of God's Spirit as the inheritance I am promised.

Thursday 8th May   John 6:44–47

J esus said to the people: "No one can come to me unless drawn by the Father who sent me; and I will raise that person up on the last day. It is written in the prophets: 'They will all be taught by God'; everyone who has listened to the Father and learned from him comes to me. Not that anyone has seen the Father except the one who is from God; he has seen the Father. Very truly, I tell you, whoever believes has eternal life."

- When you feel drawn to something good, it is God who is drawing you. The drawing may be felt as a tug on the heart, or as a good idea. Perhaps it is a kind word that gives courage.
- God draws me to what is true, to what is life-giving, to what is loving. I am being drawn all the time, and so is everyone else. This is how God works in our world.

Friday 9th May   **John 6:52–59**

The Jews then disputed among themselves, saying, "How can this man give us his flesh to eat?" So Jesus said to them, "Very truly, I tell you, unless you eat the flesh of the Son of Man and drink his blood, you have no life in you. Those who eat my flesh and drink my blood have eternal life, and I will raise them up on the last day; for my flesh is true food and my blood is true drink. Those who eat my flesh and drink my blood abide in me, and I in them. Just as the living Father sent me, and I live because of the Father, so whoever eats me will live because of me."

- People in love live out of their relationship. What keeps Jesus going is his relationship with his Father. What will keep me going is my relationship with Jesus.
- Every time I pray, I meet Jesus, and the bonds between us grow stronger, even though nothing much seems to happen on the outside.

Saturday 10th May   **John 6:66–69**

Because of his teaching many of his disciples turned back and no longer went about with him. So Jesus asked the twelve, "Do you also wish to go away?" Simon Peter answered him, "Lord, to whom can we go? You have the words of eternal life. We have come to believe and know that you are the Holy One of God."

- Peter finds that Jesus' words are "words of eternal life." What does this mean? A new and better world is opening up for him, the world of God. He is beginning to see things as Jesus sees them. He is learning to love people as Jesus loves them.
- What is happening for me?

Something to think and pray about each day this week:

At the heart

A Jewish boy, the only son of his devout parents, was a most biddable child, with one exception: he resisted learning the Torah. To his parents, nothing could have been more distressing.

The Chief Rabbi was to visit their Synagogue. They decided to ask him to visit their home also. He did, and after the meal the parents expressed to him their concern about their son.

The Rabbi asked permission to place his arms around the boy. The parents agreed, moving aside. They watched and waited, expecting to hear some word of advice from the Rabbi to the boy. But the only word they heard was silence as they watched their son rest close to the Rabbi's heart.

The next day the boy began to study the Torah. His passion for God's word grew. Years later he himself became a wise and loving Rabbi. Many asked him whence his knowledge came. He simply said, "I put my ear close to the Chief Rabbi's heart and in that moment I heard the heartbeat of God."

In the Gospel of John the beloved disciple has his ear on Jesus' heart. It is a privileged place. But I too am a beloved disciple, so I can do likewise. Only in silence can I hear the Lord's heartbeat.

The Presence of God
At any time of the day or night we can call on Jesus.
He is always waiting, listening for our call.
What a wonderful blessing.
No phone needed, no emails, just a whisper.

Freedom
I need to rise above the noise;
the noise that interrupts, that separates,
the noise that isolates.
I need to listen to God again.

Consciousness
Help me, Lord, to be more conscious of your presence.
Teach me to recognize your presence in others.
Fill my heart with gratitude for the times your love
has been shown to me through the care of others.

The Word
I read the Word of God slowly, a few times over, and I listen
to what God is saying to me. (Please turn to your scripture on
the following pages. Inspiration points are there should you
need them. When you are ready, return here to continue.)

Conversation
Do I notice myself reacting as I pray with the Word of God?
Do I feel challenged, comforted, angry?
Imagining Jesus sitting or standing by me,
I speak out my feelings, as one trusted friend to another.

Conclusion
Glory be to the Father, and to the Son, and to the Holy Spirit,
As it was in the beginning, is now and ever shall be,
World without end. Amen

Sunday 11th May,
Fourth Sunday of Easter   John 10:1–6

Jesus said to the people, "Very truly, I tell you, anyone who does not enter the sheepfold by the gate but climbs in by another way is a thief and a bandit. The one who enters by the gate is the shepherd of the sheep. The gatekeeper opens the gate for him, and the sheep hear his voice. He calls his own sheep by name and leads them out. When he has brought out all his own, he goes ahead of them, and the sheep follow him because they know his voice. They will not follow a stranger, but they will run from him because they do not know the voice of strangers." Jesus used this figure of speech with them, but they did not understand what he was saying to them.

- It is sometimes suggested that the image of sheep is a negative one, unworthy of human dignity. Especially now, in my time of prayer, I ask God to help me leave aside cynicism or flattery and receive only the word that is for my good.
- Though modern life places great emphasis on individual choice, there are many forces driving us all in the same direction. I pray that I may trust where God is leading me.

Monday 12th May   John 10:7–10

So Jesus again said to the Pharisees, "Very truly, I tell you, I am the gate for the sheep. All who came before me are thieves and bandits; but the sheep did not listen to them. I am the gate. Whoever enters by me will be saved, and will come in and go out and find pasture. The thief comes only to steal and kill and destroy. I came that they may have life, and have it abundantly."

- Thieves and bandits bring distractions and disturbances. Jesus wants us not just to be free of these but he promises us life to the full. I take care not to let my energy be dissipated by attention to what is not life-giving, but ask Jesus to lead me to abundant life.

Tuesday 13th May   **John 10:22–30**

At that time the festival of the Dedication took place in Jerusalem. It was winter, and Jesus was walking in the temple, in the portico of Solomon. So the Jews gathered around him and said to him, "How long will you keep us in suspense? If you are the Messiah, tell us plainly." Jesus answered, "I have told you, and you do not believe. The works that I do in my Father's name testify to me; but you do not believe, because you do not belong to my sheep. My sheep hear my voice. I know them, and they follow me. I give them eternal life, and they will never perish. No one will snatch them out of my hand. What my Father has given me is greater than all else, and no one can snatch it out of the Father's hand. The Father and I are one."

- The Temple was of key importance to the Jews. They cherished it and died for it. They restored it when it was desecrated.
- Jesus is the new Temple—God's presence among them. But the Jews will reject him. Why? Has God come too close? Lord, may I put you firmly at the heart of my life and believe that in meeting you I am meeting God.

Wednesday 14th May,
St Matthias, Apostle   **John 15:9–14**

Jesus said to his disciples, "As the Father has loved me, so I have loved you; abide in my love. If you keep my commandments, you will abide in my love, just as I have kept my Father's commandments and abide in his love. I have said these things to you so that my joy may be in you, and that your joy may be complete. This is my commandment, that you love one another as I have loved you. No one has greater love than this, to lay down one's life for one's friends. You are my friends if you do what I command you."

- "Nothing is more practical than finding God, that is, than falling in love in a quite absolute, final way. What you are in love with, what seizes your imagination, will affect everything. It will decide what will get you out of bed in the mornings, what you will do with your evenings, how you spend your weekends, what you read, who you know, what breaks your heart, and what amazes you with joy and gratitude. Fall in love, stay in love, and it will decide everything." (Pedro Arrupe SJ)

- Allow yourself to fall in love with God today.

Thursday 15th May   John 13:16–17

Jesus said to them, "Very truly, I tell you, servants are not greater than their master, nor are messengers greater than the one who sent them. If you know these things, you are blessed if you do them."

- I consider what it means to be servant or messenger. I am known, chosen, trusted and sent.
- Other disciples may outgrow their masters, but the disciples of Jesus do not. He is, after all, the Son of God!

Friday 16th May   John 14:1–6

Jesus said to his disciples, "Do not let your hearts be troubled. Believe in God, believe also in me. In my Father's house there are many dwelling places. If it were not so, would I have told you that I go to prepare a place for you? And if I go and prepare a place for you, I will come again and will take you to myself, so that where I am, there you may be also. And you know the way to the place where I am going." Thomas said to him, "Lord, we do not know where you are going. How can we know the way?" Jesus said to him, "I am the way, and the truth, and the life. No one comes to the Father except through me.

- Jesus knows we do experience many heartaches. He sympathizes with us. He says, "Do not let your hearts be troubled." He never abandons us. We are destined for a blessed future, because he will come again and take us to himself.
- Lord, I often wonder what way to go in life. May I always turn to you for guidance, and whatever way I choose, may I try to live out of your commandment to love.

Saturday 17th May   **John 14:7–9**

J esus said to Thomas, "If you know me, you will know my Father also. From now on you do know him and have seen him." Philip said to him, "Lord, show us the Father, and we will be satisfied." Jesus said to him, "Have I been with you all this time, Philip, and you still do not know me? Whoever has seen me has seen the Father."

• How did Philip feel when Jesus used his name? How do I feel when Jesus gently breathes my name?

• Prayer in Jesus' name means that Jesus supports all prayer which is in tune with his values. Lord, let me develop your mindset.

Something to think and pray about each day this week:

Our mother's touch
In a time of plague, oxen were dragging wagons full of fresh corpses to the lime-pits outside the village. There is no one to bless their burial because the parish priest has already died from his sick-calls. The little village juggler begins to fear for his life. How will his wife and his small child manage if he catches the plague? He decides to pray.

So he steals into the parish church and kneels in front of the altar; but he hasn't a prayer. What can he say to God Almighty, that stern magistrate? Instead, he stands in front of a statue of Our Lady. "I shall pray in my own words to the Virgin Mother. She was a villager too. I shall do what I do best. I shall juggle for her!" He takes the balls from his pouch and begins to throw them, there and then, in the empty Lady-chapel. First slowly, now swiftly, one, two, three, higher and higher the little juggler spins them until there are four, five, seven in the air.

Suddenly the sacristan appears, rude and red-faced. He punches the little juggler in the belly and he says: "Do you not know where you are, you ignoramus?" But the statue of Our Lady softens and smiles and laughs aloud. She leans down to the little juggler from her tilting plinth and she wipes his sweaty forehead with the palm of her hand.

The Presence of God
As I sit here, the beating of my heart,
the ebb and flow of my breathing, the movements of my mind
are all signs of God's ongoing creation of me.
I pause for a moment, and become aware
of this presence of God within me.

Freedom
I ask God's help,
to be free from my own preoccupations,
to be open to God in this time of prayer,
to come to love and serve him more.

Consciousness
Knowing that God loves me unconditionally,
I look honestly over the last day, its events and my feelings.
Do I have something to be grateful for? Then I give thanks.
Is there something I am sorry for? Then I ask forgiveness.

The Word
I take my time to read the Word of God, slowly, a few times,
allowing myself to dwell on anything that strikes me. (Please
turn to your scripture on the following pages. Inspiration
points are there should you need them. When you are ready,
return here to continue.)

Conversation
Remembering that I am still in God's presence,
I imagine Jesus himself standing or sitting beside me,
and say whatever is on my mind, whatever is in my heart,
speaking as one friend to another.

Conclusion
Glory be to the Father, and to the Son, and to the Holy Spirit,
As it was in the beginning, is now and ever shall be,
World without end. Amen

Sunday 18th May,
Fifth Sunday of Easter   John 14:9–12

Jesus said, "Have I been with you all this time, Philip, and you still do not know me? Whoever has seen me has seen the Father. How can you say, 'Show us the Father'? Do you not believe that I am in the Father and the Father is in me? The words that I say to you I do not speak on my own; but the Father who dwells in me does his works. Believe me that I am in the Father and the Father is in me; but if you do not, then believe me because of the works themselves. Very truly, I tell you, the one who believes in me will also do the works that I do and, in fact, will do greater works than these, because I am going to the Father."

- Jesus does not just want to help me, to give me insight or advice. He wants to draw me into the very heart of life, the source of goodness; he invites me to be with him "in the Father."
- Prayer does not remove me from the world, but deepens my ability to live in it with savour, calm and purpose. My words and actions can bring peace, justice and hope.

Monday 19th May   John 14:21–26

Jesus said to his disciples: "They who have my command-ments and keep them are those who love me; and those who love me will be loved by my Father, and I will love them and reveal myself to them." Judas (not Iscariot) said to him, "Lord, how is it that you will reveal yourself to us, and not to the world?" Jesus answered him, "Those who love me will keep my word, and my Father will love them, and we will come to them and make our home with them. Whoever does not love me does not keep my words; and the word that you hear is not mine, but is from the Father who sent me. I have said these things to you while I am still with you. The Advocate, the Holy Spirit, whom the Father will send in my name, will teach you everything, and remind you of all that I have said to you."

- I imagine the Father and the Son deciding to come to me. Why do they do this? What do they think and say about me as they travel? What gifts do they choose for me? What do they find when they arrive?

- I am the focus of a great love. The Spirit of divine love comes to abide in me. Does the Spirit find a warm welcome in me or do I ignore my guest? Am I a good pupil who wants to learn?

Tuesday 20th May   John 14:27, 31

Jesus said to his disciples, "Peace I leave with you; my peace I give to you. I do not give to you as the world gives. Do not let your hearts be troubled, and do not let them be afraid. Rise, let us be on our way."

- I may not recognize the peace that Jesus gives immediately; it is not like the peace that the world gives and a troubled or fearful heart may miss the blessing.
- I take some time to dive deeper, beneath the surface concerns of my life, to acknowledge the peace about which Jesus speaks.

Wednesday 21st May   John 15:1–5

Jesus said to his disciples, "I am the true vine, and my Father is the vine-grower. He removes every branch in me that bears no fruit. Every branch that bears fruit he prunes to make it bear more fruit. You have already been cleansed by the word that I have spoken to you. Abide in me as I abide in you. Just as the branch cannot bear fruit by itself unless it abides in the vine, neither can you unless you abide in me. I am the vine, you are the branches. Those who abide in me and I in them bear much fruit, because apart from me you can do nothing."

- What happens when I pray with *Sacred Space*? Jesus' word cleanses me. I may, for instance, think that I am of little importance, but if I struggle to believe that I am an intimate friend of Jesus, my self-image is cleansed.
- If I am hard of heart, his command about love for others cleanses me. Reading *Sacred Space* is then a daily washing, a spring cleaning of my heart.

Thursday 22nd May　　　　　　　　**John 15:9–11**

Jesus said to his disciples, "As the Father has loved me, so I
have loved you; abide in my love. If you keep my commandments, you will abide in my love, just as I have kept my Father's
commandments and abide in his love. I have said these things
to you so that my joy may be in you, and that your joy may be
complete."

- I take some time to savour the word "abide": a dwelling; a place
  of rest; where I am restored; where I am known, loved and given
  heart. Do I find that I abide in *Sacred Space*?
- Jesus says that my joy is incomplete and invites me to fulfilment.
  I make sure that I bring whatever makes me happy before God in
  my time of prayer.

Friday 23rd May　　　　　　　　**John 15:12–14**

Jesus said to his disciples: "This is my commandment, that
you love one another as I have loved you. No one has greater
love than this, to lay down one's life for one's friends. You are
my friends if you do what I command you."

- I need only to abide with Jesus to see what his love means.
- As I give my life over to God, I may look for credit or recognition.
  God sees what I do. Is that enough for me?

Saturday 24th May　　　　　　　　**John 15:18–20**

Jesus said to his disciples: "If the world hates you, be aware
that it hated me before it hated you. If you belonged to the
world, the world would love you as its own. Because you do not
belong to the world, but I have chosen you out of the world—
therefore the world hates you. Remember the word that I said
to you, 'Servants are not greater than their master.' If they persecuted me, they will persecute you; if they kept my word, they
will keep yours also."

- None of us likes to be hated, but we are told not to expect an
  easy life in following Jesus. He doesn't promise that we will be

successful when we stand for the truth, but we are to be available, faithful and loving.

- The struggle to witness to the Gospel will deepen the companionship between Jesus and ourselves. "We are in this together."

Something to think and pray about each day this week:

Listening, with Mary

May is Our Lady's month. She offers us a profound image of receptive silence. She is a woman wrapped in silence. She receives the Word fully, because she is all space for it. She ponders the Word and brings forth fruit.

It would be good that each day we might, even for a little space, be wrapped in silence. Then our lives would be more fruitful. Monks and contemplatives take their cue from Mary. They spend a lifetime trying to become silent and to listen.

Think of the hush in the huge auditorium when the great pianist sits at the piano and begins to play softly. The music plays, not simply in the piano but in the hearts of the audience. They become one with the music, while the music lasts. They come away, changed.

Prayer can be like that: we try to hear the music of God, music that is soundless.

So we ask for the gift of listening hearts; hearts in which the Word can fall like a seed, and take root and grow in fresh and broken soil. There it will bear much fruit, though we know not how.

Hail Mary!

The Presence of God
Dear Jesus, today I call on you in a special way.
Mostly I come asking for favors.
Today I'd like just to be in Your presence.
Let my heart respond to Your Love.

Freedom
'I am free.'
When I look at these words in writing
They seem to create in me a feeling of awe.
Yes, a wonderful feeling of freedom.
Thank You, God.

Consciousness
Lord, You gave me the night to rest in sleep.
In my waking hours may I not forget your goodness to me.
Guide me to share your blessings with others.

The Word
I read the Word of God slowly, a few times over, and I listen
to what God is saying to me. (Please turn to your scripture on
the following pages. Inspiration points are there should you
need them. When you are ready, return here to continue.)

Conversation
Dear Jesus, I can open up my heart to you.
I can tell you everything that troubles me.
I know You care about all the concerns in my life.
Teach me to live in the knowledge
that You who care for me today,
will care for me tomorrow and all the days of my life.

Conclusion
Glory be to the Father, and to the Son, and to the Holy Spirit,
As it was in the beginning, is now and ever shall be,
World without end. Amen

Sunday 25th May,
Sixth Sunday of Easter John 14:15–18

Jesus said to his disciples, "If you love me, you will keep my commandments. And I will ask the Father, and he will give you another Advocate, to be with you forever. This is the Spirit of truth, whom the world cannot receive, because it neither sees him nor knows him. You know him, because he abides with you, and he will be in you. I will not leave you orphaned; I am coming to you."

- Love is evident in action rather than words. I do not need to rely on my own resources but turn to God who promises to help me.
- Like a bargain-hunter or a bird-spotter, I train my heart to recognize the ways of God. In this time of quiet God teaches me to see my world differently; I don't act in it alone but am accompanied by God's ever-present Spirit.

Monday 26th May John 15:26–16:4

Jesus said to his disciples, "When the Advocate comes, whom I will send to you from the Father, the Spirit of truth who comes from the Father, he will testify on my behalf. You also are to testify because you have been with me from the beginning. I have said these things to you to keep you from stumbling. They will put you out of the synagogues. Indeed, an hour is coming when those who kill you will think that by doing so they are offering worship to God. And they will do this because they have not known the Father or me. But I have said these things to you so that when their hour comes you may remember that I told you about them. I did not say these things to you from the beginning, because I was with you."

- In these days before Pentecost, I ask God to sharpen my hope and to strengthen my faith.
- I pray with compassion for all who do not know God. I give thanks for all who do good without knowing its source. I pray for the change of heart of those who do evil.

Tuesday 27th May   **John 16:5–11**

Jesus said to his disciples, "But now I am going to him who sent me; yet none of you asks me, 'Where are you going?' But because I have said these things to you, sorrow has filled your hearts. Nevertheless I tell you the truth: it is to your advantage that I go away, for if I do not go away, the Advocate will not come to you; but if I go, I will send him to you. And when he comes, he will prove the world wrong about sin and righteousness and judgement: about sin, because they do not believe in me; about righteousness, because I am going to the Father and you will see me no longer; about judgement, because the ruler of this world has been condemned."

- Jesus answers the question that the disciples did not ask. Sometimes my spoken prayers seem not to be answered but Jesus addresses the questions that may be deeper in my heart.
- Jesus has the good of the disciples at heart; his presence, his words and his departing are all for their good. Help me, Jesus, to see how you work always for my growth.

Wednesday 28th May   **John 16:12–15**

Jesus said, "I still have many things to say to you, but you cannot bear them now. When the Spirit of truth comes, he will guide you into all the truth; for he will not speak on his own, but will speak whatever he hears, and he will declare to you the things that are to come. He will glorify me, because he will take what is mine and declare it to you. All that the Father has is mine. For this reason I said that he will take what is mine and declare it to you."

- It is impossible to assimilate in a short period of time all that Jesus has to teach us. As our journey through life continues, the Holy Spirit gradually unfolds God's message at appropriate times in our lives.
- What is the Good Spirit trying to say to me today?

Thursday 29th May John 16:16–20

Jesus said to his disciples, "A little while, and you will no longer see me, and again a little while, and you will see me." Then some of his disciples said to one another, "What does he mean by saying to us, 'A little while, and you will no longer see me, and again a little while, and you will see me'; and 'Because I am going to the Father'?" They said, "What does he mean by this 'a little while'? We do not know what he is talking about." Jesus knew that they wanted to ask him, so he said to them, "Are you discussing among yourselves what I meant when I said, 'A little while, and you will no longer see me, and again a little while, and you will see me'? Very truly, I tell you, you will weep and mourn, but the world will rejoice; you will have pain, but your pain will turn into joy."

- Perhaps I can recognize where Jesus has, at times, been hidden from me and, at other times, revealed.
- Jesus does not promise removal of suffering immediately. I pray for patience with pain, that I learn to wait this "little while."

Friday 30th May John 16:20–23

Jesus said to his disciples, "Very truly, I tell you, you will weep and mourn, but the world will rejoice; you will have pain, but your pain will turn into joy. When a woman is in labor, she has pain, because her hour has come. But when her child is born, she no longer remembers the anguish because of the joy of having brought a human being into the world. So you have pain now; but I will see you again, and your hearts will rejoice, and no one will take your joy from you. On that day you will ask nothing of me. Very truly, I tell you, if you ask anything of the Father in my name, he will give it to you."

- Childbirth was a traditional biblical metaphor for the sufferings that were to herald the age of the Messiah. Giving birth to a renewed world will always entail suffering.
- Jesus, I ask you now to help me to remain with you always, to be close to you with a passionate heart, and to accept patiently whatever you want of me. And make me a joyous person!

Saturday 31st May,
Visitation of the Virgin Mary   Luke 1:39–45

In those days Mary set out and went with haste to a Judean town in the hill country, where she entered the house of Zechariah and greeted Elizabeth. When Elizabeth heard Mary's greeting, the child leaped in her womb. And Elizabeth was filled with the Holy Spirit and exclaimed with a loud cry, "Blessed are you among women, and blessed is the fruit of your womb. And why has this happened to me, that the mother of my Lord comes to me? For as soon as I heard the sound of your greeting, the child in my womb leaped for joy. And blessed is she who believed that there would be a fulfillment of what was spoken to her by the Lord."

- Mary reveals God's activity in our world. God scatters the arrogant, pulls down the mighty, sends the rich away empty. This is not to punish them but to shock them into a change of heart and behavior towards the poor.
- Father, give me an intimate knowledge of the many gifts I have received. Filled with gratitude may I use these gifts in the service of your beloved poor.

Something to think and pray about each day this week:

Entering into silence

Pope Benedict XVI wrote about the importance of silence and the relationship between silence and word. He says that there can be no meaningful communication without silence. Silence speaks! Silence can be the most eloquent expression of our closeness to, our solidarity with and our attentiveness towards another person. Our silence can express respect and love, because by silence we listen and give priority to the other.

The God of biblical revelation communicates to us in the mystery of silence. This is manifested especially in the mystery of the Cross of Christ: "The eloquence of God's love speaks in the silence of the Cross." Just as God can express himself to us in his silence, we in turn discover in silence the possibility of speaking with God and about God. We must allow our silence to mature into contemplation.

Silence sustains the word and gives it room to move, as a swan glides over water. After listening, we must let the circles of the word ripple outward to their furthest shore. Silence can carve out an inner space in us to enable God to dwell there, so that his word will remain within us. Then love for him will take roots and inspire our life.

Sacred Space does all this: we enter our prayer in silence, and only slowly move toward the Word. We then allow it to seep into us and transform us from within.

The Presence of God

I remind myself that, as I sit here now,
God is gazing on me with love and holding me in being.
I pause for a moment and think of this.

Freedom

I need to rise above the noise;
the noise that interrupts, that separates,
the noise that isolates.
I need to listen to God again.

Consciousness

In God's loving presence I unwind the past day,
starting from now and looking back, moment by moment.
I gather in all the goodness and light, in gratitude.
I attend to the shadows and what they say to me,
seeking healing, courage, forgiveness.

The Word

I take my time to read the Word of God, slowly, a few times,
allowing myself to dwell on anything that strikes me. (Please
turn to your scripture on the following pages. Inspiration
points are there should you need them. When you are ready,
return here to continue.)

Conversation

Do I notice myself reacting as I pray with the Word of God?
Do I feel challenged, comforted, angry?
Imagining Jesus sitting or standing by me,
I speak out my feelings, as one trusted friend to another.

Conclusion

Glory be to the Father, and to the Son, and to the Holy Spirit,
As it was in the beginning, is now and ever shall be,
World without end. Amen

Sunday 1st June,
Ascension   Matthew 28:16–20

Now the eleven disciples went to Galilee, to the mountain to which Jesus had directed them. When they saw him, they worshipped him; but some doubted. And Jesus came and said to them, "All authority in heaven and on earth has been given to me. Go therefore and make disciples of all nations, baptizing them in the name of the Father and of the Son and of the Holy Spirit, and teaching them to obey everything that I have commanded you. And remember, I am with you always, to the end of the age."

- Some disciples doubted, yet Jesus seems to have spoken to them all. Jesus sends me, recognising my hesitations and weakness.
- I take these words of Jesus— "I am with you always"—and let them settle in my heart. What do they mean for me today?

Monday 2nd June   John 16:29–33

The disciples said to Jesus, "Yes, now you are speaking plainly, not in any figure of speech! Now we know that you know all things, and do not need to have anyone question you; by this we believe that you came from God." Jesus answered them, "Do you now believe? The hour is coming, indeed it has come, when you will be scattered, each one to his home, and you will leave me alone. Yet I am not alone because the Father is with me. I have said this to you, so that in me you may have peace. In the world you face persecution. But take courage; I have conquered the world!"

- The disciples proclaim their faith in Jesus but these same men will scatter when he is arrested and crucified. Yet Jesus never despairs of them, or of me.
- When I face opposition and rejection, it is hard to keep faith. In such moments, Father, give me your courage and peace.

Tuesday 3rd June   John 17:6–10

Jesus said, "I have made your name known to those whom you gave me from the world. They were yours, and you gave them to me, and they have kept your word. Now they know that everything you have given me is from you; for the words that you gave to me I have given to them, and they have received them and know in truth that I came from you; and they have believed that you sent me. I am asking on their behalf; I am not asking on behalf of the world, but on behalf of those whom you gave me, because they are yours. All mine are yours, and yours are mine; and I have been glorified in them."

- To know God means intimacy with God, the kind of intimacy that couples enjoy with one another. To be enveloped by this intimacy is to experience something of what eternal life will be like.
- God, protect me and those I love. Keep me in the hollow of your hand, and draw me ever more deeply into your friendship.

Wednesday 4th June   John 17:11–19

Jesus said, "And now I am no longer in the world, but they are in the world, and I am coming to you. Holy Father, protect them in your name that you have given me, so that they may be one, as we are one. While I was with them, I protected them in your name that you have given me. I guarded them, and not one of them was lost except the one destined to be lost, so that the scripture might be fulfilled. But now I am coming to you, and I speak these things in the world so that they may have my joy made complete in themselves. I have given them your word, and the world has hated them because they do not belong to the world, just as I do not belong to the world. I am not asking you to take them out of the world, but I ask you to protect them from the evil one. They do not belong to the world, just as I do not belong to the world. Sanctify them in the truth; your word is truth. As you have sent me into the world, so I have sent them into the world. And for their sakes I sanctify myself, so that they also may be sanctified in truth."

- The words for "joy" occur 335 times in the Bible. It is God's gift to us. God does not want us to be sorrowful.
- Is Jesus' joy complete in me?

Thursday 5th June   **John 17:20–23**

J esus looked up to heaven and said, "Father, I ask not only on behalf of these, but also on behalf of those who will believe in me through their word, that they may all be one. As you, Father, are in me and I am in you, may they also be in us, so that the world may believe that you have sent me. The glory that you have given me I have given them, so that they may be one, as we are one, I in them and you in me, that they may become completely one, so that the world may know that you have sent me and have loved them even as you have loved me."

- There are over 300 references to love in the New Testament. Love is God's greatest gift to us. By our mutual love we reveal God's love to the world.
- Pagans said to one another: in the time of the Early Church: "See how these Christians love one another!" They were impressed by this mystery and at least some came to believe in Jesus.

Friday 6th June   **John 21:15–17**

W hen they had finished breakfast, Jesus said to Simon Peter, "Simon son of John, do you love me more than these?" He said to him, "Yes, Lord; you know that I love you." Jesus said to him, "Feed my lambs." A second time he said to him, "Simon son of John, do you love me?" He said to him, "Yes, Lord; you know that I love you." Jesus said to him, "Tend my sheep." He said to him the third time, "Simon son of John, do you love me?" Peter felt hurt because he said to him the third time, "Do you love me?" And he said to him, "Lord, you know everything; you know that I love you." Jesus said to him, "Feed my sheep."

- Three times Jesus gently asks Peter, "Do you love me?" He does not admonish him for his betrayals. Because he loves, Peter is re-instated, and given a great responsibility to care for the early Christian community.
- If Jesus were to ask me, "Do you love me?" how would I respond? Many women and men, down the ages, have given their lives for Christ. How would I feel if I were asked to do the same? Can I at least be a good follower of Jesus?

Saturday 7th June　　　　　　　　　　　**John 21:20–25**

Peter turned and saw the disciple whom Jesus loved following them; he was the one who had reclined next to Jesus at the supper and had said, "Lord, who is it that is going to betray you?" When Peter saw him, he said to Jesus, "Lord, what about him?" Jesus said to him, "If it is my will that he remain until I come, what is that to you? Follow me!" So the rumor spread in the community that this disciple would not die. Yet Jesus did not say to him that he would not die, but, "If it is my will that he remain until I come, what is that to you?" This is the disciple who is testifying to these things and has written them, and we know that his testimony is true. But there are also many other things that Jesus did; if every one of them were written down, I suppose that the world itself could not contain the books that would be written.

- The Beloved Disciple is anonymous so he can stand for me! He is the authority behind the community's story about Jesus, and about his continuing presence among Christians.
- I thank this quiet figure, and I ask that I too may faithfully proclaim the Christian story as a parent or teacher, or in humble conversation with friends.

Something to think and pray about each day this week:

Growing awareness

May has come and gone. But has Mary also come and gone, without much notice on our part? This would be truly a deep loss. Mary shows us what human beings are capable of by saying Yes. Her story dramatises the entrance of divine love into human life. In the Annunciation, divine and human intersect in vulnerable trust.

Mary's unique moment is repeated in us when we too allow God to meet with us directly. This of course can be dangerous, life-changing. I may be asked to let go of something, as Mary was, and to take on something else, as she was. It can all be very humdrum, but such moments carry the quiet beat of angels' wings, and leave deep peace behind.

A little old lady in a run-down suburb confided in me. "It can be heaven," she said, "by our bus stop." She was caught by the beauty of simple things—a sunny afternoon, the precious stones of a street, people going by unaware that they are the images of God.

Everyday reality can be our sanctuary lamp, if we have eyes to see and ears to hear. It can be hard for us to endure the glittering brevity of a truly beautiful spring day. Yet the earth persists in trying to get across to us that we are to be mystics.

The Presence of God

I remind myself that, as I sit here now,
God is gazing on me with love and holding me in being.
I pause for a moment and think of this.

Freedom

I need to rise above the noise;
the noise that interrupts, that separates,
the noise that isolates.
I need to listen to God again.

Consciousness

In God's loving presence I unwind the past day,
starting from now and looking back, moment by moment.
I gather in all the goodness and light, in gratitude.
I attend to the shadows and what they say to me,
seeking healing, courage, forgiveness.

The Word

I take my time to read the Word of God, slowly, a few times,
allowing myself to dwell on anything that strikes me. (Please
turn to your scripture on the following pages. Inspiration
points are there should you need them. When you are ready,
return here to continue.)

Conversation

Do I notice myself reacting as I pray with the Word of God?
Do I feel challenged, comforted, angry?
Imagining Jesus sitting or standing by me,
I speak out my feelings, as one trusted friend to another.

Conclusion

Glory be to the Father, and to the Son, and to the Holy Spirit,
As it was in the beginning, is now and ever shall be,
World without end. Amen

Sunday 8th June,
Pentecost   John 20:19–23

When it was evening on that day, the first day of the week, and the doors of the house where the disciples had met were locked for fear of the Jews, Jesus came and stood among them and said, "Peace be with you." After he said this, he showed them his hands and his side. Then the disciples rejoiced when they saw the Lord. Jesus said to them again, "Peace be with you. As the Father has sent me, so I send you." When he had said this, he breathed on them and said to them, "Receive the Holy Spirit. If you forgive the sins of any, they are forgiven them; if you retain the sins of any, they are retained."

- I listen to Jesus say to me, "Peace be with you." I bring before him those aspects of my life most in need of peace and hear him say again, "Peace be with you."
- Jesus speaks of peace but shows his hands and feet: he reminds me that there is a cost to being a presence of peace in the world.

Monday 9th June   Matthew 5:1-9

When Jesus saw the crowds, he went up the mountain; and after he sat down, his disciples came to him. Then he began to speak, and taught them, saying: "Blessed are the poor in spirit, for theirs is the kingdom of heaven. Blessed are those who mourn, for they will be comforted. Blessed are the meek, for they will inherit the earth. Blessed are those who hunger and thirst for righteousness, for they will be filled. Blessed are the merciful, for they will receive mercy. Blessed are the pure in heart, for they will see God. Blessed are the peacemakers, for they will be called children of God."

- The Incarnation is a powerful mission statement by God. Jesus follows it by announcing his own goals in the Beatitudes: they offer us a divine perspective in life. The Beatitudes are prophetic rather than profit-based. They speak of freedom and selflessness, not of worldly success, as the way to happiness.

Tuesday 10th June   **Matthew 5:14-16**

Jesus said to the disciples, "You are the light of the world. A city built on a hill cannot be hidden. No one after lighting a lamp puts it under the bushel basket, but on the lampstand, and it gives light to all in the house. In the same way, let your light shine before others, so that they may see your good works and give glory to your Father in heaven."

- Light does not change a room: it enables us to see what is in it. It helps us appreciate what is good and beautiful, and saves us from pitfalls. We are children of the light: our lives are illumined by Jesus, the light of the world (John 8:12).
- This light helps us to see the hidden hope of glory that is in us. So we can rejoice even in the darkness of the world.

Wednesday 11th June   **Matthew 5:17–19**

Jesus said to the crowds, "Do not think that I have come to abolish the law or the prophets; I have come not to abolish but to fulfill. For truly I tell you, until heaven and earth pass away, not one letter, not one stroke of a letter, will pass from the law until all is accomplished. Therefore, whoever breaks one of the least of these commandments, and teaches others to do the same, will be called least in the kingdom of heaven; but whoever does them and teaches them will be called great in the kingdom of heaven."

- The primary role of a prophet was to teach, reminding people of God's message and calling them back when they strayed. Jesus is the great Prophet, bringing meaning and direction to my life.
- When I pray the Gospels, Jesus is present, helping me to see my best way forward.

Thursday 12th June   **Matthew 5:20–26**

Jesus said to the crowds, "For I tell you, unless your righteous-ness exceeds that of the scribes and Pharisees, you will never enter the kingdom of heaven. You have heard that it was said to those of ancient times, 'You shall not murder'; and 'whoever murders shall be liable to judgment.' But I say to you that if you are angry with a brother or sister, you will be liable to judgment; and if you insult a brother or sister, you will be liable to the council; and if you say, 'You fool,' you will be liable to the hell of fire. So when you are offering your gift at the altar, if you remember that your brother or sister has something against you, leave your gift there before the altar and go; first be reconciled to your brother or sister, and then come and offer your gift."

• The Pharisees were mainly concerned about the love of God rather than love of neighbour. But for Jesus the two are linked intimately. He draws attention to the importance of right relationships with God and others.
• Reconciliation and forgiveness are at the heart of all relationships. Am I known as a reconciler?

Friday 13th June, St Anthony of Padua Matthew 5:27–32

Jesus said, "You have heard that it was said, 'You shall not commit adultery.' But I say to you that everyone who looks at a woman with lust has already committed adultery with her in his heart. If your right eye causes you to sin, tear it out and throw it away; it is better for you to lose one of your members than for your whole body to be thrown into hell. And if your right hand causes you to sin, cut it off and throw it away; it is better for you to lose one of your members than for your whole body to go into hell. "It was also said, 'Whoever divorces his wife, let him give her a certificate of divorce.' But I say to you that anyone who divorces his wife, except on the ground of unchastity, causes her to commit adultery; and whoever marries a divorced woman commits adultery."

• With these words of Jesus we bring to our prayer people who experience difficulties in marriage and in their family commitments.
• Prayer is not the time for long thoughts on adultery or divorce, but a time to pray for light, guidance and strength for ourselves and for all we know who may be in family or marital difficulties.

Saturday 14th June   **Matthew 5:33–37**

Jesus said to the crowds, "Again, you have heard that it was said to those of ancient times, 'You shall not swear falsely, but carry out the vows you have made to the Lord.' But I say to you, Do not swear at all, either by heaven, for it is the throne of God, or by the earth, for it is his footstool, or by Jerusalem, for it is the city of the great King. And do not swear by your head, for you cannot make one hair white or black. Let your word be 'Yes, Yes' or 'No, No'; anything more than this comes from the evil one."

- Children can embarrass us by their honesty in telling of things as they are. Jesus calls for sincerity, simplicity and respect in what we say or promise. He challenges ambiguity and political correctness. Jesus was never ambiguous.
- His response to all God's promises and demands is "Yes!" Can God rely on me in this way?

Something to think and pray about each day this week:

Saints of today

The doctrine of the Communion of Saints is felt by many to be a dusty irrelevance. Rightly understood, however, this doctrine can galvanize energy enough to change the world, because it emphasizes the power of companionship to forward the common good.

But what are "saints"? First it meant "ordinary" members of the early Christian communities, still living in our present world. Only later the term was reserved for virtuous people who had "gone to heaven."

So what then were "saints"? It is hard to believe that the first Christians were much better than you or me. If they were different it was in their keener awareness that something wonderful had happened to them. They were won over by what had been done for them by Jesus. Full of gratitude, these ordinary folk were trying to live out together in their daily lives the command to love. They often failed in this, but they were trying to be a network of grateful and altruistic people.

So let us revive the original dynamism of the term. We are the "Communion of saints." Think of us as "A Network of Good People" who draw strength from our companionship in Christ, and who illuminate the darkness of the age.

The early Christians were beacons of light in a bleak landscape. The *Sacred Space* community can be the same.

The Presence of God

For a few moments, I think of God's veiled presence in things:
in the elements, giving them existence;
in plants, giving them life; in animals, giving them sensation;
and finally, in me, giving me all this and more,
making me a temple, a dwelling-place of the Spirit.

Freedom

God is not foreign to my freedom.
Instead the Spirit breathes life into my most intimate desires,
gently nudging me towards all that is good.
I ask for the grace to let myself be enfolded by the Spirit.

Consciousness

Knowing that God loves me unconditionally,
I can afford to be honest about how I am.
How has the last day been, and how do I feel now?
I share my feelings openly with the Lord.

The Word

I take my time to read the Word of God, slowly, a few times,
allowing myself to dwell on anything that strikes me. (Please
turn to your scripture on the following pages. Inspiration
points are there should you need them. When you are ready,
return here to continue.)

Conversation

How has God's Word moved me? Has it left me cold?
Has it consoled me or moved me to act in a new way?
I imagine Jesus standing or sitting beside me,
I turn and share my feelings with him.

Conclusion

Glory be to the Father, and to the Son, and to the Holy Spirit,
As it was in the beginning, is now and ever shall be,
World without end. Amen

Sunday 15th June,
The Most Holy Trinity   John 3:16–17

Jesus said to Nicodemus, "For God so loved the world that he gave his only Son, so that everyone who believes in him may not perish but may have eternal life. Indeed, God did not send the Son into the world to condemn the world, but in order that the world might be saved through him."

- I allow myself to be drawn into the mystery that is the Trinity. Jesus has often told me that his desire for me is that I share fully in their life. I allow myself to be present to this wonder and, just for now, avoid trying to figure it out.
- In love for me, God desires my salvation, my being made whole.

Monday 16th June   Matthew 5:38–42

Jesus said to the crowds, "You have heard that it was said, 'An eye for an eye and a tooth for a tooth.' But I say to you, Do not resist an evildoer. But if anyone strikes you on the right cheek, turn the other also; and if anyone wants to sue you and take your coat, give your cloak as well; and if anyone forces you to go one mile, go also the second mile. Give to everyone who begs from you, and do not refuse anyone who wants to borrow from you."

- The law and duty provide basic guidelines but won't be enough for a disciple and certainly not enough for one who wants to be a friend of Jesus. Where do I need more generosity or freedom to respond to the vision that Jesus put before me?
- Do I use laws and rules to protect my security or to promote justice for others?

Tuesday 17th June   Matthew 5:43–48

Jesus said to the crowds, "You have heard that it was said, 'You shall love your neighbor and hate your enemy.' But I say to you, Love your enemies and pray for those who persecute you, so that you may be children of your Father in heaven; for he makes his sun rise on the evil and on the good, and sends rain on the righteous and on the unrighteous. For if you love those who love you, what reward do you have? Do not even the tax collectors do the same? And if you greet only your brothers and sisters, what more are you doing than others? Do not even the Gentiles do the same? Be perfect, therefore, as your heavenly Father is perfect."

- God's unconditional love extends to enemies. That challenges neat categories and personal preferences. It is only with his heart that we can love in a way that otherwise is humanly impossible.
- Holiness means imitating God and trying to be as generous as we can. His mercy and graciousness is radical, disproportionate, and outrageous. Is mine perhaps a little more cautious?

Wednesday 18th June   Matthew 6:1–4

Jesus said to the disciples, "Beware of practicing your piety before others in order to be seen by them; for then you have no reward from your Father in heaven. So whenever you give alms, do not sound a trumpet before you, as the hypocrites do in the synagogues and in the streets, so that they may be praised by others. Truly I tell you, they have received their reward. But when you give alms, do not let your left hand know what your right hand is doing, so that your alms may be done in secret; and your Father who sees in secret will reward you."

- Almsgiving, prayer and fasting are three classical expressions of piety. Each has an important place in our relationship with God and each other. But they can be motivated by selfishness or by generosity. Key to our choices is where our hearts are.
- Is my heart set on God alone? Do I sometimes set out to receive praise and admiration?

Thursday 19th June   Matthew 6:7–15

Jesus said, "When you are praying, do not heap up empty phrases as the Gentiles do; for they think that they will be heard because of their many words. Do not be like them, for your Father knows what you need before you ask him. Pray then in this way: Our Father in heaven, hallowed be your name. Your kingdom come. Your will be done, on earth as it is in heaven. Give us this day our daily bread. And forgive us our debts, as we also have forgiven our debtors. And do not bring us to the time of trial, but rescue us from the evil one. For if you forgive others their trespasses, your heavenly Father will also forgive you; but if you do not forgive others, neither will your Father forgive your trespasses."

- Prayer begins and ends with God. The Father's will was a guiding light to Jesus. His relationship with Abba was at the heart of his prayer of thanksgiving. So he shows us how to pray.
- In our relationship with God we ask that God's will be done in us, while acknowledging our weakness and our capacity to lose direction.

Friday 20th June   Matthew 6:19–23

Jesus said to his disciples, "Do not store up for yourselves treasures on earth, where moth and rust consume and where thieves break in and steal; but store up for yourselves treasures in heaven, where neither moth nor rust consumes and where thieves do not break in and steal. For where your treasure is, there your heart will be also. So, if your eye is healthy, your whole body will be full of light; but if your eye is unhealthy, your whole body will be full of darkness. If then the light in you is darkness, how great is the darkness!"

- Greed can blind us so that we see only what we want to see. Vision and light give hope.
- Healthy vision makes you aware of the challenges of life and the cost of good decisions, and it gives clarity on the path to take in the darkness of life.

Saturday 21st June   Matthew 6:28–34

Jesus said to his disciples, "Consider the lilies of the field, how they grow; they neither toil nor spin, yet I tell you, even Solomon in all his glory was not clothed like one of these. But if God so clothes the grass of the field, which is alive today and tomorrow is thrown into the oven, will he not much more clothe you—you of little faith? Therefore do not worry, saying,

'What will we eat?' or 'What will we drink?' or 'What will we wear?' For it is the Gentiles who strive for all these things; and indeed your heavenly Father knows that you need all these things. But strive first for the kingdom of God and his right-eousness, and all these things will be given to you as well. So do not worry about tomorrow, for tomorrow will bring worries of its own. Today's trouble is enough for today."

- The core of Jesus' message is the Kingdom; not a kingdom of power and control but one in which love and justice color all relationships.
- When we look back at life, we see that God has provided and guided us through challenging times. Most of what we worried about never happened. Where am I being called to trust more now?

Something to think and pray about each day this week:

The way ahead
The prayer for the 50th International Eucharistic Congress, held in Ireland in 2012, still shows us the way:

Lord Jesus, you were sent by the Father to gather together those who are scattered. You came among us, doing good and bringing healing, announcing the Word of salvation and giving the Bread which lasts forever. Be our companion on life's pilgrim way.

May your Holy Spirit inflame our hearts, enliven our hope and open our minds, so that together with our sisters and brothers in faith we may recognize you in the Scriptures and in the breaking of bread.

May your Holy Spirit transform us into one body and lead us to walk humbly on the earth in justice and love, as witnesses of your resurrection.

In communion with Mary may all praise, honor and blessing be to the Father through you, in the Holy Spirit and in the Church, now and forever. Amen.

This prayer calls for action! The Father, Son and Spirit transform us, bring us to life and gather us as one. Plenty of work for the Trinity there!

We in turn are to allow ourselves to be led by the Spirit. We are to go out into the world as living witnesses of the resurrection. We are to love everyone as Jesus did, and we are to be committed to social justice, as he was. Plenty of work still to be done!

The Presence of God

At any time of the day or night we can call on Jesus.
He is always waiting, listening for our call.
What a wonderful blessing.
No phone needed, no emails, just a whisper.

Freedom

Lord, grant me the grace to be free from the excesses
of this life.
Let me not get caught up with the desire for wealth.
Keep my heart and mind free to love and serve you.

Consciousness

I exist in a web of relationships—links to nature, people, God.
I trace out these links, giving thanks for the life that flows
through them.
Some links are twisted or broken: I may feel regret, anger,
disappointment.
I pray for the gift of acceptance and forgiveness.

The Word

God speaks to each one of us individually. I need to listen to
what he is saying to me. (Please turn to your scripture on the
following pages. Inspiration points are there should you need
them. When you are ready, return here to continue.)

Conversation

Remembering that I am still in God's presence,
I imagine Jesus himself standing or sitting beside me,
and say whatever is on my mind, whatever is in my heart,
speaking as one friend to another.

Conclusion

Glory be to the Father, and to the Son, and to the Holy Spirit,
As it was in the beginning, is now and ever shall be,
World without end. Amen

Sunday 22nd June,
Feast of the Body and Blood of Christ   John 6:51–58

Jesus said to the crowd, "I am the living bread that came down from heaven. Whoever eats of this bread will live forever; and the bread that I will give for the life of the world is my flesh." The Jews then disputed among themselves, saying, "How can this man give us his flesh to eat?" So Jesus said to them, "Very truly, I tell you, unless you eat the flesh of the Son of Man and drink his blood, you have no life in you. Those who eat my flesh and drink my blood have eternal life, and I will raise them up on the last day; for my flesh is true food and my blood is true drink. Those who eat my flesh and drink my blood abide in me, and I in them."

- My mind may have questions about what Jesus says but my prayer draws me to listen to him, heart to heart. He leads me to appreciate the closeness to which he calls me.
- "Eat," "live" and "abide" are all words that belong to the home. Jesus invites me to bring anything in my life that is unsettled or out of place, that it may find its home in him.

Monday 23rd June   Matthew 7:1–5

Jesus said to the crowds, "Do not judge, so that you may not be judged. For with the judgment you make you will be judged, and the measure you give will be the measure you get. Why do you see the speck in your neighbor's eye, but do not notice the log in your own eye? Or how can you say to your neighbor, 'Let me take the speck out of your eye,' while the log is in your own eye? You hypocrite, first take the log out of your own eye, and then you will see clearly to take the speck out of your neighbor's eye."

- The judgements we make of others use a particular vocabulary; the limited words and narrow vision that we use can prevent us from being open to broader realities. Jesus reminds us that if we measure others wrongly—or at all—we limit ourselves.
- If I call to mind times when I have been judged unfairly, I ask God that I may do so with a sense of peace and calm, learning

only how I might become more loving and tolerant in my attitudes to others.

Tuesday 24th June,
Birth of St John the Baptist   Luke 1:57–64

Now the time came for Elizabeth to give birth, and she bore a son. Her neighbors and relatives heard that the Lord had shown his great mercy to her, and they rejoiced with her. On the eighth day they came to circumcise the child, and they were going to name him Zechariah after his father. But his mother said, "No; he is to be called John." They said to her, "None of your relatives has this name." Then they began motioning to his father to find out what name he wanted to give him. He asked for a writing tablet and wrote, "His name is John." And all of them were amazed. Immediately his mouth was opened and his tongue freed, and he began to speak, praising God.

- The birth of a long-awaited child to older parents is an occasion of great joy. The unexpected has happened. We celebrate the birth of a promised child.
- Apart from Jesus and Mary, John is the only person whose birth and death we celebrate. He is given a new name, because God has a special mission for him.
- I too have a new name, my baptismal name. What is my mission?

Wednesday 25th June   Matthew 7:15–20

Jesus told the crowds, "Beware of false prophets, who come to you in sheep's clothing but inwardly are ravenous wolves. You will know them by their fruits. Are grapes gathered from thorns, or figs from thistles? In the same way, every good tree bears good fruit, but the bad tree bears bad fruit. A good tree cannot bear bad fruit, nor can a bad tree bear good fruit. Every tree that does not bear good fruit is cut down and thrown into the fire. Thus you will know them by their fruits."

- A tree does not go bad overnight. Rather, decay tends to begin from within and it takes time before it becomes evident. Outward appearances may be good but loss of fruitfulness is observed.

- On the other hand, growth in goodness is evident. We have the potential for good and the Lord desires we develop it. By our fruits others will know us.

Thursday 26th June   Matthew 7:24–29

Jesus said to his disciples, "Everyone then who hears these words of mine and acts on them will be like a wise man who built his house on rock. The rain fell, the floods came, and the winds blew and beat on that house, but it did not fall, because it had been founded on rock. And everyone who hears these words of mine and does not act on them will be like a foolish man who built his house on sand. The rain fell, and the floods came, and the winds blew and beat against that house, and it fell—and great was its fall!" Now when Jesus had finished saying these things, the crowds were astounded at his teaching, for he taught them as one having authority, and not as their scribes.

- A sandy base gives an unreliable foundation. The message applies to our faith lives, too, as we seek to engage more fully with Jesus. The word of God is the rock we are to build on.
- Knowing the Lord and his word helps us to recognize God's way and to be open to God's will for us. It helps us live and speak with conviction as Jesus did.

Friday 27th June,
Feast of the Sacred Heart   Matthew 11:25–30

At that time Jesus said, "I thank you, Father, Lord of heaven and earth, because you have hidden these things from the wise and the intelligent and have revealed them to infants; yes, Father, for such was your gracious will. All things have been handed over to me by my Father; and no one knows the Son except the Father, and no one knows the Father except the Son and anyone to whom the Son chooses to reveal him. Come to me, all you that are weary and are carrying heavy burdens, and I will give you rest. Take my yoke upon you, and learn from me; for I am gentle and humble in heart, and you will find rest for your souls. For my yoke is easy, and my burden is light."

- The deeds of lovers may seem foolish to us but to themselves they are full of meaning. Cost, time and effort are of little concern. Love means reaching out, being with and desiring to bring happiness to the other.

- Today is a feast of love, of God's immense love for us shown in the total self-giving of Jesus. Even in death, he gave till there was no more to give.

Saturday 28th June   Matthew 8:5–13

When he entered Capernaum, a centurion came to him, appealing to him and saying, "Lord, my servant is lying at home paralyzed, in terrible distress." And he said to him, "I will come and cure him." The centurion answered, "Lord, I am not worthy to have you come under my roof; but only speak the word, and my servant will be healed. For I also am a man under authority, with soldiers under me; and I say to one, 'Go,' and he goes, and to another, 'Come,' and he comes, and to my slave, 'Do this,' and the slave does it." When Jesus heard him, he was amazed and said to those who followed him, "Truly I tell you, in no one in Israel have I found such faith. I tell you, many will come from east and west and will eat with Abraham and Isaac and Jacob in the kingdom of heaven, while the heirs of the kingdom will be thrown into the outer darkness, where there will be weeping and gnashing of teeth." And to the centurion Jesus said, "Go; let it be done for you according to your faith." And the servant was healed in that hour."

- Jesus was not ready for this expression of faith but appreciated it as a sign of God at work. I pray that I may be open to detecting signs of faith around me.

- The centurion displayed a great compassion for his servant. I allow my heart to be moved as I think of those in need. I bring their needs before God.

Something to think and pray about each day this week:

The challenge of God's mercy

St. John records the drama of a woman being dragged to her death by stoning, on a capital charge of adultery.

The woman was spared, due to Jesus' intervention but it appears that early on, some male editors deleted the episode for "pastoral reasons." Did they fear that Jesus' extravagance of mercy might be misinterpreted by the fragile Christian flock as licence to sin?

There is suspicion too over another disappearing text which also seemed to go too far in forgiveness and mercy. Christ's cry, "Father, forgive them, for they know not what they do!" is omitted in some versions of Luke's passion narrative. Did some scribes reason that God is merciful, but not to the point of madness? Did they argue that Jesus' murder must be avenged, else society would fall apart? Why should anyone try to be good, if these murderers were going to be so easily forgiven?

Thus, the wonder of divine extravagance is reduced to manageable human proportions by small minds.

Under pressure, Jesus invites the sinless among the crowd to cast the first stone. The men all go away, one after the other, empty-handed and mute. The drift starts with those who have learned, even in the late hours of their life, and beyond all academic credentials, the divine benefits of doubting themselves. What were their thoughts for the rest of that day?

The Presence of God
God is with me, but more,
God is within me, giving me existence.
Let me dwell for a moment on God's life-giving presence
in my body, my mind, my heart
and in the whole of my life.

Freedom
God is not foreign to my freedom.
Instead the Spirit breathes life into my most intimate desires,
gently nudging me towards all that is good.
I ask for the grace to let myself be enfolded by the Spirit.

Consciousness
How am I really feeling? Light-hearted? Heavy-hearted?
I may be very much at peace, happy to be here.
Equally, I may be frustrated, worried or angry.
I acknowledge how I really am. It is the real me that the
Lord loves.

The Word
I read the Word of God slowly, a few times over, and I listen
to what God is saying to me. (Please turn to your scripture on
the following pages. Inspiration points are there should you
need them. When you are ready, return here to continue.)

Conversation
How has God's Word moved me? Has it left me cold?
Has it consoled me or moved me to act in a new way?
I imagine Jesus standing or sitting beside me,
I turn and share my feelings with him.

Conclusion
Glory be to the Father, and to the Son, and to the Holy Spirit,
As it was in the beginning, is now and ever shall be,
World without end. Amen

Sunday 29th June,
Ss Peter & Paul, Apostles   Matthew 16:13–17

Now when Jesus came into the district of Caesarea Philippi, he asked his disciples, "Who do people say that the Son of Man is?" And they said, "Some say John the Baptist, but others Elijah, and still others Jeremiah or one of the prophets." He said to them, "But who do you say that I am?" Simon Peter answered, "You are the Messiah, the Son of the living God." And Jesus answered him, "Blessed are you, Simon son of Jonah! For flesh and blood has not revealed this to you, but my Father in heaven."

- The disciples were familiar with the gossip about Jesus. Jesus leads them to put aside external voices. The only question for me is, "Who do I say Jesus is?" as I put aside gossip and other opinions.
- I proclaim Jesus by the way I live. My words and actions, my attitudes and choices demonstrate who influences me.

Monday 30th June   Matthew 8:18–22

Now when Jesus saw great crowds around him, he gave orders to go over to the other side. A scribe then approached and said, "Teacher, I will follow you wherever you go." And Jesus said to him, "Foxes have holes, and birds of the air have nests; but the Son of Man has nowhere to lay his head." Another of his disciples said to him, "Lord, first let me go and bury my father." But Jesus said to him, "Follow me, and let the dead bury their own dead."

- Did the scribe want to follow Jesus because he saw him as a celebrity who could attract great crowds and perform so many healings? What is Jesus' attitude to fame, power and privilege?
- Imagine that the Lord of Creation has nowhere to lay his head! Is he challenging me to be freer about my possessions? I pray for a generous spirit, so that I can truly follow him.

Tuesday 1st July   Matthew 8:23–27

And when Jesus got into the boat, his disciples followed him. A windstorm arose on the sea, so great that the boat was being swamped by the waves; but he was asleep. And they went and woke him up, saying, "Lord, save us! We are perishing!" And he said to them, "Why are you afraid, you of little faith?" Then he got up and rebuked the winds and the sea; and there was a dead calm. They were amazed, saying, "What sort of man is this, that even the winds and the sea obey him?"

• After an exhausting day beset by crowds, Jesus was able to sleep peacefully in a boat so swamped by waves that the disciples thought they were going under. It is from that inner peace that he calms the fears of his friends, and equally reassures the threatened church.

• When I feel tossed by storms, Lord, may I call on you with confidence.

Wednesday 2nd July   Matthew 8:28–34

When he came to the other side, to the country of the Gadarenes, two demoniacs coming out of the tombs met him. They were so fierce that no one could pass that way. Suddenly they shouted, "What have you to do with us, Son of God? Have you come here to torment us before the time?" Now a large herd of swine was feeding at some distance from them. The demons begged him, "If you cast us out, send us into the herd of swine." And he said to them, "Go!" So they came out and entered the swine; and suddenly, the whole herd rushed down the steep bank into the lake and perished in the water. The swineherds ran off, and on going into the town, they told the whole story about what had happened to the demoniacs. Then the whole town came out to meet Jesus; and when they saw him, they begged him to leave their neighborhood.

• The real sign here is not the stampede of pigs, but that Jesus is the Son of God and can overcome the powers of evil.

• Because the townspeople cannot cope with divine power, they ask Jesus to leave. But Jesus has won a fundamental victory over evil and has established the reign of God. By staying close to Jesus, we have nothing to fear from the devil or the world.

Thursday 3rd July,
St Thomas, Apostle   John 20:24–29

Thomas (who was called the Twin), one of the twelve, was not with them when Jesus came. So the other disciples told him, "We have seen the Lord." But he said to them, "Unless I see the mark of the nails in his hands, and put my finger in the mark of the nails and my hand in his side, I will not believe." A week later his disciples were again in the house, and Thomas was with them. Although the doors were shut, Jesus came and stood among them and said, "Peace be with you." Then he said to Thomas, "Put your finger here and see my hands. Reach out your hand and put it in my side. Do not doubt but believe." Thomas answered him, "My Lord and my God!" Jesus said to him, "Have you believed because you have seen me? Blessed are those who have not seen and yet have come to believe."

- Thomas moves from disbelief to the wonderful affirmation on which the Gospel of John is centred: "My Lord and my God!"
- We are blessed when we believe in the constant personal presence of the living Jesus, even though we do not see him.

Friday 4th July   Matthew 9:9–13

As Jesus was walking along, he saw a man called Matthew sitting at the tax booth; and he said to him, "Follow me." And he got up and followed him. And as he sat at dinner in the house, many tax collectors and sinners came and were sitting with him and his disciples. When the Pharisees saw this, they said to his disciples, "Why does your teacher eat with tax collectors and sinners?" But when he heard this, he said, "Those who are well have no need of a physician, but those who are sick. Go and learn what this means, 'I desire mercy, not sacrifice.' For I have come to call not the righteous but sinners."

- Matthew, as a tax collector for the Roman army of occupation, would have been hated by everybody; he was a moral and social outcast. What a boost to his self-esteem that Jesus sees good in him and wants him to become part of this exciting new movement!
- No matter how I may see myself, Jesus sees me too as a friend.

Saturday 5th July   **Matthew 9:14–17**

Then the disciples of John came to him, saying, "Why do we and the Pharisees fast often, but your disciples do not fast?" And Jesus said to them, "The wedding guests cannot mourn as long as the bridegroom is with them, can they? The days will come when the bridegroom is taken away from them, and then they will fast. No one sews a piece of unshrunk cloth on an old cloak, for the patch pulls away from the cloak, and a worse tear is made. Neither is new wine put into old wineskins; otherwise, the skins burst, and the wine is spilled, and the skins are destroyed; but new wine is put into fresh wineskins, and so both are preserved."

- Jesus uses wedding imagery to let us know how intimate his relationship is with us. It's a time to be joyful. The bridegroom's absence will be brief—Jesus will die—but he will return to be close to us always, bringing love, joy and peace.
- Lord, let me respond joyously to your intimacy with me. Life with you is a love affair!

Something to think and pray about each day this week:

Working on God's project
What is God up to in our world, and how does it matter to me?

The divine project is an all-embracing network of good people, human and divine. This demands our human collaboration to succeed. When we believe this, energy and excitement replace our boredom and dullness. The brute facts of the human story are re-interpreted as either strengthening or fragmenting the network of humankind which God is building with our help.

When we join in with God, we learn to pray deeply for the world, instead of reacting cynically to human failures. When challenges come, instead of saying, "Not my problem" we can each ask: "What ought I do?" We begin to see our task as that of supporting a God who labors mightily with us for the wretched of the world. Every person becomes important to us: no one can be written out of the Great Story, because the bad as well as the good are woven into God's epic.

Today the internet creates temporary networks of good people in response to disasters. Saint Paul's statement is now true in a new way: "If one part of the body hurts, all the other parts hurt with it" (1 Cor 12:26).

Wherever people are inclusive and for-one-another, a network of loving relationships is present, and becomes a transient image of the final project of God.

The Presence of God

To be present is to arrive as one is and open up to the other.
At this instant, as I arrive here, God is present waiting for me.
God always arrives before me, desiring to connect with me
even more than my most intimate friend.
I take a moment and greet my loving God.

Freedom

Everything has the potential to draw forth from me a fuller
love and life.
Yet my desires are often fixed, caught, on illusions of
fulfillment.
I ask that God, through my freedom, may orchestrate
my desires in a vibrant loving melody rich in harmony.

Consciousness

Knowing that God loves me unconditionally,
I can afford to be honest about how I am.
How has the last day been, and how do I feel now?
I share my feelings openly with the Lord.

The Word

I take my time to read the Word of God, slowly, a few times,
allowing myself to dwell on anything that strikes me. (Please
turn to your scripture on the following pages. Inspiration
points are there should you need them. When you are ready,
return here to continue.)

Conversation

What feelings are rising in me
as I pray and reflect on God's Word?
I imagine Jesus himself sitting or standing beside me,
and open my heart to him.

Conclusion

Glory be to the Father, and to the Son, and to the Holy Spirit,
As it was in the beginning, is now and ever shall be,
World without end. Amen

Sunday 6th July,
Fourteenth Sunday in Ordinary Time
Matthew 11:25–30

Jesus said, "I thank you, Father, Lord of heaven and earth, because you have hidden these things from the wise and the intelligent and have revealed them to infants; yes, Father, for such was your gracious will. All things have been handed over to me by my Father; and no one knows the Son except the Father, and no one knows the Father except the Son and anyone to whom the Son chooses to reveal him. Come to me, all you that are weary and are carrying heavy burdens, and I will give you rest. Take my yoke upon you, and learn from me; for I am gentle and humble in heart, and you will find rest for your souls. For my yoke is easy, and my burden is light."

- I approach the Scripture not only with my mind, trying to figure out and understand. The word of God is spoken to my heart and comes to life when I respect the insights that God gives to me in simple ways.
- I know it is easy to feel weighed down when I struggle on my own. I consider what it is like to carry my burdens with Jesus' help. He promises that his attitudes of humility and gentleness will make a difference.

Monday 7th July
Matthew 9:18–26

While Jesus was speaking, suddenly a leader of the synagogue came in and knelt before him, saying, "My daughter has just died; but come and lay your hand on her, and she will live." And Jesus got up and followed him, with his disciples. Suddenly a woman who had been suffering from hemorrhages for twelve years came up behind him and touched the fringe of his cloak, for she said to herself, "If I only touch his cloak, I will be made well." Jesus turned, and seeing her he said, "Take heart, daughter; your faith has made you well." And instantly the woman was made well. When Jesus came to the leader's house and saw the flute players and the crowd making a commotion, he said, "Go away; for the girl is not dead but sleeping." And they laughed at him. But when the crowd had been put outside, he went in and took her by the hand, and the girl got up. And the report of this spread throughout that district.

- Whom do I identify with in this crowded scene? Am I like the desperate leader, or the sick woman? Or am I like the people who laughed at Jesus because they had no faith in him? Or do I ask Jesus just to let me touch him, or to take me by the hand and bring me to life?
- Lest anyone think her cure was magic, Jesus tells the woman that it is her faith that has saved her. How strong is my faith in him?

Tuesday 8th July   Matthew 9:35–38

Then Jesus went about all the cities and villages, teaching in their synagogues, and proclaiming the good news of the kingdom, and curing every disease and every sickness. When he saw the crowds, he had compassion for them, because they were harassed and helpless, like sheep without a shepherd. Then he said to his disciples, "The harvest is plentiful, but the laborers are few; therefore ask the Lord of the harvest to send out laborers into his harvest."

- Jesus wants us to pray for more labourers to bring in the plentiful harvest. The lack of labourers, then as now, is a problem, but it is also an opportunity and a challenge.
- Do I play my part in bringing in the Lord's harvest? Or do I leave that to others?

Wednesday 9th July   Matthew 10:1–7

Then Jesus summoned his twelve disciples and gave them authority over unclean spirits, to cast them out, and to cure every disease and every sickness. These are the names of the twelve apostles: first, Simon, also known as Peter, and his brother Andrew; James son of Zebedee, and his brother John; Philip and Bartholomew; Thomas and Matthew the tax collector; James son of Alphaeus, and Thaddaeus; Simon the Cananaean, and Judas Iscariot, the one who betrayed him. These twelve Jesus sent out with the following instructions: "Go nowhere among the Gentiles, and enter no town of the Samaritans, but go rather to the lost sheep of the house of Israel. As you go, proclaim the good news, 'The kingdom of heaven has come near.'"

- This address captures the essence of the apostles' mission. The basic message is that the reign of God is coming close. To establish it, however, is an enormous challenge to the envoys that Jesus sends out. But Jesus goes before us as we travel.
- Do I bring good news wherever I go?

Thursday 10th July   Matthew 10:7–14

Jesus said to the Twelve, "As you go, proclaim the good news, 'The kingdom of heaven has come near.' Cure the sick, raise the dead, cleanse the lepers, cast out demons. You received without payment; give without payment. Take no gold, or silver, or copper in your belts, no bag for your journey, or two tunics, or sandals, or a staff; for laborers deserve their food. Whatever town or village you enter, find out who in it is worthy, and stay there until you leave. As you enter the house, greet it. If the house is worthy, let your peace come upon it; but if it is not worthy, let your peace return to you. If anyone will not welcome you or listen to your words, shake off the dust from your feet as you leave that house or town."

- The disciples are to travel light and adopt a simple lifestyle. Because they bring gifts—healing and peace—they are entitled to the traditional warm welcome of the Jewish people.
- Am I known as a hospitable person who welcomes others as coming from God into my life?

Friday 11th July   Matthew 10:16–20

"See, I am sending you out like sheep into the midst of wolves; so be wise as serpents and innocent as doves. Beware of them, for they will hand you over to councils and flog you in their synagogues; and you will be dragged before governors and kings because of me, as a testimony to them and the Gentiles. When they hand you over, do not worry about how you are to speak or what you are to say; for what you are to say will be given to you at that time; for it is not you who speak, but the Spirit of your Father speaking through you."

- What an assignment! Jesus' disciples are to proclaim to the religious and secular powers of this world that a new order of things is drawing near.
- Inevitably, betrayal, persecution, imprisonment and torture will be their lot. Even so, they are to speak out boldly in all simplicity, confident in the Holy Spirit.

Saturday 12th July   Matthew 10:26–28

Jesus said to the Twelve: "So have no fear of them; for nothing is covered up that will not be uncovered, and nothing secret that will not become known. What I say to you in the dark, tell in the light; and what you hear whispered, proclaim from the housetops. Do not fear those who kill the body but cannot kill the soul; rather fear him who can destroy both soul and body in hell."

- The underlying message of these various sayings of Jesus is encouragement. When events go against us, we are to remain confident, trusting in God's care.
- We are not to be deterred in the face of opposition. Why? Because Jesus is with us always.

Something to think and pray about each day this week:

With empty hands

What is God trying to make of us in the diminishment of our later years? Can the often bitter water of these years ever become wine? Old age is terrifying to most of us: we need help to navigate it well. Occasionally we meet wisdom figures who have come to terms with the reality of their own ageing. What characterises them? They are just themselves; they are not "difficult"—or at least not for long. Love flows through them to those around, even if they've had a stroke and can hardly talk. If you can find such people, try to be like them: you will be a blessing for the world.

Some level of experience of God as being good is needed in order to face the final stage of our journey. Our current stage of development required us to let go of previous, comfortable stages. While we may have resisted, something—or Someone!—was pushing us on till eventually we had to let go. This pushing was for our good. We became more loving, which is what true human development is about.

This process continues in our final years. The final push and letting go—our dying—will bring us something incomparably better than we now have. Only with empty hands can we grasp the huge gift offered to us—eternal joy. A wise and good God orchestrates our ageing.

The Presence of God

What is present to me is what has a hold on my becoming.
I reflect on the presence of God always there in love,
amidst the many things that have a hold on me.
I pause and pray that I may let God
affect my becoming in this precise moment.

Freedom

There are very few people
who realize what God would make of them
if they abandoned themselves into his hands,
and let themselves be formed by his grace. (St Ignatius)
I ask for the grace to trust myself totally to God's love.

Consciousness

In the presence of my loving Creator,
I look honestly at my feelings over the last day,
the highs, the lows and the level ground.
Can I see where the Lord has been present?

The Word

God speaks to each one of us individually. I need to listen to
what he is saying to me. (Please turn to your scripture on the
following pages. Inspiration points are there should you need
them. When you are ready, return here to continue.)

Conversation

What is stirring in me as I pray?
Am I consoled, troubled, left cold?
I imagine Jesus himself standing or sitting at my side,
and share my feelings with him.

Conclusion

Glory be to the Father, and to the Son, and to the Holy Spirit,
As it was in the beginning, is now and ever shall be,
World without end. Amen

Sunday 13th July,
Fifteenth Sunday in Ordinary Time   Matthew 13:3–9

And Jesus told the people many things in parables, saying: "Listen! A sower went out to sow. And as he sowed, some seeds fell on the path, and the birds came and ate them up. Other seeds fell on rocky ground, where they did not have much soil, and they sprang up quickly, since they had no depth of soil. But when the sun rose, they were scorched; and since they had no root, they withered away. Other seeds fell among thorns, and the thorns grew up and choked them. Other seeds fell on good soil and brought forth grain, some a hundredfold, some sixty, some thirty. Let anyone with ears listen!"

- There are words of Jesus that have found root in me, that flourish and give life: I thank God for them as I recognize again how God's Spirit is present and active in my life.
- Jesus knew that there would be many threats to his word, many situations in which it would not be fruitful. With him, I pay attention to where there is life and growth.

Monday 14th July   Matthew 10:34–39, 11:1

Jesus said to the Twelve, "Do not think that I have come to bring peace to the earth; I have not come to bring peace, but a sword. For I have come to set a man against his father, and a daughter against her mother, and a daughter-in-law against her mother-in-law; and one's foes will be members of one's own household. Whoever loves father or mother more than me is not worthy of me; and whoever loves son or daughter more than me is not worthy of me; and whoever does not take up the cross and follow me is not worthy of me. Those who find their life will lose it, and those who lose their life for my sake will find it." Now when Jesus had finished instructing his twelve disciples, he went on from there to teach and proclaim his message in their cities.

- If Jesus sometimes uses shocking words, it is to jolt us into realizing what he is about. He does not endorse armed conflict, but he warns that we have to struggle to put him first, before family ties.

Divisions will occur according as people are forced to decide for him or against him.

- I pray that he give me the courage I need to stand with him despite losing things I hold dear.

Tuesday 15th July   Matthew 11:20–22

Then Jesus began to reproach the cities in which most of his deeds of power had been done, because they did not repent. "Woe to you, Chorazin! Woe to you, Bethsaida! For if the deeds of power done in you had been done in Tyre and Sidon, they would have repented long ago in sackcloth and ashes. But I tell you, on the day of judgment it will be more tolerable for Tyre and Sidon than for you."

- In Matthew's gospel, people show great enthusiasm for Jesus, on the level of getting him to cure their sick. But discipleship must go beyond this. I must ask: "Lord, what do you need me to do to further the kingdom of God in my part of the world?"
- Again Jesus uses shocking language, as he tries to break through complacency and smugness. Am I a self-satisfied Christian, or do I allow the daily gospel to challenge me?

Wednesday 16th July   Matthew 11:25–27

At that time Jesus said, "I thank you, Father, Lord of heaven and earth, because you have hidden these things from the wise and the intelligent and have revealed them to infants; yes, Father, for such was your gracious will. All things have been handed over to me by my Father; and no one knows the Son except the Father, and no one knows the Father except the Son and anyone to whom the Son chooses to reveal him."

- Here we get a privileged insight into Jesus' prayer. He speaks directly to his Father, and his prayer is full of gratitude. I take a few moments to listen to him praying. Then I ask him to enliven my prayer.
- Do I speak to God as a loving Father? Is gratitude and wonder part of my prayer?

Thursday 17th July   **Matthew 11:28–30**

Jesus said, "Come to me, all you that are weary and are carrying heavy burdens, and I will give you rest. Take my yoke upon you, and learn from me; for I am gentle and humble in heart, and you will find rest for your souls. For my yoke is easy, and my burden is light."

- Jesus issues a gracious invitation: "Come to me!" Let me listen to Jesus whispering that call to me. He uses my name; his face shows his love; the tone of his voice is one of purest welcome. I relax in this.
- Perhaps I may use the phrase as my mantra today.

Friday 18th July   **Matthew 12:1–8**

At that time Jesus went through the grainfields on the sabbath; his disciples were hungry, and they began to pluck heads of grain and to eat. When the Pharisees saw it, they said to him, "Look, your disciples are doing what is not lawful to do on the sabbath." He said to them, "Have you not read what David did when he and his companions were hungry? He entered the house of God and ate the bread of the Presence, which it was not lawful for him or his companions to eat, but only for the priests. Or have you not read in the law that on the sabbath the priests in the temple break the sabbath and yet are guiltless? I tell you, something greater than the temple is here. But if you had known what this means, 'I desire mercy and not sacrifice,' you would not have condemned the guiltless. For the Son of Man is lord of the sabbath."

- Jesus is like a big brother who defends his bewildered disciples against attack from the Pharisees. Lord, let me take courage from this. I am not alone in my struggles: you are always at my side, watching out for me.
- Jesus is very sure about God's love. For him, God is on our side: God would rather see us fed than go hungry. God's great concern is love: all law must serve the law of love. Is this how I live—putting love before all else?

Saturday 19th July Matthew 12:14–21

But the Pharisees went out and conspired against him, how to destroy him. When Jesus became aware of this, he departed. Many crowds followed him, and he cured all of them, and he ordered them not to make him known. This was to fulfill what had been spoken through the prophet Isaiah: "Here is my servant, whom I have chosen, my beloved, with whom my soul is well pleased. I will put my Spirit upon him, and he will proclaim justice to the Gentiles. He will not wrangle or cry aloud, nor will anyone hear his voice in the streets. He will not break a bruised reed or quench a smoldering wick until he brings justice to victory. And in his name the Gentiles will hope."

- Powerful people were out to destroy Jesus from the beginning, beginning with Herod. Why is this? Because Jesus poses a threat to all who put themselves in the place of God, by living as they please, and dominating others.
- I pray for the powerful who destroy the loving relationships which are meant to hold our fragile world together.

july 20–26

Something to think and pray about each day this week:

With all my being

The body is not irrelevant to prayer. Monks know this: their desire is for God, and they pray with their bodies as they stand and sit and sing the psalms each day. They also believe that bodily work, with the intention of serving God, is prayer. Ignatius of Loyola would enthusiastically agree. Augustine remarks that those who sing, pray twice. With the sign of the Cross we bless our bodies. We receive the host in our hands at communion and then eat it. We go on pilgrimage, which is a bodily prayer, with its abandonment of creature comforts.

Truly the body prays, because it is as human persons and not as angels, that we meet our God. You won't hear God saying: "Now, when you pray, please forget your body. I'm interested only in your soul!" The psalmist was right to say: "Let all my being bless his holy name."

His Father had been the desire of Jesus' whole being, body and soul, throughout his life, even when he was busy or sleeping. The Father is our desire too. Concentration of mind may lapse during my time of prayer, but my body is still there. If someone asked me what I was doing, I'd say, "I don't know, and I'd love to be somewhere else, but I just want God, and this is the best I can do to show it."

The Presence of God

Jesus waits silent and unseen to come into my heart.
I will respond to His call.
He comes with His infinite power and love
May I be filled with joy in His presence.

Freedom

A thick and shapeless tree-trunk would never believe
that it could become a statue, admired as a miracle of
sculpture,
and would never submit itself to the chisel of the sculptor,
who sees by her genius what she can make of it. (St Ignatius)
I ask for the grace to let myself be shaped by my loving
Creator.

Consciousness

Knowing that God loves me unconditionally,
I look honestly over the last day, its events and my feelings.
Do I have something to be grateful for? Then I give thanks.
Is there something I am sorry for? Then I ask forgiveness.

The Word

I read the Word of God slowly, a few times over, and I listen
to what God is saying to me. (Please turn to your scripture on
the following pages. Inspiration points are there should you
need them. When you are ready, return here to continue.)

Conversation

Do I notice myself reacting as I pray with the Word of God?
Do I feel challenged, comforted, angry?
Imagining Jesus sitting or standing by me,
I speak out my feelings, as one trusted friend to another.

Conclusion

Glory be to the Father, and to the Son, and to the Holy Spirit,
As it was in the beginning, is now and ever shall be,
World without end. Amen

218

Sunday 20th July,
Sixteenth Sunday in Ordinary Time   Matthew 13:24–30

Jesus put before them another parable: "The kingdom of heaven may be compared to someone who sowed good seed in his field; but while everybody was asleep, an enemy came and sowed weeds among the wheat, and then went away. So when the plants came up and bore grain, then the weeds appeared as well. And the slaves of the householder came and said to him, 'Master, did you not sow good seed in your field? Where, then, did these weeds come from?' He answered, 'An enemy has done this.' The slaves said to him, 'Then do you want us to go and gather them?' But he replied, 'No; for in gathering the weeds you would uproot the wheat along with them. Let both of them grow together until the harvest; and at harvest time I will tell the reapers, Collect the weeds first and bind them in bundles to be burned, but gather the wheat into my barn.'"

- The idea that good and bad might coexist troubles the tidy mind. Jesus does not encourage a simplistic approach but calls us to humility and patience as we allow God to work in our lives.
- There are "weeds" in my life for sure, but they are not the measure of the harvest that God values in me. I ask for help that my habits and choices may give growth to what is good and true.

Monday 21st July   Matthew 12:38–42

Then some of the scribes and Pharisees said to him, "Teacher, we wish to see a sign from you." But he answered them, "An evil and adulterous generation asks for a sign, but no sign will be given to it except the sign of the prophet Jonah. For just as Jonah was three days and three nights in the belly of the sea monster, so for three days and three nights the Son of Man will be in the heart of the earth. The people of Nineveh will rise up at the judgment with this generation and condemn it, because they repented at the proclamation of Jonah, and see, something greater than Jonah is here! The queen of the South will rise up at the judgment with this generation and condemn it, because she came from the ends of the earth to listen to the wisdom of Solomon, and see, something greater than Solomon is here!

- Undoubtedly Jesus was like many people whose spiritual beauty, at once very secret and very striking, dazzles some and escapes others. He points us away from externals towards what is deeper.
- Christ transforms the person who is attracted to him.

Tuesday 22nd July   Matthew 12:46–50

While he was still speaking to the crowds, his mother and his brothers were standing outside, wanting to speak to him. Someone told him, "Look, your mother and your brothers are standing outside, wanting to speak to you." But to the one who had told him this, Jesus replied, "Who is my mother, and who are my brothers?" And pointing to his disciples, he said, "Here are my mother and my brothers! For whoever does the will of my Father in heaven is my brother and sister and mother."

- Jesus always draws a deeper meaning from casual situations. The lesson here is positive: he is emphasising that everyone can be part of the divine family.
- I tell Jesus how grateful I am to be included, and I ask to be alert to the fact that others are not strangers: they are my sisters and brothers. This changes every encounter I have!

Wednesday 23rd July   Matthew 13:1–9

Jesus told them many things in parables, saying: "Listen! A sower went out to sow. And as he sowed, some seeds fell on the path, and the birds came and ate them up. Other seeds fell on rocky ground, where they did not have much soil, and they sprang up quickly, since they had no depth of soil. But when the sun rose, they were scorched; and since they had no root, they withered away. Other seeds fell among thorns, and the thorns grew up and choked them. Other seeds fell on good soil and brought forth grain, some a hundredfold, some sixty, some thirty. Let anyone with ears listen!"

- Just as a river flows from the source and may water lands many miles away, our love and goodness can influence people in future generations. The love we share may be shared further with others.
- We leave in God's hands the fruits of our goodness.

Thursday 24th July   **Matthew 13:10–13**

Then the disciples came and asked Jesus, "Why do you speak to them in parables?" He answered, "To you it has been given to know the secrets of the kingdom of heaven, but to them it has not been given. For to those who have, more will be given, and they will have an abundance; but from those who have nothing, even what they have will be taken away. The reason I speak to them in parables is that 'seeing they do not perceive, and hearing they do not listen, nor do they understand.'"

- Jesus speaks in parables so that his meaning may take root in me: only I can, in my prayer, receive the word of God that is addressed to me. I quiet the voices of my habits and standard responses, listening for the whisper that speaks to my heart.
- Jesus offers me more than parables, strengthening my faith, building me up in love, and nurturing my hope.

Friday 25th July,
St James, Apostle   **Matthew 20:20–23**

Then the mother of the sons of Zebedee came to him with her sons, and kneeling before him, she asked a favor of him. And he said to her, "What do you want?" She said to him, "Declare that these two sons of mine will sit, one at your right hand and one at your left, in your kingdom." But Jesus answered, "You do not know what you are asking. Are you able to drink the cup that I am about to drink?" They said to him, "We are able." He said to them, "You will indeed drink my cup, but to sit at my right hand and at my left, this is not mine to grant, but it is for those for whom it has been prepared by my Father."

- Jesus is saying: "You all want to be great? Fine! You will indeed become great—by serving others." And so it was.
- In my prayer, I let him ask me about my quality of service. This is what measures my closeness to him.

Saturday 26th July   **Matthew 13:24–30**

He put before them another parable: "The kingdom of heaven may be compared to someone who sowed good seed in his field; but while everybody was asleep, an enemy came and sowed weeds among the wheat, and then went away. So when the plants came up and bore grain, then the weeds appeared as well. And the slaves of the householder came and said to him, 'Master, did you not sow good seed in your field? Where, then, did these weeds come from?' He answered, 'An enemy has done this.' The slaves said to him, 'Then do you want us to go and gather them?' But he replied, 'No; for in gathering the weeds you would uproot the wheat along with them. Let both of them grow together until the harvest; and at harvest time I will tell the reapers, Collect the weeds first and bind them in bundles to be burned, but gather the wheat into my barn.'"

- The "weeds" are a species of wild wheat, sometimes known as "false wheat." Only at harvest time can the farmer distinguish the real from the false. Jesus is saying that good and bad are mixed together in this world and indeed in each one of us.
- We must be patient with others and with ourselves: none of us is yet perfect.

Something to think and pray about each day this week:

Building God's family

Some years ago a Dublin family decided to bring a child home from the local orphanage for Christmas day. When the father arrived a small girl was sitting waiting for him. "Are you all set?" he asked. "No" she said fiercely, "I won't come without my little brother!" So he negotiated that, and the pair had a great day. The family loved them so much that they adopted both.

Ruth Burrows uses the image of an orphanage to highlight the relationship that exists between God and ourselves. A couple might run an orphanage, she says, and devote themselves daily to their charges. Perhaps they spare themselves nothing in their love and care. Yet, when each day is done, the couple retire to their private family life with their own children, delegating the orphans to the good care of someone else. The orphans get to know where they live and the fun they have together, their holidays, their friends, their birthday celebrations. But from this they are excluded.

Not so with God, Ruth Burrows insists. God has no hidden private life to which we have no access. We are brought into God's family circle; we are his beloved children. God shares everything with us. Hence Jesus' promise: "I will not leave you orphans," and his request: "Father, I want those you have given me to be where I am." We are family!

The Presence of God

As I sit here, the beating of my heart,
the ebb and flow of my breathing, the movements of my mind
are all signs of God's ongoing creation of me.
I pause for a moment, and become aware
of this presence of God within me.

Freedom

I ask for the grace
to let go of my own concerns
and be open to what God is asking of me,
to let myself be guided and formed by my loving Creator.

Consciousness

How do I find myself today?
Where am I with God? With others?
Do I have something to be grateful for? Then I give thanks.
Is there something I am sorry for? Then I ask forgiveness.

The Word

I take my time to read the Word of God, slowly, a few times,
allowing myself to dwell on anything that strikes me. (Please
turn to your scripture on the following pages. Inspiration
points are there should you need them. When you are ready,
return here to continue.)

Conversation

Remembering that I am still in God's presence,
I imagine Jesus himself standing or sitting beside me,
and say whatever is on my mind, whatever is in my heart,
speaking as one friend to another.

Conclusion

Glory be to the Father, and to the Son, and to the Holy Spirit,
As it was in the beginning, is now and ever shall be,
World without end. Amen

Sunday 27th July, Seventeenth Sunday in Ordinary Time

Matthew 13:44–52

Jesus said to the disciples, "The kingdom of heaven is like treasure hidden in a field, which someone found and hid; then in his joy he goes and sells all that he has and buys that field. "Again, the kingdom of heaven is like a merchant in search of fine pearls; on finding one pearl of great value, he went and sold all that he had and bought it."

- Think about this hidden treasure: it inspires, enlivens and opens horizons of new plans and dreams. Not everyone should be told about it but the excitement that it brings cannot always be hidden.
- Perhaps God looks at me and sees a hidden treasure, wondering when I might discover it.

Monday 28th July   Matthew 13:31–35

He put before them another parable: "The kingdom of heaven is like a mustard seed that someone took and sowed in his field; it is the smallest of all the seeds, but when it has grown it is the greatest of shrubs and becomes a tree, so that the birds of the air come and make nests in its branches." He told them another parable: "The kingdom of heaven is like yeast that a woman took and mixed in with three measures of flour until all of it was leavened." Jesus told the crowds all these things in parables; without a parable he told them nothing. This was to fulfil what had been spoken through the prophet: "I will open my mouth to speak in parables; I will proclaim what has been hidden from the foundation of the world."

- The mustard seed and the yeast symbolise the growth brought about by Jesus' ministry. We are meant to be struck with wonder that one man, Jesus, could bring about the salvation of the world. I ask that I may never try to domesticate God, nor reduce his greatness to what is small and manageable.
- God is overflowing goodness: let me trust that and rejoice in it.

Tuesday 29th July   **Matthew 13:36–43**

His disciples approached Jesus, saying, "Explain to us the parable of the weeds of the field." He answered, "The one who sows the good seed is the Son of Man; the field is the world, and the good seed are the children of the kingdom; the weeds are the children of the evil one, and the enemy who sowed them is the devil; the harvest is the end of the age, and the reapers are angels. Just as the weeds are collected and burned up with fire, so will it be at the end of the age. The Son of Man will send his angels, and they will collect out of his kingdom all causes of sin and all evildoers, and they will throw them into the furnace of fire, where there will be weeping and gnashing of teeth. Then the righteous will shine like the sun in the kingdom of their Father. Let anyone with ears listen!"

- We must live in a world where good and evil are intertwined. Jesus warns that only at the end of time will all be resolved.
- In the meantime we are not to despair in the face of evil, but to trust that God can bring good out of human evil. I ask that by the end of history all of us may shine together like the sun.

Wednesday 30th July   **Matthew 13:44–46**

Jesus said to the disciples, "The kingdom of heaven is like treasure hidden in a field, which someone found and hid; then in his joy he goes and sells all that he has and buys that field. "Again, the kingdom of heaven is like a merchant in search of fine pearls; on finding one pearl of great value, he went and sold all that he had and bought it."

- In the Lord's Prayer, we ask that the kingdom will come among us and within us. But that requires our co-operation.
- The kingdom should be our greatest and most important possession. It means that my values are the values of God. Is that how I see it? Would anyone know?

Thursday 31st July,
St Ignatius Loyola   Matthew 13:47–53

Jesus said, "Again, the kingdom of heaven is like a net that was thrown into the sea and caught fish of every kind; when it was full, they drew it ashore, sat down, and put the good into baskets but threw out the bad. So it will be at the end of the age. The angels will come out and separate the evil from the righteous and throw them into the furnace of fire, where there will be weeping and gnashing of teeth. Have you understood all this?" They answered, "Yes." And he said to them, "Therefore every scribe who has been trained for the kingdom of heaven is like the master of a household who brings out of his treasure what is new and what is old."

- Will judgment be a final division of good and bad? The early Church held the hope that somehow, by the goodness of God, we will all be saved. I must work and pray for this.
- Sometimes we have little patience with old ways and customs. But the storehouse of the kingdom contains many treasures.

Friday 1st August   Matthew 13:54–58

Jesus came to his home town and began to teach the people in their synagogue, so that they were astounded and said, "Where did this man get this wisdom and these deeds of power? Is not this the carpenter's son? Is not his mother called Mary? And are not his brothers James and Joseph and Simon and Judas? And are not all his sisters with us? Where then did this man get all this?" And they took offense at him. But Jesus said to them, "Prophets are not without honor except in their own country and in their own house." And he did not do many deeds of power there, because of their unbelief.

- Faith is necessary for "deeds of power"—either our own faith or that of those who pray for us. Without faith, Jesus' hands are tied and his power is limited.
- I pray for greater faith: "I believe, Lord, help my unbelief."

Saturday 2nd August   **Matthew 14:1–12**

At that time Herod the ruler heard reports about Jesus; and he said to his servants, "This is John the Baptist; he has been raised from the dead, and for this reason these powers are at work in him." For Herod had arrested John, bound him, and put him in prison on account of Herodias, his brother Philip's wife, because John had been telling him, "It is not lawful for you to have her." Though Herod wanted to put him to death, he feared the crowd, because they regarded him as a prophet. But when Herod's birthday came, the daughter of Herodias danced before the company, and she pleased Herod so much that he promised on oath to grant her whatever she might ask. Prompted by her mother, she said, "Give me the head of John the Baptist here on a platter." The king was grieved, yet out of regard for his oaths and for the guests, he commanded it to be given; he sent and had John beheaded in the prison. The head was brought on a platter and given to the girl, who brought it to her mother. His disciples came and took the body and buried it; then they went and told Jesus.

• This is a story about negative emotions—fear, passion, hatred, lack of respect. These can so overwhelm us that we ignore their consequences.

• Self-control isn't popular in our world. But it is a gift of the Spirit: perhaps I need to pray for it?

Something to think and pray about each day this week:

The image of God

In the Book of Job God speaks from the heart of a storm. This impresses upon poor Job that God is the Almighty One, before whom all creatures should be silent. Job acknowledges that he has spoken out of turn; he says, "My words have been frivolous: what can I reply? I had better lay my hand over my mouth" (Job 40:4). God is presented here as the Creator who is totally different from his creatures, and who is to be respected and obeyed.

Is this our image of God? The issue arises for us when we make a serious effort to pray. Images shape the atmosphere of our prayer. There are two related questions: "Who is God for me?" and, "Who am I for God?" These two questions arise either explicitly or implicitly because our prayer time is a meeting with God. "Who is this God whom I am meeting? What is God like? What is my perception of God?" And on the other hand, "Who am I for God? What does God see in me? How is God regarding me?" There is a lifelong spiritual journey encompassed within these two broad questions, for I am always needing to grow in my perception of who God is for me, and I am also needing to see myself through God's eyes.

Saint Teresa says: "Gaze on him, who gazes on you lovingly and humbly."

The Presence of God
I pause for a moment
and reflect on God's life-giving presence
in every part of my body, in everything around me,
in the whole of my life.

Freedom
I ask for the grace to believe
in what I could be and do
if I only allowed God, my loving Creator,
to continue to create me, guide me and shape me.

Consciousness
In God's loving presence I unwind the past day,
starting from now and looking back, moment by moment.
I gather in all the goodness and light, in gratitude.
I attend to the shadows and what they say to me,
seeking healing, courage, forgiveness.

The Word
God speaks to each one of us individually. I need to listen to
what he is saying to me. (Please turn to your scripture on the
following pages. Inspiration points are there should you need
them. When you are ready, return here to continue.)

Conversation
How has God's Word moved me? Has it left me cold?
Has it consoled me or moved me to act in a new way?
I imagine Jesus standing or sitting beside me,
I turn and share my feelings with him.

Conclusion
Glory be to the Father, and to the Son, and to the Holy Spirit,
As it was in the beginning, is now and ever shall be,
World without end. Amen

Sunday 3rd August,
Eighteenth Sunday in Ordinary Time   Matthew 14:13–21

Now when Jesus heard of the death of John the Baptist, he withdrew from there in a boat to a deserted place by himself. But when the crowds heard it, they followed him on foot from the towns. When he went ashore, he saw a great crowd; and he had compassion for them and cured their sick. When it was evening, the disciples came to him and said, "This is a deserted place, and the hour is now late; send the crowds away so that they may go into the villages and buy food for themselves." Jesus said to them, "They need not go away; you give them something to eat." They replied, "We have nothing here but five loaves and two fish." And he said, "Bring them here to me." Then he ordered the crowds to sit down on the grass. Taking the five loaves and the two fish, he looked up to heaven, and blessed and broke the loaves, and gave them to the disciples, and the disciples gave them to the crowds. And all ate and were filled; and they took up what was left over of the broken pieces, twelve baskets full. And those who ate were about five thousand men, besides women and children.

- Jesus' first response on hearing of the death of John the Baptist was to withdraw to a quiet place. He was able, however, to change his plan to meet the needs of the people.
- I pray for the same freedom: to know what I need and to seek it, remaining ready to turn aside to serve the greater good.

Monday 4th August   Matthew 14:25–32

Early in the morning he came walking towards them on the lake. But when the disciples saw him walking on the lake, they were terrified, saying, "It is a ghost!" And they cried out in fear. But immediately Jesus spoke to them and said, "Take heart, it is I; do not be afraid." Peter answered him, "Lord, if it is you, command me to come to you on the water." He said, "Come." So Peter got out of the boat, started walking on the water, and came towards Jesus. But when he noticed the strong wind, he became frightened, and beginning to sink, he cried out, "Lord, save me!" Jesus immediately reached out his hand and caught him, saying to him, "You of little faith, why did you doubt?" When they got into the boat, the wind ceased. And those in the boat worshipped him, saying, "Truly you are the Son of God."

- Peter always responded energetically and fully, risking everything. His faltering seems to have begun when he took his eyes off Jesus. Then he realized that he couldn't rely just on himself.
- Jesus made his way to the boat where the disciples were having some trouble. Intent on their own efforts, they did not realize he was there. I do what I can, as a disciple, but try not to forget that the one I follow is very near.

Tuesday 5th August   **Matthew 15:1, 1–2, 10–14**
Then Pharisees and scribes came to Jesus from Jerusalem and said, "Why do your disciples break the tradition of the elders? For they do not wash their hands before they eat." Then he called the crowd to him and said to them, "Listen and understand: it is not what goes into the mouth that defiles a person, but it is what comes out of the mouth that defiles." Then the disciples approached and said to him, "Do you know that the Pharisees took offence when they heard what you said?" He answered, "Every plant that my heavenly Father has not planted will be uprooted. Let them alone; they are blind guides of the blind. And if one blind person guides another, both will fall into a pit."

- Have you ever thought of yourself as a plant, planted by God? What sort of plant would you like to be—a rose or a cactus, a common plant, or perhaps something more exotic?
- Or a sunflower which is said to face always toward the sun? What does our gardening God think of us?

Wednesday 6th August,
Transfiguration of the Lord   **Matthew 17:1–9**
Six days later, Jesus took with him Peter and James and his brother John and led them up a high mountain, by

themselves. And he was transfigured before them, and his face shone like the sun, and his clothes became dazzling white. Suddenly there appeared to them Moses and Elijah, talking with him. Then Peter said to Jesus, "Lord, it is good for us to be here; if you wish, I will make three dwellings here, one for you, one for Moses, and one for Elijah." While he was still speaking, suddenly a bright cloud overshadowed them, and from the cloud a voice said, "This is my Son, the Beloved; with him I am well pleased; listen to him!" When the disciples heard this, they fell to the ground and were overcome by fear. But Jesus came and touched them, saying, "Get up and do not be afraid." And when they looked up, they saw no one except Jesus himself alone. As they were coming down the mountain, Jesus ordered them, "Tell no one about the vision until after the Son of Man has been raised from the dead."

- This revelation came after an arduous climb "up a high mountain." It reveals Jesus' importance. Am I willing to work hard, perhaps in prayer, to get to know Jesus more deeply?
- Impulsive Peter wanted to honour Jesus, Moses and Elijah. It took the voice to silence him and to reveal that Jesus is the one that matters. As a disciple, do I always try to listen to Jesus?

Thursday 7th August   **Matthew 16:13–16**

Now when Jesus came into the district of Caesarea Philippi, he asked his disciples, "Who do people say that the Son of Man is?" And they said, "Some say John the Baptist, but others Elijah, and still others Jeremiah or one of the prophets." He said to them, "But who do you say that I am?" Simon Peter answered, "You are the Messiah, the Son of the living God."

- At Caesarea there was a shrine to Pan, the god of shepherds and flocks. Imperial power was also embedded in the name. But now God's chosen shepherd is acknowledged: he will carry out God's purposes.
- The person of Jesus, not the law of the past, would be the centre of the new community. Is it so in my local church?

Friday 8th August   **Matthew 16:24–26**

Then Jesus told his disciples, "If any want to become my followers, let them deny themselves and take up their cross and follow me. For those who want to save their life will lose it, and those who lose their life for my sake will find it. For what will it profit them if they gain the whole world but forfeit their life? Or what will they give in return for their life?"

- Being a disciple is costly. He speaks about taking myself out of the centre of the picture so that Jesus and his cause is "the" essential.
- This means that we carry the cross of the injustice and violence of the world as he did. We can let this human reality enter our prayer—praying both for those who suffer needlessly and that we can be people who feel the pain of others in such a way as to improve and redeem their lives.

Saturday 9th August   **Matthew 17:14–20**

When they came to the crowd, a man came to Jesus, knelt before him, and said, "Lord, have mercy on my son, for he is an epileptic and he suffers terribly; he often falls into the fire and often into the water. And I brought him to your disciples, but they could not cure him." Jesus answered, "You faithless and perverse generation, how much longer must I be with you? How much longer must I put up with you? Bring him here to me." And Jesus rebuked the demon, and it came out of him, and the boy was cured instantly. Then the disciples came to Jesus privately and said, "Why could we not cast it out?" He said to them, "Because of your little faith. For truly I tell you, if you have faith the size of a mustard seed, you will say to this mountain, 'Move from here to there,' and it will move; and nothing will be impossible for you."

- Not surprisingly, Jesus can get quite frustrated at our perversity and lack of faith. In what areas of my life do I show these qualities of non-responsiveness? What can I do about them?
- Jesus has no doubt that if we had enough faith we could move mountains. In other words, if my relationship with the Father were as strong as Jesus' was, the power of God could flow freely through me and achieve great things. Do I want this?

Something to think and pray about each day this week:

Growing in faith

The youthful John Henry Newman was captivated by the phrase "Growth is the only evidence of life." He had a sense that faith is a continuing discovery, not simply a dogged adherence to static truths about God. Faith, he would say, is a life, and it moves ever onward. Faith is a commitment to Another, and like falling in love, it is meant to be an adventure which engages the whole person, and forever. Intellectual engagement is not enough; the heart, the person, must be caught and transformed.

The word "creed" comes from two small Latin words: *Cor do*, which mean: "I give my heart." Faith involves a relationship: on one side is a generous and concerned God who gives us everything. On the other side is myself, who have nothing to give except my yearning heart.

In prayer we express that hunger, and that is a great thing. We may worry that the "younger generation" has little sense of the great truths of the faith. But what we can offer them is a witness that God is the most important person in our own lives, that we are in love with God and God with us. We become living witnesses to something which they are searching for.

The Presence of God

"The world is charged with the grandeur of God" (Gerard Manley Hopkins).
I dwell for a moment on the presence of God
around me, in every part of my body,
and deep within my being.

Freedom

"In these days, God taught me
as a schoolteacher teaches a pupil" (St Ignatius).
I remind myself that there are things God has to teach me yet,
and ask for the grace to hear them and let them change me.

Consciousness

Help me, Lord, to be more conscious of your presence.
Teach me to recognize your presence in others.
Fill my heart with gratitude for the times your love
has been shown to me through the care of others.

The Word

I read the Word of God slowly, a few times over, and I listen
to what God is saying to me. (Please turn to your scripture on
the following pages. Inspirations points are there should you
need them. When you are ready, return here to continue.)

Conversation

What feelings are rising in me
as I pray and reflect on God's Word?
I imagine Jesus himself sitting or standing beside me,
and open my heart to him.

Conclusion

Glory be to the Father, and to the Son, and to the Holy Spirit,
As it was in the beginning, is now and ever shall be,
World without end. Amen

Sunday 10th August, Nineteenth Sunday in Ordinary Time

Matthew 14:22–33

Jesus made the disciples get into the boat and go on ahead to the other side, while he dismissed the crowds. And after he had dismissed the crowds, he went up the mountain by himself to pray. When evening came, he was there alone, but by this time the boat, battered by the waves, was far from the land, for the wind was against them. And early in the morning he came walking toward them on the sea. But when the disciples saw him walking on the sea, they were terrified, saying, "It is a ghost!" And they cried out in fear. But immediately Jesus spoke to them and said, "Take heart, it is I; do not be afraid." Peter answered Jesus, "Lord, if it is you, command me to come to you on the water." He said, "Come." So Peter got out of the boat, started walking on the water, and came towards Jesus. But when he noticed the strong wind, he became frightened, and beginning to sink, he cried out, "Lord, save me!" Jesus immediately reached out his hand and caught him, saying to him, "You of little faith, why did you doubt?" When they got into the boat, the wind ceased. And those in the boat worshipped him, saying, "Truly you are the Son of God."

- Time apart at prayer did not close Jesus to the world, but inspired him to go to the help of the troubled disciples. The time that I spend at prayer builds me up in my relationship with God and strengthens me to act in God's name.
- Peter had courage when his eyes were on Jesus, but foundered when he focused on himself and his situation. I ask God to help me to keep Jesus before me.

Monday 11th August

Matthew 17:22–27

As they were gathering in Galilee, Jesus said to them, "The Son of Man is going to be betrayed into human hands, and they will kill him, and on the third day he will be raised." And they were greatly distressed. When they reached Capernaum, the collectors of the temple tax came to Peter and said, "Does your teacher not pay the temple tax?" He said, "Yes, he does." And when he came home, Jesus spoke of it first, asking, "What do you think, Simon? From whom do kings of the earth take toll or tribute? From their children or from others?" When Peter said, "From others." Jesus said to him, "Then the children are free. However, so that we do not give offence to them, go to the lake and cast a hook; take the first fish that comes up; and when you open its mouth, you will find a coin; take that and give it to them for you and me."

- Living in faith I may, like Jesus, be ready for all my actions and words to be weighed and evaluated.
- Jesus did not discuss everything freely in public but waited until he was alone with the disciples. I need time before I speak; time to reflect and time to consider where my words might be best used.

Tuesday 12th August   Matthew 18:1–5

At that time the disciples came to Jesus and asked, "Who is the greatest in the kingdom of heaven?" He called a child, whom he put among them, and said, "Truly I tell you, unless you change and become like children, you will never enter the kingdom of heaven. Whoever becomes humble like this child is the greatest in the kingdom of heaven. Whoever welcomes one such child in my name welcomes me."

- Because we are competitive we are anxious to know who is the best, the cleverest, the greatest. Status means a great deal to us.
- Jesus shocks the disciples by saying that without the humility and simplicity of little children, we are not even in the race.

Wednesday 13th August   Matthew 18:19–20

Jesus said, "Again, truly I tell you, if two of you agree on earth about anything you ask, it will be done for you by my Father in heaven. For where two or three are gathered in my name, I am there among them."

- Jesus promises guidance and his presence to his followers for all ages. If we gather in his name, he is with us. The "in his name" means openness to his word and the traditions faithfully handed on by his community of followers.

- It means openness to asking for wisdom and guidance and the humility to admit that none of us has all the answers.

Thursday 14th August   Matthew 18:21–19:1

Then Peter came and said to him, "Lord, if another member of the church sins against me, how often should I forgive? As many as seven times?" Jesus said to him, "Not seven times, but, I tell you, seventy-seven times." "For this reason the kingdom of heaven may be compared to a king who wished to settle accounts with his slaves. When he began the reckoning, one who owed him ten thousand talents was brought to him; and, as he could not pay, his lord ordered him to be sold, together with his wife and children and all his possessions, and payment to be made. So the slave fell on his knees before him, saying, 'Have patience with me, and I will pay you everything.' And out of pity for him, the lord of that slave released him and forgave him the debt. But that same slave, as he went out, came upon one of his fellow-slaves who owed him a hundred denarii; and seizing him by the throat, he said, 'Pay what you owe.' Then his fellow slave fell down and pleaded with him, 'Have patience with me, and I will pay you.' But he refused; then he went and threw him into prison until he should pay the debt. When his fellow-slaves saw what had happened, they were greatly distressed, and they went and reported to their lord all that had taken place. Then his lord summoned him and said to him, 'You wicked slave! I forgave you all that debt because you pleaded with me. Should you not have had mercy on your fellow-slave, as I had mercy on you?' And in anger his lord handed him over to be tortured until he should pay his entire debt. So my heavenly Father will also do to every one of you, if you do not forgive your brother or sister from your heart." When Jesus had finished saying these things, he left Galilee and went to the region of Judea beyond the Jordan.

- I use my imagination and allow myself to be drawn into this story; I think of how I am forgiven and consider how well I offer that forgiveness to others.

- I ask God to help me to see and appreciate how forgiving God is towards me.

Friday 15th August,
Assumption of the Virgin Mary   Luke 1:46–56

And Mary said, "My soul magnifies the Lord, and my spirit rejoices in God my Savior, for he has looked with favor on the lowliness of his servant. Surely, from now on all generations will call me blessed; for the Mighty One has done great things for me, and holy is his name. His mercy is for those who fear him from generation to generation. He has shown strength with his arm; he has scattered the proud in the thoughts of their hearts. He has brought down the powerful from their thrones, and lifted up the lowly; he has filled the hungry with good things, and sent the rich away empty. He has helped his servant Israel, in remembrance of his mercy, according to the promise he made to our ancestors, to Abraham and to his descendants forever." And Mary remained with Elizabeth about three months and then returned to her home.

- Mary was a woman of faith. Elizabeth praises her, not because she has conceived the Christ, but because she believed the angel's words. Let us pray to her for the strong faith we need in these troubled times. God can do what *we* think impossible.
- Mary passes on the praise to God. No false humility here—just an acknowledgment of the truth. God is the author of every good in my life. Let me ponder this.

Saturday 16th August   Matthew 19:13–15

Then little children were being brought to Jesus in order that he might lay his hands on them and pray. The disciples spoke sternly to those who brought them; but Jesus said, "Let the little children come to me, and do not stop them; for it is to such as these that the kingdom of heaven belongs." And he laid his hands on them and went on his way.

- How Jesus loved little children! He rejoiced in their innocence and gaiety. He looked into their eyes and saw the purity of their souls and the trust of their hearts. I pray for children who have been abused in any way.

- "The kingdom of heaven belongs to such as these." But I have lost my innocence; my trust in God is shaky; I don't experience much joy in life. Help me, Lord, to become again like a trusting little child before you, for nothing is impossible for you. Amen.

Sacred Space

Something to think and pray about each day this week:

Transforming the world

There is a growing sense that "our" world—which of course, actually belongs to God—has its place in the final scheme of things. This should be a source of joy to us. For much of Christian history, matter was suspect. So we were taught that after death the "separated soul" enjoys the beatific vision, the body being added in for our enjoyment only at the last day.

Now, however, we speak of the transformation of matter by the Incarnation: the unity of the human person is acknowledged, and resurrection is understood as the rising of the total person to life with God.

This brings into focus the final transformation of the cosmos. We are "children of this world" in Karl Rahner's term, and through the Incarnation God has become forever part of the material universe, most obviously through the Eucharist, when the most ordinary things, bread and wine, become Christ's own body. This invests our ecological concerns with grace and hope. We feel that what we have destroyed will never be restored to us.

But God, who by a single word created our cosmos with its vast array, can with another word restore what we have disfigured, and make all bloom again. Christian hope is for the long haul! Not only are we precious to God, but our world is also, and both will be made glorious in God's good time.

The Presence of God

As I sit here, God is present,
breathing life into me and into everything around me.
For a few moments, I sit silently,
and become aware of God's loving presence.

Freedom

If God were trying to tell me something, would I know?
If God were reassuring me or challenging me, would I notice?
I ask for the grace to be free of my own preoccupations
and open to what God may be saying to me.

Consciousness

How am I really feeling? Light-hearted? Heavy-hearted?
I may be very much at peace, happy to be here.
Equally, I may be frustrated, worried or angry.
I acknowledge how I really am. It is the real me that the
Lord loves.

The Word

I take my time to read the Word of God, slowly, a few times,
allowing myself to dwell on anything that strikes me. (Please
turn to your scripture on the following pages. Inspiration
points are there should you need them. When you are ready,
return here to continue.)

Conversation

What is stirring in me as I pray?
Am I consoled, troubled, left cold?
I imagine Jesus himself standing or sitting at my side,
and share my feelings with him.

Conclusion

Glory be to the Father, and to the Son, and to the Holy Spirit,
As it was in the beginning, is now and ever shall be,
World without end. Amen

Sunday 17th August,
Twentieth Sunday in Ordinary Time   Matthew 15:21–28

J esus left that place and went away to the district of Tyre and Sidon. Just then a Canaanite woman from that region came out and started shouting, "Have mercy on me, Lord, Son of David; my daughter is tormented by a demon." But he did not answer her at all. And his disciples came and urged him, saying, "Send her away, for she keeps shouting after us." He answered, "I was sent only to the lost sheep of the house of Israel." But she came and knelt before him, saying, "Lord, help me." He answered, "It is not fair to take the children's food and throw it to the dogs." She said, "Yes, Lord, yet even the dogs eat the crumbs that fall from their masters' table." Then Jesus answered her, "Woman, great is your faith! Let it be done for you as you wish." And her daughter was healed instantly.

- Even when the woman appeared to get a No from Jesus she persisted, showing the depth of her desire.
- I realize that my prayer often falters when I see no answer. Do I sometimes give up easily, not giving the energy, time or attention that demonstrates my sincerity?

Monday 18th August   Matthew 19:16–22

T hen someone came to Jesus and said, "Teacher, what good deed must I do to have eternal life?" And he said to him, "Why do you ask me about what is good? There is only one who is good. If you wish to enter into life, keep the command-ments." He said to him, "Which ones?" And Jesus said, "You shall not murder; You shall not commit adultery; You shall not steal; You shall not bear false witness; Honor your father and mother; also, You shall love your neighbor as yourself." The young man said to him, "I have kept all these; what do I still lack?" Jesus said to him, "If you wish to be perfect, go, sell your possessions, and give the money to the poor, and you will have treasure in heaven; then come, follow me." When the young man heard this word, he went away grieving, for he had many possessions.

- The rich young man has tried to be "good," but still feels something lacking, some "good deed" which will give him peace. Does that sound familiar? His is a religion of deeds rather than of relationships. And mine?
- Jesus lets him know that it is our love for him that matters most, not what we do. "Come, follow me!" Lord, make me a true disciple, help me to love you more and more.

Tuesday 19th August   **Matthew 19:23–26**

Jesus said to his disciples, "Truly I tell you, it will be hard for a rich person to enter the kingdom of heaven. Again I tell you, it is easier for a camel to go through the eye of a needle than for someone who is rich to enter the kingdom of God." When the disciples heard this, they were greatly astounded and said, "Then who can be saved?" But Jesus looked at them and said, "For mortals it is impossible, but for God all things are possible."

- These words also apply to spiritual "possessions." If we depend on our prayers and "good deeds" to get us into heaven, we may be in for a shock. They won't give us first place!
- We are saved because God is good, not because we have some goodness of our own, independent of God.

Wednesday 20th August   **Matthew 20:1–16**

Jesus said to his disciples, "For the kingdom of heaven is like a landowner who went out early in the morning to hire laborers for his vineyard. After agreeing with the laborers for the usual daily wage, he sent them into his vineyard. When he went out about nine o'clock, he saw others standing idle in the marketplace; and he said to them, 'You also go into the vineyard, and I will pay you whatever is right.' So they went. When he went out again about noon and about three o'clock, he did the same. And about five o'clock he went out and found others standing around; and he said to them, 'Why are you standing here idle all day?' They said to him, 'Because no one has hired us.' He said to them, 'You also go into the vineyard.' When evening came, the owner of the vineyard said to his manager, 'Call the laborers and give them their pay, beginning with the last and then going to the first.' When those hired about five o'clock came, each of them received the usual daily wage. Now when the first came, they thought they would receive more; but each of them also received the usual daily wage. And when they received it, they grumbled against the landowner, saying, 'These last worked only one hour, and you have made them equal to us who have borne the burden of the day and the scorching heat.' But he replied to one of them, 'Friend, I am doing you no wrong; did you not agree with me for the usual daily wage? Take what belongs to you and go; I choose to give to this last the same as I give to you. Am I not allowed to do what I choose with what belongs to me? Or are you envious because I am generous?' So the last will be first, and the first will be last."

- We tend to forget that the workers who started late had been "standing idle all day" waiting to be employed. They too had borne the "scorching heat" and were fearful of going home with empty hands. The generosity of the vineyard owner saves them. The story reveals the lavish generosity of God.

- "Are you envious because I am generous?" Do I feel envious of some who have been given a talent that I do not have? But God tells no one any story but their own. Lord, you know best: let me say a simple "Amen" to the way you are guiding my life.

Thursday 21st August Matthew 22:1–2, 8–14

Once more Jesus spoke to them in parables, saying: "The kingdom of heaven may be compared to a king who gave a wedding banquet for his son. Then he said to his slaves, 'The wedding is ready. Go therefore into the main streets, and invite everyone you find to the wedding banquet.' Those slaves went out into the streets and gathered all whom they found, both good and bad; so the wedding hall was filled with guests. But when the king came in to see the guests, he noticed a man there who was not wearing a wedding robe, and he said to him, 'Friend, how did you get in here without a wedding robe?' And he was speechless. Then the king said to the attendants, 'Bind him hand and foot, and throw him into the outer darkness, where there will be weeping and gnashing of teeth.' For many are called, but few are chosen."

- This generous king not only invited everyone to the wedding of his son, but also supplied suitable clothes for the banquet. One stubborn man refused the clothes and also refused to defend himself. He was defiant.
- The kingdom of heaven comes with a huge price—the suffering and death of Jesus. If we put on the "wedding robe" of our salvation, then we can enjoy God's banquet. Lord, let me not imagine that I do not need all that you have done for me!

Friday 22nd August — Matthew 22:34–40

When the Pharisees heard that Jesus had silenced the Sadducees, they gathered together, and one of them, a lawyer, asked him a question to test him. "Teacher, which commandment in the law is the greatest?" He said to him, "'You shall love the Lord your God with all your heart, and with all your soul, and with all your mind.' This is the greatest and first commandment. And a second is like it: 'You shall love your neighbor as yourself.' On these two commandments hang all the law and the prophets."

- I have a treasure in my heart, which is the limitless love of God for me. But I must share it with my needy neighbour.
- I ask to be a true escort of God's grace to others.

Saturday 23rd August — Matthew 23:1–12

Then Jesus said to the crowds and to his disciples, "The scribes and the Pharisees sit on Moses' seat; therefore, do whatever they teach you and follow it; but do not do as they do, for they do not practice what they teach. They tie up heavy burdens, hard to bear, and lay them on the shoulders of others; but they themselves are unwilling to lift a finger to move them. They do all their deeds to be seen by others; for they make their phylacteries broad and their fringes long. They love to have the place of honour at banquets and the best seats in the synagogues, and to be greeted with respect in the marketplaces, and to have people call them rabbi. You are not to be called rabbi, for you have one teacher, and you are all students. And call no one your father on earth, for you have one Father—the one in heaven. Nor are you to be called instructors, for you have one instructor, the Messiah. The greatest among you will be your servant. All who exalt themselves will be humbled, and all who humble themselves will be exalted."

- Hypocrisy means play-acting, being untrue to oneself. Jesus' harshest words are reserved for this vice. He sums it up very succinctly as "They do not practise what they preach." Do I?
- It is easy to see the hypocrisy of others, particularly of those in authority, but I need to be constantly vigilant about my own deceptions, the small lies I tell. I can change only myself. Lord, make me live transparently in the truth.

Sacred Space

Something to think and pray about each day this week:

The nature of prayer

I am inclined to believe that all people pray at some time. I recall the observation of a diplomat's wife who, tired of the bland exchanges at diplomatic gatherings, decided to begin asking those she met, "What place has prayer in your life?" To her pleasant surprise she discovered that despite differences of cultures and religions, most prayed and reached out to a higher power to ask for help or to express gratitude.

Prayer seems to start when we acknowledge that we are not in complete control and that we are faced with a certain puzzlement about our own life. Prayer is natural.

Those who build on this inner urge for meaning, make time for prayer. Either we use prayers composed by others, such as the psalms, or we talk in our own words about our needs and concerns, trusting that we are being heard. But if we persevere, we come to a point where we sense that there must be more to prayer than only the saying of prayers.

If I want to know that I am being heard, I will need to go beyond formulas and discover how to listen, how to pick up the signals that are coming from this God who wants to play an active part in my praying. Such a development takes time, however, because prayer, like any good relationship, is a long journey and is learnt by doing.

The Presence of God

As I sit here with these words in front of me, God is here.
Around me, in my sensations, in my thoughts and deep
within me.
I pause for a moment, and become aware
of God's life-giving presence.

Freedom

I need to rise above the noise;
the noise that interrupts, that separates,
the noise that isolates.
I need to listen to God again.

Consciousness

Knowing that God loves me unconditionally,
I can afford to be honest about how I am.
How has the last day been, and how do I feel now?
I share my feelings openly with the Lord.

The Word

God speaks to each one of us individually. I need to listen to
what he is saying to me. (Please turn to your scripture on the
following pages. Inspiration points are there should you need
them. When you are ready, return here to continue.)

Conversation

Do I notice myself reacting as I pray with the Word of God?
Do I feel challenged, comforted, angry?
Imagining Jesus sitting or standing by me,
I speak out my feelings, as one trusted friend to another.

Conclusion

Glory be to the Father, and to the Son, and to the Holy Spirit,
As it was in the beginning, is now and ever shall be,
World without end. Amen

Sunday 24th August, Twenty-first Sunday in Ordinary Time

Matthew 16:13–20

Now when Jesus came into the district of Caesarea Philippi, he asked his disciples, "Who do people say that the Son of Man is?" And they said, "Some say John the Baptist, but others Elijah, and still others Jeremiah or one of the prophets." He said to them, "But who do you say that I am?" Simon Peter answered, "You are the Messiah, the Son of the living God." And Jesus answered him, "Blessed are you, Simon son of Jonah! For flesh and blood has not revealed this to you, but my Father in heaven. And I tell you, you are Peter, and on this rock I will build my church, and the gates of Hades will not prevail against it. I will give you the keys of the kingdom of heaven, and whatever you bind on earth will be bound in heaven, and whatever you loose on earth will be loosed in heaven." Then he sternly ordered the disciples not to tell anyone that he was the Messiah.

- Jesus asks about what others say, but it is what Peter says that is important to him. I may come to prayer motivated to pray for others but God wants to be in touch with me personally. Prayer is my heart and God's heart in conversation.
- Jesus was not, for Peter, just another great or admirable figure. He was the one who could change his life. How do I let Jesus reconfigure my priorities?

Monday 25th August   Matthew 23:13–17

Jesus said to the people, "But woe to you, scribes and Pharisees, hypocrites! For you lock people out of the kingdom of heaven. For you do not go in yourselves, and when others are going in, you stop them. Woe to you, scribes and Pharisees, hypocrites! For you cross sea and land to make a single convert, and you make the new convert twice as much a child of hell as yourselves. Woe to you, blind guides, who say, 'Whoever swears by the sanctuary is bound by nothing, but whoever swears by the gold of the sanctuary is bound by the oath.' You blind fools! For which is greater, the gold or the sanctuary that has made the gold sacred?"

- Jesus continues his seven-fold condemnation of bad leaders. He wants people to be free, whereas bad leaders have a disastrous impact on those they are meant to serve.
- The phrase "blind guides" is a warning to authority figures in the Christian church. In his life and death Jesus protests against all forms of domination in the name of religion. He gives us eyes to look on God and then to act rightly. This is what prayer means.

Tuesday 26th August   Matthew 23:23–24

Jesus said, "Woe to you, scribes and Pharisees, hypocrites! For you tithe mint, dill, and cummin, and have neglected the weightier matters of the law: justice and mercy and faith. It is these you ought to have practiced without neglecting the others. You blind guides! You strain out a gnat but swallow a camel!

- People are often shocked at the hypocrisy of Christians who worship God on Sundays and then tear apart their neighbour's reputation during the rest of the week. Am I ever guilty?
- Cleaning "the inside of the cup" takes constant vigilance. Lord, don't let me keep using a dirty cup, especially when I am entertaining you!

Wednesday 27th August   Matthew 23:27–28

Jesus said to the people, "Woe to you, scribes and Pharisees, hypocrites! For you are like whitewashed tombs, which on the outside look beautiful, but inside they are full of the bones of the dead and of all kinds of filth. So you also on the outside look righteous to others, but inside you are full of hypocrisy and lawlessness."

- Sometimes I'm struck by the forced smiles on the faces of the "great and good." These people are busy projecting an image which is far from the truth. But is the image which I project to others the real me?

- When making decisions, we wonder "What would the neighbours say?" But does it really matter? There is only One whose opinion really matters. God knows the truth.

Thursday 28th August   Matthew 24:42–44

Jesus said to his disciples, "Keep awake therefore, for you do not know on what day your Lord is coming. But understand this: if the owner of the house had known in what part of the night the thief was coming, he would have stayed awake and would not have let his house be broken into. Therefore you also must be ready, for the Son of Man is coming at an unexpected hour."

- An example of staying awake: when Mary received her world-shattering message from God through the angel Gabriel, she did not miss the footnote. She set off to help Elizabeth. There she met God again.
- We must not be complacent, but alert to seeking and finding God however God wishes to be found.

Friday 29th August   Matthew 25:1–13

Jesus said to his disciples, "Then the kingdom of heaven will be like this. Ten bridesmaids took their lamps and went to meet the bridegroom. Five of them were foolish, and five were wise. When the foolish took their lamps, they took no oil with them; but the wise took flasks of oil with their lamps. As the bridegroom was delayed, all of them became drowsy and slept. But at midnight there was a shout, 'Look! Here is the bridegroom! Come out to meet him.' Then all those bridesmaids got up and trimmed their lamps. The foolish said to the wise, 'Give us some of your oil, for our lamps are going out.' But the wise replied, 'No! there will not be enough for you and for us; you had better go to the dealers and buy some for yourselves.' And while they went to buy it, the bridegroom came, and those who were ready went with him into the wedding banquet; and the door was shut. Later the other bridesmaids came also, saying, 'Lord, lord, open to us.' But he replied, 'Truly I tell you, I do not know you.' Keep awake therefore, for you know neither the day nor the hour."

- Weddings are special occasions and Jesus used them as images of the kingdom of heaven. The emphasis here is on preparation. Celebrations need preparation, and the more important they are, the more prepared we need to be.
- Lord, how bright is my lamp? Help me to be watching out for the ways you come to me.

Saturday 30th August   Matthew 25:14–28

Jesus told his disciples this parable, "For it is as if a man, going on a journey, summoned his slaves and entrusted his property to them; to one he gave five talents, to another two, to another one, to each according to his ability. Then he went away. The one who had received the five talents went off at once and traded with them, and made five more talents. In the same way, the one who had the two talents made two more talents. But the one who had received the one talent went off and dug a hole in the ground and hid his master's money. After a long time the master of those slaves came and settled accounts with them. Then the one who had received the five talents came forward, bringing five more talents, saying, 'Master, you handed over to me five talents; see, I have made five more talents.' His master said to him, 'Well done, good and trustworthy slave; you have been trustworthy in a few things, I will put you in charge of many things; enter into the joy of your master.' And the one with the two talents also came forward, saying, 'Master, you handed over to me two talents; see, I have made two more talents.' His master said to him, 'Well done, good and trustworthy slave; you have been trustworthy in a few things, I will put you in charge of many things; enter into the joy of your master.' Then the one who had received the one talent also came forward, saying, 'Master, I knew that you were a harsh man, reaping where you did not sow, and gathering where you did not scatter seed; so I was afraid, and I went and hid your talent in the ground. Here you have what is yours.' But his master replied, 'You wicked and lazy slave! You knew, did you, that I reap where I did not sow, and gather where I did not scatter? Then you ought to have invested my money with the bankers, and on my return I would have received what was my own with interest. So take the talent from him, and give it to the one with the ten talents.'"

- Physical and intellectual gifts if not exercised will atrophy. Likewise our spiritual gifts! The anxiety-ridden servant with his timid inactivity suffers the paralysis of a shut mind and stinginess too.
- Discipleship requires courage and risk-taking. Lord, let me discover my unique talents and use them in whole-hearted activity and worthwhile deeds of love. Deliver me, Lord, from becoming a timid disciple through neglect, inactivity, or fear.

Sacred Space

Something to think and pray about each day this week:

The presence of God

About 11 years ago I began to study as a mature-age student and an angry one. The anger was because of a perceived absence of God in the suffering of people I have loved. I hoped that my study might resolve my problem. But as I was about to write a thesis on suffering in Job, cancer attacked me. Thus, as it turned out, the last essay I wrote was on Jesus' prayer in Gethsemane.

The night before the operation was possibly the worst experience of my life. I was alone and terrified. There was the operation ahead, the possibility that I might not come out the other side of it, and there was no escape. Then suddenly I was in Gethsemane and there was a Presence, a very powerful Presence, beside me, which lifted and supported me firmly and gently. It was not a cosy Presence but one which sustained me and gave me courage and assurance that no matter what the outcome, all would be well. That Presence was still with me when I came to after the operation.

The experience of that Presence remains with me, and I now know that God is with us always but particularly in the dark moments when there is nothing else.

So, you see, I have had the answer to my furious questions, not through reading, listening and writing, but through a personal experience which I would never have chosen, and indeed never expected.

The Presence of God

I pause for a moment, aware that God is here.
I think of how everything around me,
the air I breathe, my whole body,
is tingling with the presence of God.

Freedom

I will ask God's help,
to be free from my own preoccupations,
to be open to God in this time of prayer,
to come to love and serve him more.

Consciousness

In the presence of my loving Creator,
I look honestly at my feelings over the last day,
the highs, the lows and the level ground.
Can I see where the Lord has been present?

The Word

I read the Word of God slowly, a few times over, and I listen
to what God is saying to me. (Please turn to your scripture on
the following pages. Inspiration points are there should you
need them. When you are ready, return here to continue.)

Conversation

Remembering that I am still in God's presence,
I imagine Jesus himself standing or sitting beside me,
and say whatever is on my mind, whatever is in my heart,
speaking as one friend to another.

Conclusion

Glory be to the Father, and to the Son, and to the Holy Spirit,
As it was in the beginning, is now and ever shall be,
World without end. Amen

Sunday 31st August,
Twenty-second Sunday in Ordinary Time

Matthew 16:21–27

From that time on, Jesus began to show his disciples that he must go to Jerusalem and undergo great suffering at the hands of the elders and chief priests and scribes, and be killed, and on the third day be raised. And Peter took him aside and began to rebuke him, saying, "God forbid it, Lord! This must never happen to you." But he turned and said to Peter, "Get behind me, Satan! You are a stumbling block to me; for you are setting your mind not on divine things but on human things." Then Jesus told his disciples, "If any want to become my followers, let them deny themselves and take up their cross and follow me. For those who want to save their life will lose it, and those who lose their life for my sake will find it. For what will it profit them if they gain the whole world but forfeit their life? Or what will they give in return for their life? For the Son of Man is to come with his angels in the glory of his Father, and then he will repay everyone for what has been done."

- Jesus tells us that hard choices have to be made. I pray that I may remain generous at such times and not become resentful or bitter.
- My prayer will help me to recognize the cross that God needs me to carry. Like Jesus in the Garden of Gethsemane, I pray that God's will be done.

Monday 1st September

Luke 4:16–22

When he came to Nazareth, where he had been brought up, he went to the synagogue on the sabbath day, as was his custom. He stood up to read, and the scroll of the prophet Isaiah was given to him. He unrolled the scroll and found the place where it was written: "The Spirit of the Lord is upon me, because he has anointed me to bring good news to the poor. He has sent me to proclaim release to the captives and recovery of sight to the blind, to let the oppressed go free, to proclaim the year of the Lord's favor." And he rolled up the scroll, gave it back to the attendant, and sat down. The eyes of all in the synagogue were fixed on him. Then he began to say to them, "Today this scripture has been fulfilled in your hearing." All spoke well of him and were amazed at the gracious words that came from his mouth.

- Filled with the very wind of God, Jesus begins his springtime ministry back in his hometown. He is full of loving compassion, liberation, and healing. The word receives a mixed reception: amazement and rejection.
- Lord, in what spirit do I receive your daily word? Is it with amazement or with indifference and apathy?

Tuesday 2nd September   Luke 4:31–37

He went down to Capernaum, a city in Galilee, and was teaching them on the sabbath. They were astounded at his teaching, because he spoke with authority. In the synagogue there was a man who had the spirit of an unclean demon, and he cried out with a loud voice, "Let us alone! What have you to do with us, Jesus of Nazareth? Have you come to destroy us? I know who you are, the Holy One of God." But Jesus rebuked him, saying, "Be silent, and come out of him!" When the demon had thrown him down before them, he came out of him without having done him any harm. They were all amazed and kept saying to one another, "What kind of utterance is this? For with authority and power he commands the unclean spirits, and out they come!" And a report about him began to reach every place in the region.

- Unlike the rabbis of his day who must look outside themselves for validation, Jesus carries his authority within himself. He is the expert: people recognize this and are amazed and astounded!
- Liberation comes to a man possessed of a demon. The spirit of evil retreats from the spirit of good in Jesus. Lord, may my daily encounter with you in *Sacred Space* enable me to speak with a power and authority that is rooted in your living word.

Wednesday 3rd September   Luke 4:40–44

As the sun was setting, all those who had any who were sick with various kinds of diseases brought them to Jesus; and he laid his hands on each of them and cured them. Demons also came out of many, shouting, "You are the Son of God!" But he rebuked them and would not allow them to speak, because they knew that he was the Messiah. At daybreak he departed and went into a deserted place. And the crowds were looking for him; and when they reached him, they wanted to prevent him from leaving them. But he said to them, "I must proclaim the good news of the kingdom of God to the other cities also; for I was sent for this purpose." So he continued proclaiming the message in the synagogues of Judea.

- Health is such a priceless gift, Lord. When I am well may I use this gift in the service of others.

- Lord, today I bring to you my many friends who are sick in mind, body or spirit. Lay your healing hands upon them and renew their spirits.

Thursday 4th September   Luke 5:4–11

When Jesus had finished speaking, he said to Simon, "Put out into the deep water and let down your nets for a catch." Simon answered, "Master, we have worked all night long but have caught nothing. Yet if you say so, I will let down the nets." When they had done this, they caught so many fish that their nets were beginning to break. So they signaled their partners in the other boat to come and help them. And they came and filled both boats, so that they began to sink. But when Simon Peter saw it, he fell down at Jesus' knees, saying, "Go away from me, Lord, for I am a sinful man!" For he and all who were with him were amazed at the catch of fish that they had taken; and so also were James and John, sons of Zebedee, who were partners with Simon. Then Jesus said to Simon, "Do not be afraid; from now on you will be catching people." When they had brought their boats to shore, they left everything and followed him.

- An adventure is about to unfold, an encounter that is radical and life-changing. Simon the fisherman, called by Jesus to go beyond his comfort zone, puts the boat of his life out into deep waters. From that moment forward his entire life is hooked on Jesus.
- Lord, you call me daily to an adventure of faith with you. You are the captain of the boat of my life, and I am your crew. Grant me the courage to take risks, knowing that you are always with me.

Friday 5th September   Luke 5:33–39

Then the Pharisees and the scribes said to Jesus, "John's disciples, like the disciples of the Pharisees, frequently fast and pray, but your disciples eat and drink." Jesus said to them, "You cannot make wedding guests fast while the bridegroom is with them, can you? The days will come when the bridegroom will be taken away from them, and then they will fast in those days." He also told them a parable: "No one tears a piece from a new garment and sews it on an old garment; otherwise the new will be torn, and the piece from the new will not match the old. And no one puts new wine into old wineskins; otherwise the new wine will burst the skins and will be spilled, and the skins will be destroyed. But new wine must be put into fresh wineskins."

- Fasting has its place, but not during a wedding celebration. The religion of the Pharisees and Scribes was anxiety-ridden, full of doom and gloom. Jesus invites his hearers to celebrate the joy of what God is doing. Shrivelled wineskins can never hold the abundance of this joy-filled message.
- Lord, our Church is sorely in need of new wineskins. Grant me an elasticity of heart and mind, so that I can be ever open to the freshness and power of your word.

Saturday 6th September   1 Corinthians 4:9–14

For I think that God has exhibited us apostles as last of all, as though sentenced to death, because we have become a spectacle to the world, to angels and to mortals. We are fools for the sake of Christ, but you are wise in Christ. We are weak, but you are strong. You are held in honour, but we in disrepute. To the present hour we are hungry and thirsty, we are poorly clothed and beaten and homeless, and we grow weary from the work of our own hands. When reviled, we bless; when persecuted, we endure; when slandered, we speak kindly. We have become like the rubbish of the world, the dregs of all things, to this very day.

- I bring to my prayer those who may have difficulties with me and with what I believe. I pray for them and ask for a softness of heart and a real desire for their good.
- I pray for all those who believe themselves to be less than who God has made them to be.

Sacred Space

Something to think and pray about each day this week:

Towards a privileged place

There is a certain similarity between how I am in myself and how I perceive God. To observe rules and right behavior is good, but it is not a place at which to remain, else I will see God only as lawgiver and critical accountant, and I will be preoccupied by performance.

There is more. God invites me beyond a life lived by commandments, even if they be divine. My Creator is inviting me into a personal relationship of love. I am invited to awaken to the deep truth of what it means to be a creature, namely, that my Creator is loving me continuously into existence. I am attractive and important in God's eyes, precious to him. To accept this truth brings a big shift in my perception of who I am and who God is. A new level of relationship with God comes into view. But there is yet more.

This God wants my heart. God is giving me his heart already by loving me without reserve. God even gives me his Son, so that I can be not only a loved creature but an adopted son or daughter, who shares in the inner life of the Three Persons. It takes time and God's grace to become able to hear this in such a way that it becomes real for me. Personal prayer is a privileged place in which to hear and to develop it over a lifetime.

The Presence of God

For a few moments, I think of God's veiled presence in things:
in the elements, giving them existence;
in plants, giving them life; in animals, giving them sensation;
and finally, in me, giving me all this and more,
making me a temple, a dwelling-place of the Spirit.

Freedom

God is not foreign to my freedom.
Instead the Spirit breathes life into my most intimate desires,
gently nudging me towards all that is good.
I ask for the grace to let myself be enfolded by the Spirit.

Consciousness

Knowing that God loves me unconditionally,
I look honestly over the last day, its events and my feelings.
Do I have something to be grateful for? Then I give thanks.
Is there something I am sorry for? Then I ask forgiveness.

The Word

I take my time to read the Word of God, slowly, a few times,
allowing myself to dwell on anything that strikes me. (Please
turn to your scripture on the following pages. Inspiration
points are there should you need them. When you are ready,
return here to continue.)

Conversation

How has God's Word moved me? Has it left me cold?
Has it consoled me or moved me to act in a new way?
I imagine Jesus standing or sitting beside me,
I turn and share my feelings with him.

Conclusion

Glory be to the Father, and to the Son, and to the Holy Spirit,
As it was in the beginning, is now and ever shall be,
World without end. Amen

Sunday 7th September,
Twenty-third Sunday
in Ordinary Time

Matthew 18:15–17

Jesus said, "If another member of the church sins against you, go and point out the fault when the two of you are alone. If the member listens to you, you have regained that one. But if you are not listened to, take one or two others along with you, so that every word may be confirmed by the evidence of two or three witnesses. If the member refuses to listen to them, tell it to the church; and if the offender refuses to listen even to the church, let such a one be to you as a Gentile and a tax collector."

- Jesus does not imagine a life full of harmony and companionship, but acknowledges the need for forgiveness, patience and humility. I pray that I may live in a way that forgives freely and repents readily.
- Matthew describes a "safety net," a bottom line, an emergency drill. I can give thanks if life is usually less acrimonious. This itself is a sign that the Spirit of God is present and active; helping, healing, bringing wholeness.

Monday 8th September,
Birthday of the
Blessed Virgin Mary

Matthew 1:16, 18–23

Now the birth of Jesus the Messiah took place in this way. When his mother Mary had been engaged to Joseph, but before they lived together, she was found to be with child from the Holy Spirit. Her husband Joseph, being a righteous man and unwilling to expose her to public disgrace, planned to dismiss her quietly. But just when he had resolved to do this, an angel of the Lord appeared to him in a dream and said, "Joseph, son of David, do not be afraid to take Mary as your wife, for the child conceived in her is from the Holy Spirit. She will bear a son, and you are to name him Jesus, for he will save his people from their sins." All this took place to fulfill what had been spoken by the Lord through the prophet: "Look, the virgin shall conceive and bear a son, and they shall name him Emmanuel," which means, "God is with us."

- We contemplate here a major crisis in the life of Joseph. Hopes and expectations dashed, how is he to respond to this moral dilemma? Just when he has come to a reasonable decision, a divine intervention awakens him to trust the deeper action of "Another" at work.
- Lord, at a personal level I grapple with upheavals and feel overwhelmed at times. In the midst of such nightmare scenarios, give me eyes to see you. Wake me up to trust in your faithful presence, you who are God-with-us.

Tuesday 9th September   Luke 6:12–16

Now during those days he went out to the mountain to pray; and he spent the night in prayer to God. And when day came, he called his disciples and chose twelve of them, whom he also named apostles: Simon, whom he named Peter, and his brother Andrew, and James, and John, and Philip, and Bartholomew, and Matthew, and Thomas, and James son of Alphaeus, and Simon, who was called the Zealot, and Judas son of James, and Judas Iscariot, who became a traitor.

- Luke's gospel highlights the centrality of prayer in the life and mission of Jesus. His decisions and choices emerge from lengthy periods of communion with the one he calls "Abba."
- Lord, I come to you in this time of prayer to take your touch. Let me hear again your call to me. Let me sense your power at work in and through me.

Wednesday 10th September   Luke 6:20–23

Then Jesus looked up at his disciples and said: "Blessed are you who are poor, for yours is the kingdom of God. Blessed are you who are hungry now, for you will be filled. Blessed are you who weep now, for you will laugh. Blessed are you when people hate you, and when they exclude you, revile you, and defame you on account of the Son of Man. Rejoice on that day and leap for joy, for surely your reward is great in heaven; for that is what their ancestors did to the prophets."

- The beatitudes are a series of bombshells. They are revolutionary. Each beatitude challenges our comfortable, carefully constructed value systems.
- Lord, to be filled with blessedness demands a transformation from within, a conversion of heart and mind. Do not let me tame your word. May I live a simple and uncluttered way of life in solidarity with the poor.

Thursday 11th September　　　　　　　**Luke 6:27, 32–36**

"But I say to you that listen, if you love those who love you, what credit is that to you? For even sinners love those who love them. If you do good to those who do good to you, what credit is that to you? For even sinners do the same. If you lend to those from whom you hope to receive, what credit is that to you? Even sinners lend to sinners, to receive as much again. But love your enemies, do good, and lend, expecting nothing in return. Your reward will be great, and you will be children of the Most High; for he is kind to the ungrateful and the wicked. Be merciful, just as your Father is merciful."

- Jesus, the love you speak of is not just emotion: it is a commitment of the will. It is extravagant and limitless, and it includes us all, good and bad alike. "The measure of love is to love without measure."
- Lord, I am the focus of your indiscriminate love. Grant me a profound appreciation of this limitless gift. Transformed by this love, may I in turn show unrestricted loving to others-especially to my enemies!

Friday 12th September　　　　　　　**1 Corinthians 9:19, 22–27**

For though I am free with respect to all, I have made myself a slave to all, so that I might win more of them. To the weak I became weak, so that I might win the weak. I have become all things to all people, so that I might by any means save some. I do it all for the sake of the gospel, so that I may share in its blessings. Do you not know that in a race the runners all compete, but only one receives the prize? Run in such a way that you may win it. Athletes exercise self-control in all things; they do it to receive a perishable garland, but we an imperishable one. So I do not run aimlessly, nor do I box as though beating the air; but I punish my body and enslave it, so that after proclaiming to others I myself should not be disqualified.

- Considering the runners in the stadium, I bring myself to God for healing, encouragement and strength. I listen for the advice that God has for me, imagining a coach who knows my strengths and weaknesses well.

- The endeavour and commitment of athletes speaks to me of their single-mindedness. As I bring my desires to God, I ask for the focus that I need to serve God wholeheartedly.

Saturday 13th September   Luke 6:46–49

Jesus said to the people, "Why do you call me 'Lord, Lord', and do not do what I tell you? I will show you what someone is like who comes to me, hears my words, and acts on them. That one is like a man building a house, who dug deeply and laid the foundation on rock; when a flood arose, the river burst against that house but could not shake it, because it had been well built. But the one who hears and does not act is like a man who built a house on the ground without a foundation. When the river burst against it, immediately it fell, and great was the ruin of that house."

- Even the strongest building needs care and repair. I work with God to make a worthy dwelling, a refuge, a place from which to set forth.

- The foundations of a building are often its least recognized feature, usually hidden and seemingly insignificant. My "faith foundations" may not be known to many but are cherished by God to whom I bring them now in prayer, that they may be blessed and strengthened.

Something to think and pray about each day this week:

This magnificent God
John Henry Newman reminds us that the human mind works with shadows and images until it finally emerges into the full light of truth. "We see now only dimly." Human language is woefully inadequate to express our faith. St Thomas Aquinas, who wrote a million words on things divine, said we merely stammer in speaking of God. But at the same time let us take heart from Vatican II's image of the pilgrim Church. Pilgrims edge along difficult paths, using all available helps to arrive at their destination. At crossroads they discuss the path that seems most promising. The French theologian Henri de Lubac uses the image of swimming: with each stroke you push a volume of water behind you as you move toward your objective, but without that water you would never get there. Words do not present "the real thing" but they hint at it.

As we approach the world of divine mystery an amber light glows: it does not forbid entry but advises us to proceed with caution. When we ponder the twists and turns in every human life, the boundaries which we place around God's redeeming creativity are burst open. God works silently, taking into account every awkward knot that we insert into the divine tapestry. The author Liz Gilbert, asked what kind of God she believed in, said: "I believe in a magnificent God!"

The Presence of God

Jesus waits silent and unseen to come into my heart.
I will respond to His call.
He comes with His infinite power and love
May I be filled with joy in His presence.

Freedom

Everything has the potential to draw forth from me a fuller love and life.
Yet my desires are often fixed, caught, on illusions of fulfillment.
I ask that God, through my freedom, may orchestrate
my desires in a vibrant loving melody rich in harmony.

Consciousness

How do I find myself today?
Where am I with God? With others?
Do I have something to be grateful for? Then I give thanks.
Is there something I am sorry for? Then I ask forgiveness.

The Word

God speaks to each one of us individually. I need to listen to what he is saying to me. (Please turn to your scripture on the following pages. Inspiration points are there should you need them. When you are ready, return here to continue.)

Conversation

What feelings are rising in me
as I pray and reflect on God's Word?
I imagine Jesus himself sitting or standing beside me,
and open my heart to him.

Conclusion

Glory be to the Father, and to the Son, and to the Holy Spirit,
As it was in the beginning, is now and ever shall be,
World without end. Amen

Sunday 14th September,
Triumph of the Holy Cross   John 3:13–17

Jesus said, "And just as Moses lifted up the serpent in the wilderness, so must the Son of Man be lifted up, that whoever believes in him may have eternal life. For God so loved the world that he gave his only Son, so that everyone who believes in him may not perish but may have eternal life. Indeed, God did not send the Son into the world to condemn the world, but in order that the world might be saved through him."

- The cross reveals the vast breadth and width of God's love. It reverses all human values. Once a symbol of shame, it becomes the symbol of glory. The love revealed is not exclusive, for just a few. It embraces the whole world.
- Lord, divine love doesn't count the cost; it gives liberally. True lovers offer everything to their beloveds. The cross is the icon of great faith, hope and love. As I gaze on it, may I be lifted up into all that is true, good and beautiful.

Monday 15th September   Luke 7:1–10

After Jesus had finished all his sayings in the hearing of the people, he entered Capernaum. A centurion there had a slave whom he valued highly, and who was ill and close to death. When he heard about Jesus, he sent some Jewish elders to him, asking him to come and heal his slave. When they came to Jesus, they appealed to him earnestly, saying, "He is worthy of having you do this for him, for he loves our people, and it is he who built our synagogue for us." And Jesus went with them, but when he was not far from the house, the centurion sent friends to say to him, "Lord, do not trouble yourself, for I am not worthy to have you come under my roof; therefore I did not presume to come to you. But only speak the word, and let my servant be healed. For I also am a man set under authority, with soldiers under me; and I say to one, 'Go,' and he goes, and to another, 'Come,' and he comes, and to my slave, 'Do this,' and the slave does it." When Jesus heard this he was amazed at him, and turning to the crowd that followed him, he said,

"I tell you, not even in Israel have I found such faith." When those who had been sent returned to the house, they found the slave in good health.

- A gentile centurion holding authority in Palestine has much to teach us about real humanity. Instead of throwing the slave out to die, he uses his position to save him. Sensitive to Jewish customs, he turns to Jewish elders to intercede with Jesus. He is a humble and faith-filled man. Jesus' inclusive love is revealed here.
- Lord, though I am unworthy, you daily knock at the door of my heart. Sweep out the chambers of my heart that I may be free to reach out without discrimination to others, as you did.

Tuesday 16th September   Luke 7:11–15

Soon afterwards he went to a town called Nain, and his disciples and a large crowd went with him. As he approached the gate of the town, a man who had died was being carried out. He was his mother's only son, and she was a widow; and with her was a large crowd from the town. When the Lord saw her, he had compassion for her and said to her, "Do not weep." Then he came forward and touched the bier, and the bearers stood still. And he said, "Young man, I say to you, rise!" The dead man sat up and began to speak, and Jesus gave him to his mother.

- This scene reveals the pathos of human life—a funeral procession for an only son, whose mother is a widow. Without her son, she is unprotected and has no place in a patriarchal world. Jesus risks legal impurity and defilement in order to help her.
- Jesus, you reveal a God who comes close to us: you heal our brokenness with kindness and compassion. I live in a broken and tearful world. When the suffering of life threatens to overwhelm me, help me to notice that you are watching, and that you "come forward" with your compassion and power to raise me up.

Wednesday 17th September   Luke 7:31–35

Jesus said to the people, "To what then will I compare the people of this generation, and what are they like? They are like children sitting in the market-place and calling to one another, 'We played the flute for you, and you did not dance; we wailed, and you did not weep.' For John the Baptist has come eating no bread and drinking no wine, and you say, 'He has a demon;' the Son of Man has come eating and drinking, and you say, 'Look, a glutton and a drunkard, a friend of tax-collectors and sinners!' Nevertheless, wisdom is vindicated by all her children."

- Jesus exposes the perversity, contrariness and stubbornness of heart of the Pharisees and Scribes. Unlike the tax-collectors and sinners, they refuse to recognize God's presence in Jesus. No appeal of his penetrates their hearts. So they miss the moment of grace.
- Lord, I too can be contrary of heart, blind and deaf to your truth. I go through periods of negativity and complaint, when nothing seems to please me. Come to me in my poverty of spirit. Help me!

Thursday 18th September   Luke 7:36–38

One of the Pharisees asked Jesus to eat with him, and he went into the Pharisee's house and took his place at the table. And a woman in the city, who was a sinner, having learned that he was eating in the Pharisee's house, brought an alabaster jar of ointment. She stood behind him at his feet, weeping, and began to bathe his feet with her tears and to dry them with her hair. Then she continued kissing his feet and anointing them with the ointment.

- This is a story of extravagance and generosity. The ointment was expensive, and so was the alabaster jar. The woman whom nobody wanted near the feast was extravagant in love.
- Somehow Jesus' forgiving love had got through to her and she responded as best she knew—giving something really expensive —her way of giving all. Jesus saw beyond the sin and behind the oil to the love. That would conquer all in the end.

Friday 19th September   1 Corinthians 15:19–20

If for this life only we have hoped in Christ, we are of all people most to be pitied. But in fact Christ has been raised from the dead, the first fruits of those who have died.

- Our hope in Christ is not for this life only: we look forward to being brought to a fullness of life in Christ.
- Human history is often told in terms of failure, conflict and death. The resurrection of Jesus draws my attention to the real direction and meaning of my life: I am made to be with God in whom completeness is to be found.

Saturday 20th September   Luke 8:4–10

When a great crowd gathered and people from town after town came to Jesus, he said in a parable: "A sower went out to sow his seed; and as he sowed, some fell on the path and was trampled on, and the birds of the air ate it up. Some fell on the rock; and as it grew up, it withered for lack of moisture. Some fell among thorns, and the thorns grew with it and choked it. Some fell into good soil, and when it grew, it produced a hundredfold." As he said this, he called out, "Let anyone with ears to hear listen!" Then his disciples asked him what this parable meant. He said, "To you it has been given to know the secrets of the kingdom of God; but to others I speak in parables, so that 'looking they may not perceive, and listening they may not understand.'"

- The fruitfulness of the seed is determined by the quality of the soil. Similarly the fruitfulness of the word of God is determined by our openness of heart. We grow at our own pace. God is patient with this growth.
- God, grant me a heart of flesh to receive your holy Word. Each day may I spend time listening to the song of the seed which you plant in my heart. May it transform me ever more fully into the likeness of your Son.

september 21–27

Something to think and pray about each day this week:

Making sense of life

John, happily married and a successful businessman, came to me to ask if I would accompany him on his inner journey. I knew already that he had made the *Spiritual Exercises of St Ignatius* in their daily life form, and that prayer had by now put down roots in his daily life.

During our first conversation, I asked him, "What is prayer like for you now?" He recalled a chat-show in which Yehudi Menuhin, the world-renowned virtuoso violinist, was being interviewed. When asked, "Is music good for your health?" Menuhin answered with warmth and solemnity, "Music co-ordinates my life." John then said to me, "Prayer coordinates my life."

John was telling me that his business was not the centre of his life. Something else was: he called it prayer. By this he meant his personal relationship with Jesus of which prayer was an essential expression. Just as Menuhin could not make sense of his life without music, my friend could not make sense of his life without regularly meeting with the One who loved him. Time had to be found for it even in a busy schedule, because it gave meaning to everything else—his marriage, his business, his reaching out to others, his leisure times. Prayer was a privileged time and space where he was at home with his Lord. There he found depth and energy, and guidance for his choices. Prayer was indeed coordinating his life.

The Presence of God
'I stand at the door and knock,' says the Lord.
What a wonderful privilege
that the Lord of all creation desires to come to me.
I welcome His presence.

Freedom
Lord, grant me the grace to be free from the excesses of
this life.
Let me not get caught up with the desire for wealth.
Keep my heart and mind free to love and serve you.

Consciousness
'There is a time and place for everything,' as the saying goes.
Lord, grant that I may always desire
to spend time in your presence. To hear your call.

The Word
God speaks to each one of us individually. I need to listen to
what he is saying to me. (Please turn to your scripture on the
following pages. Inspiration points are there should you need
them. When you are ready, return here to continue.)

Conversation
The gift of speech is a wonderful gift.
May I use this gift with kindness.
May I be slow to utter harsh words,
hurtful words, and words spoken in anger.

Conclusion
Glory be to the Father, and to the Son, and to the Holy Spirit,
As it was in the beginning, is now and ever shall be,
World without end. Amen

Sunday 21st September,
Twenty-fifth Sunday in Ordinary Time   Matthew 20:1–16

And Jesus said, "For the kingdom of heaven is like a landowner who went out early in the morning to hire laborers for his vineyard. After agreeing with the laborers for the usual daily wage, he sent them into his vineyard. When he went out about nine o'clock, he saw others standing idle in the marketplace; and he said to them, 'You also go into the vineyard, and I will pay you whatever is right.' So they went. When he went out again about noon and about three o'clock, he did the same. And about five o'clock he went out and found others standing around; and he said to them, 'Why are you standing here idle all day?' They said to him, 'Because no one has hired us.' He said to them, 'You also go into the vineyard.' When evening came, the owner of the vineyard said to his manager, 'Call the laborers and give them their pay, beginning with the last and then going to the first.' When those hired about five o'clock came, each of them received the usual daily wage. Now when the first came, they thought they would receive more; but each of them also received the usual daily wage. And when they received it, they grumbled against the landowner, saying, 'These last worked only one hour, and you have made them equal to us who have borne the burden of the day and the scorching heat.' But he replied to one of them, 'Friend, I am doing you no wrong; did you not agree with me for the usual daily wage? Take what belongs to you and go; I choose to give to this last the same as I give to you. Am I not allowed to do what I choose with what belongs to me? Or are you envious because I am generous?' So the last will be first, and the first will be last."

- The human mind suspects injustice, while the heart of God sees only an opportunity to be generous. Help me, Lord, to let go of my presumptions so that I may see as you do and act freely from a full heart.
- The generosity of God calls us to be generous too; any judgement that is based on nationality, income or education is just too narrow and shuts God out.
- Imagine the joy and appreciation that a late-arriving worker would experience.

Monday 22nd September   Luke 8:16–18

Jesus said to his disciples, "No one after lighting a lamp hides it under a jar, or puts it under a bed, but puts it on a lampstand, so that those who enter may see the light. For nothing is hidden that will not be disclosed, nor is anything secret that will not become known and come to light. Then pay attention to how you listen; for to those who have, more will be given; and from those who do not have, even what they seem to have will be taken away."

- The gospel calls us to live in light and truth, no matter what the cost. "Secret discipleship is a contradiction in terms, for either the secrecy kills the discipleship or the discipleship kills the secrecy."
- Lord, when the wick of my lamp flickers and fades, strengthen its beam and let me be again a light-bearer, a beacon of hope to all whom I daily encounter.

Tuesday 23rd September   Luke 8:19–21

Then his mother and his brothers came to him, but they could not reach him because of the crowd. And he was told, "Your mother and your brothers are standing outside, wanting to see you." But he said to them, "My mother and my brothers are those who hear the word of God and do it."

- Luke's audience knew that the cost of receiving Jesus' word led them into opposition and family ruptures. Choices had to be made between Jesus and family. Jesus comes first. Everyone who hears and acts on his word is a relative of Jesus.
- Lord, fidelity to your word is the only basis for my Christian identity. As I daily sit at your feet in *Sacred Space*, may I draw nourishment from listening to you and may I reveal you through my actions.

Wednesday 24th September   Luke 9:1–6

Jesus called the twelve together and gave them power and authority over all demons and to cure diseases, and he sent them out to proclaim the kingdom of God and to heal. He said to them, "Take nothing for your journey, no staff, nor bag, nor bread, nor money—not even an extra tunic. Whatever house you enter, stay there, and leave from there. Wherever they do not welcome you, as you are leaving that town shake the dust off your feet as a testimony against them." They departed and went through the villages, bringing the good news and curing diseases everywhere.

- Jesus gives the twelve some road tips for the journey. He asks them to travel lightly, unencumbered by the baggage of material things. They are to walk the path of simplicity, openness and trust. They are to be flexible and available.
- Lord, today our world is blessed with technologies of which you knew nothing. May the medium of *Sacred Space* help me to rediscover the heart of discipleship—an absolute reliance on your providence and the freedom that follows from trusting in you.

Thursday 25th September   **Luke 9:7–9**

Now Herod the ruler heard about all that had taken place, and he was perplexed, because it was said by some that John had been raised from the dead, by some that Elijah had appeared, and by others that one of the ancient prophets had arisen. Herod said, "John I beheaded; but who is this about whom I hear such things?" And he tried to see him.

- Herod is perplexed and anxious. He tries to see Jesus, but more from fear and bad conscience than from genuine desire. A true disciple has a faith-filled desire to know Jesus and to grow in an ever-deepening relationship with him.
- Lord, faith is a pre-requisite for sight. Only by truly accepting you and embracing your way can I hope to see you. Lord, may I know you more clearly, love you more dearly, and follow you more closely, day by day.

Friday 26th September   **Luke 9:18–22**

Once when Jesus was praying alone, with only the disciples near him, he asked them, "Who do the crowds say that I am?" They answered, "John the Baptist; but others, Elijah; and still others, that one of the ancient prophets has arisen." He said to them, "But who do you say that I am?" Peter answered, "The Messiah of God." He sternly ordered and commanded them not to tell anyone, saying, "The Son of Man must undergo great suffering, and be rejected by the elders, chief priests, and scribes, and be killed, and on the third day be raised."

- This is a crucial moment in Jesus' life. He asks the question which lies at the heart of Christian faith: "Who do you say I am?"
- Lord, I too, like Peter, must embark on a personal discovery of who you are. Give me the grace to walk this faith-journey. May I not keep you at arm's length by putting a protective shield around myself, but help me rather to daily embrace you on the path of discipleship, with its pains and joys.

Saturday 27th September   Ecclesiastes 12:1–6

Remember your creator in the days of your youth, before the days of trouble come, and the years draw near when you will say, "I have no pleasure in them"; before the sun and the light and the moon and the stars are darkened and the clouds return with the rain; on the day when the guards of the house tremble, and the strong men are bent, and the women who grind cease working because they are few, and those who look through the windows see dimly; when the doors on the street are shut, and the sound of the grinding is low, and one rises up at the sound of a bird, and all the daughters of song are brought low; when one is afraid of heights, and terrors are in the road; the almond tree blossoms, the grasshopper drags itself along and desire fails; because all must go to their eternal home, and the mourners will go about the streets.

- The words of the sage seem downbeat and negative yet they echo what it is given to us as news every day. I take care not to let this negative outlook become part of my way of thinking and talking.
- I keep in mind all those who are distressed, whose hope is challenged. I consider what I might do to lift the heart of someone I know.

Something to think and pray about each day this week:

The mystery of God's goodness

How do you reconcile belief in the providence of God with the awful things that happen? Should we abandon the notion of divine providence or deny the truth of the tragedies that hit us? Does it comfort a mother whose baby dies, to say, "It was all for the best: God wanted to have the little angel for himself?"

The theologian Balthasar says that the little word "and" is central to a rich grasp of Christianity. Jesus is God and human! God is Three and yet One! And so forth. So let us look today at the goodness of divine providence. Next week we will ask if suffering and evil can co-exist with this goodness. Can these opposites be joined by the word "and"? If they can, we get the light we need to live by.

Firstly, the goodness of God is shown in God's creation: its beauty and wonder enthral us. God sustains us in existence out of love, and this shows itself in all the good that surrounds us. It is good to notice and thank God for this.

Next we see the awesome generosity and care of God for us in the life, death and resurrection of his Son, because all of this is done for us. On this basis early Christians affirmed that God is love. Liturgy speaks of God "from whom comes all that is good." Overall, we can truly affirm that God is good, indeed very good.

The Presence of God
I remind myself that, as I sit here now,
God is gazing on me with love and holding me in being.
I pause for a moment and think of this.

Freedom
Lord, grant me the grace to be free from the excesses of
this life.
Let me not get caught up with the desire for wealth.
Keep my heart and mind free to love and serve you.

Consciousness
How am I really feeling? Light-hearted? Heavy-hearted?
I may be very much at peace, happy to be here.
Equally, I may be frustrated, worried or angry.
I acknowledge how I really am. It is the real me that the
Lord loves.

The Word
I take my time to read the Word of God, slowly, a few times,
allowing myself to dwell on anything that strikes me. (Please
turn to your scripture on the following pages. Inspiration
points are there should you need them. When you are ready,
return here to continue.)

Conversation
Do I notice myself reacting as I pray with the Word of God?
Do I feel challenged, comforted, angry?
Imagining Jesus sitting or standing by me,
I speak out my feelings, as one trusted friend to another.

Conclusion
Glory be to the Father, and to the Son, and to the Holy Spirit,
As it was in the beginning, is now and ever shall be,
World without end. Amen

Sunday 28th September, Twenty-sixth Sunday in Ordinary Time

Matthew 21:28–32

Jesus said, "What do you think? A man had two sons; he went to the first and said, 'Son, go and work in the vineyard today.' He answered, 'I will not'; but later he changed his mind and went. The father went to the second and said the same; and he answered, 'I go, sir'; but he did not go. Which of the two did the will of his father?" They said, "The first." Jesus said to them, "Truly I tell you, the tax collectors and the prostitutes are going into the kingdom of God ahead of you. For John came to you in the way of righteousness and you did not believe him, but the tax collectors and the prostitutes believed him; and even after you saw it, you did not change your minds and believe him."

- I review the statements and declarations I may have made. Does God find me dependable? I ask God for forgiveness for wherever I have fallen short.
- God continually invites me to fullness of life. I do not have to be downhearted by the awareness that I don't always accept the invitation, but am encouraged by the call to serve others.

Monday 29th September, Ss Michael, Gabriel and Raphael

John 1:47–51

When Jesus saw Nathanael coming toward him, he said of him, "Here is truly an Israelite in whom there is no deceit!" Nathanael asked him, "Where did you get to know me?" Jesus answered, "I saw you under the fig tree before Philip called you." Nathanael replied, "Rabbi, you are the Son of God! You are the King of Israel!" Jesus answered, "Do you believe because I told you that I saw you under the fig tree? You will see greater things than these." And he said to him, "Very truly, I tell you, you will see heaven opened and the angels of God ascending and descending upon the Son of Man."

- Jesus witnessed some aspect of Nathanael that seemed to surprise him; there are hidden and secret aspects of my life too that are known and valued by God.

- Jesus lifts Nathanael's eyes from the everyday and prompts him to think of heaven; I might consider my hoped-for destination and see how my daily concerns are brought into another perspective.

Tuesday 30th September   Luke 9:51–56

When the days drew near for him to be taken up, Jesus set his face to go to Jerusalem. And he sent messengers ahead of him. On their way they entered a village of the Samaritans to make ready for him; but they did not receive him, because his face was set toward Jerusalem. When his disciples James and John saw it, they said, Lord, do you want us to command fire to come down from heaven and consume them?" But he turned and rebuked them. Then they went on to another village.

- Jesus asserts the way of non-violence towards the unwelcoming Samaritans.
- How does his response compare with my own attitudes towards those who may not accept me for who I am? Am I always aware of God's protection and guidance in my life, each day and night?

Wednesday 1st October   Luke 9:57–62

As they were going along the road, someone said to him, "I will follow you wherever you go." And Jesus said to him, "Foxes have holes, and birds of the air have nests; but the Son of Man has nowhere to lay his head." To another he said, "Follow me." But he said, "Lord, first let me go and bury my father." But Jesus said to him, "Let the dead bury their own dead; but as for you, go and proclaim the kingdom of God." Another said, "I will follow you, Lord; but let me first say farewell to those at my home." Jesus said to him, "No one who puts a hand to the plow and looks back is fit for the kingdom of God."

- Jesus invites others to follow him. But discipleship is a radical call which requires our whole-hearted response. It involves taking up one's cross each day and following after him.
- Contrast the total commitment of Jesus to doing his Father's will with the pre-conditions and qualifications which we can make in response to his call to discipleship.

288

Thursday 2nd October   Luke 10:1–7

After this the Lord appointed seventy others and sent them on ahead of him in pairs to every town and place where he himself intended to go. He said to them, "The harvest is plentiful, but the laborers are few; therefore ask the Lord of the harvest to send out laborers into his harvest. Go on your way. See, I am sending you out like lambs into the midst of wolves. Carry no purse, no bag, no sandals; and greet no one on the road. Whatever house you enter, first say, 'Peace to this house!' And if anyone is there who shares in peace, your peace will rest on that person; but if not, it will return to you. Remain in the same house, eating and drinking whatever they provide, for the laborer deserves to be paid."

- "The kingdom of God has come near to you." Am I receptive to God's word spoken to my heart each day?
- I thank God for the help that *Sacred Space* gives me to become a true hearer of the Word.

Friday 3rd October   Luke 10:13–16

"Woe to you, Chorazin! Woe to you, Bethsaida! For if the deeds of power done in you had been done in Tyre and Sidon, they would have repented long ago, sitting in sackcloth and ashes. But at the judgment it will be more tolerable for Tyre and Sidon than for you. And you, Capernaum, will you be exalted to heaven? No, you will be brought down to Hades." "Whoever listens to you listens to me, and whoever rejects you rejects me, and whoever rejects me rejects the one who sent me."

- Do I believe that the Church today, no matter how imperfectly, continues the mission and ministry of Christ Jesus, as he received it from his heavenly Father?
- This can demand great faith.

Saturday 4th October,
St Francis of Assisi   Luke 10:21–24

Jesus rejoiced in the Holy Spirit and said, "I thank you, Father, Lord of heaven and earth, because you have hidden these things from the wise and the intelligent and have revealed them to infants; yes, Father, for such was your gracious will. All things have been handed over to me by my Father; and no one knows who the Son is except the Father, or who the Father is except the Son and anyone to whom the Son chooses to reveal him." Then turning to the disciples, Jesus said to them privately, "Blessed are the eyes that see what you see! For I tell you that many prophets and kings desired to see what you see, but did not see it, and to hear what you hear, but did not hear it."

- Why is it only to "infants" that "these things" are revealed? Perhaps because in their dependence and need they are open to be nourished. The so-called "wise and intelligent," on the other hand, do not experience such needs because of their self-sufficiency and pride.
- Which group do I belong to? What can the life of St Francis teach me about child-like faith?

Something to think and pray about each day this week:

The mystery of suffering and evil

How can we say "God is provident" when creation, for all its beauty, accommodates landslides, tsunamis, droughts and so forth? Why do we humans, and our planet, have to suffer and die? Why are there breakdowns in personal relationships, why wars, torture and oppression? Why could God not simply "zap" bad people?

The case against providence seems endless, and the reality of evil is undeniable. But while evil will always be a mystery, we have glimpses into the ways God responds.

Firstly, God's plans must be vast enough to allow evil and suffering.

Secondly, God opposes evil and suffering, and works through them to bring good out of what is bad. The passion of Jesus best reveals God at work. There alone we learn just how deeply God cares about us.

Thirdly, while we are not given immunity from suffering and death, God promises to bring us through them into eternal joy.

Fourthly, sometimes we can see how good emerges from bad. Sickness can mature us; dying can focus us on essentials; repentance and forgiveness can break open our stony hearts. So while evil remains a great mystery, enough light is thrown on it to help us to live with the paradox of how divine providence and evil can co-exist in our world.

The Presence of God
In the silence of my innermost being,
in the fragments of my yearned-for wholeness,
can I hear the whispers of God's presence?
Can I remember when I felt God's nearness?
When we walked together and I let myself be embraced by
God's love.

Freedom
I ask for the grace
to let go of my own concerns
and be open to what God is asking of me,
to let myself be guided and formed by my loving Creator.

Consciousness
I exist in a web of relationships—links to nature, people, God.
I trace out these links, giving thanks for the life that flows
through them.
Some links are twisted or broken: I may feel regret, anger,
disappointment.
I pray for the gift of acceptance and forgiveness.

The Word
The word of God comes to us through the scriptures.
May the Holy Spirit enlighten my mind and my heart to
respond to the gospel teachings. (Please turn to your scripture
on the following pages. Inspiration points are there should you
need them. When you are ready, return here to continue.)

Conversation
Remembering that I am still in God's presence,
I imagine Jesus himself standing or sitting beside me,
and say whatever is on my mind, whatever is in my heart,
speaking as one friend to another.

Conclusion
Glory be to the Father, and to the Son, and to the Holy Spirit,
As it was in the beginning, is now and ever shall be,
World without end. Amen

Sunday 5th October, Twenty-seventh Sunday in Ordinary Time

Matthew 21:42–43

Jesus said to them, "Have you never read in the scriptures: 'The stone that the builders rejected has become the cornerstone; this was the Lord's doing, and it is amazing in our eyes'? Therefore I tell you, the kingdom of God will be taken away from you and given to a people that produces the fruits of the kingdom."

- Those who think they own God's kingdom are in trouble. The reign of God is an action of grace, a yielding to the sway of God. I remember that it is a gift to be appreciated more than a property to be claimed or asserted.
- Jesus allowed himself to be the rejected stone, to be overlooked and demeaned. In what way might I learn from him?

Monday 6th October

Luke 10:25–37

Just then a lawyer stood up to test Jesus. "Teacher," he said, "what must I do to inherit eternal life?" He said to him, "What is written in the law? What do you read there?" He answered, "You shall love the Lord your God with all your heart, and with all your soul, and with all your strength, and with all your mind; and your neighbor as yourself." And he said to him, "You have given the right answer; do this, and you will live." But wanting to justify himself, he asked Jesus, "And who is my neighbor?" Jesus replied, "A man was going down from Jerusalem to Jericho, and fell into the hands of robbers, who stripped him, beat him, and went away, leaving him half dead. Now by chance a priest was going down that road; and when he saw him, he passed by on the other side. So likewise a Levite, when he came to the place and saw him, passed by on the other side. But a Samaritan while travelling came near him; and when he saw him, he was moved with pity. He went to him and bandaged his wounds, having poured oil and wine on them. Then he put him on his own animal, brought him to an inn, and took care of him. The next day he took out two denarii, gave them to the innkeeper, and said, 'Take care of him; and when I come back, I will repay you whatever more you spend'; Which of these three, do you think, was a neighbor to the man who fell into the hands of the robbers?" He said, "The one who showed him mercy." Jesus said to him, "Go and do likewise."

- This parable challenges my deep-seated presumptions and prejudices. The Samaritan showed himself to be Christ-like. He is moved with pity and shows mercy.
- How Christ-like am I in my thoughts and attitudes, words and deeds?

Tuesday 7th October — Luke 10:38–42

Now as they went on their way, Jesus entered a certain village, where a woman named Martha welcomed him into her home. She had a sister named Mary, who sat at the Lord's feet and listened to what he was saying. But Martha was distracted by her many tasks; so she came to him and asked, "Lord, do you not care that my sister has left me to do all the work by myself? Tell her then to help me." But the Lord answered her, "Martha, Martha, you are worried and distracted by many things; there is need of only one thing. Mary has chosen the better part, which will not be taken away from her."

- Jesus' main point here is about priorities. What is the more important response on this particular occasion? Mary recognizes that Jesus has far more to offer her than she could possibly offer him.
- "There is need of only one thing. Mary has chosen the better part." Jesus is highlighting here one of the fundamental requirements for being his follower: namely, to listen to the word of God, to reflect upon it, and to put it into practice.

Wednesday 8th October — Luke 11:1–4

Jesus was praying in a certain place, and after he had finished, one of his disciples said to him, "Lord, teach us to pray, as

John taught his disciples." He said to them, "When you pray, say: Father, hallowed be your name. Your kingdom come. Give us each day our daily bread. And forgive us our sins, for we ourselves forgive everyone indebted to us. And do not bring us to the time of trial."

- It is clear that prayer was essential for Jesus—for his identity and his mission. Prayer expressed Jesus' relationship with his Father. He taught his followers how to pray, and he made time for it himself, no matter what needs and demands pressed on him.
- Do I do likewise?

Thursday 9th October   Luke 11:9–10

Jesus said, "I say to you, Ask, and it will be given to you; search, and you will find; knock, and the door will be opened for you. For everyone who asks receives, and everyone who searches finds, and for everyone who knocks, the door will be opened."

- God is gracious and willing to respond to all our needs, far surpassing the natural disposition of a parent or a friend.
- May I truly believe that when I ask it will be given to me; when I search that I will find; and that when I knock, the door will be opened for me.

Friday 10th October   Luke 11:15–23

Some of the crowd said of Jesus, "He casts out demons by Beelzebul, the ruler of the demons." Others, to test him, kept demanding from him a sign from heaven. But he knew what they were thinking and said to them, "Every kingdom divided against itself becomes a desert, and house falls on house. If Satan also is divided against himself, how will his kingdom stand?—for you say that I cast out the demons by Beelzebul. Now if I cast out the demons by Beelzebul, by whom do your exorcists cast them out? Therefore they will be your judges. But if it is by the finger of God that I cast out the demons, then the kingdom of God has come to you. When a strong man, fully armed, guards his castle, his property is safe. But when one stronger than he attacks him and overpowers him, he takes away his armour in which he trusted and divides his plunder. Whoever is not with me is against me, and whoever does not gather with me scatters."

- The opposition which Jesus faced was endless. Here he argues that demons can only be cast out by "the finger of God," which symbolizes divine power. With every victory over evil the kingdom of God becomes more firmly established.
- It is said that if those in recovery from an addiction lapse into their former negative life-style, their new condition may be far worse than before. Am I resolved, with the help of God's power, to continue to progress on the path of health and growth?

Saturday 11th October   Luke 11:27–28

While Jesus was speaking, a woman in the crowd raised her voice and said to him, "Blessed is the womb that bore you and the breasts that nursed you!" But he said, "Blessed rather are those who hear the word of God and obey it!"

- Such a natural and beautiful response on the part of the woman in the crowd to Jesus! She expressed her overriding feeling very much from a feminine and maternal perspective.
- Is Jesus so real and fresh for me that I sometimes respond to him in a truly spontaneous and personal way?

october

Something to think and pray about each day this week:

Finding Jesus, finding your self
You pray in order to find Jesus and be with him. You give time to prayer because you treasure your relationship with him. But God is seeking you more than you seek him, so keep in mind that you pray in order to be found by Jesus. God thirsts for relationship with you, and is more active in your prayer than you are.

It is possible to be wanting Jesus, but in a shallow and self-centred way. I could, for instance, be seeking Jesus in order to find pleasant feelings; I could be praying on my own terms, not God's.

I can stay superficial in prayer and decline God's invitation to come deeper. I can do this by controlling my way of praying: being rigid about it, wanting to feel secure through it, instead of letting the Lord teach me how he wants me to be in his presence. I can stay in my head during prayer, thinking interesting thoughts instead of meeting the Lord. I can stay superficial, also, by being afraid to come down to the level of my heart where I am invited to trust and to let myself be loved without deserving it, and to hear the Lord's desire for me. It is even possible to stay superficial by clinging to my anxieties, anger and hurts. In short, I can stay superficial by keeping the main focus on myself.

The Presence of God
God is with me, but more,
God is within me, giving me existence.
Let me dwell for a moment on God's life-giving presence
in my body, my mind, my heart
and in the whole of my life.

Freedom
I ask for the grace to believe
in what I could be and do
if I only allowed God, my loving Creator,
to continue to create me, guide me and shape me.

Consciousness
Knowing that God loves me unconditionally,
I can afford to be honest about how I am.
How has the last day been, and how do I feel now?
I share my feelings openly with the Lord.

The Word
I read the Word of God slowly, a few times over, and I listen
to what God is saying to me. (Please turn to your scripture on
the following pages. Inspiration points are there should you
need them. When you are ready, return here to continue.)

Conversation
How has God's Word moved me? Has it left me cold?
Has it consoled me or moved me to act in a new way?
I imagine Jesus standing or sitting beside me,
I turn and share my feelings with him.

Conclusion
Glory be to the Father, and to the Son, and to the Holy Spirit,
As it was in the beginning, is now and ever shall be,
World without end. Amen

Sunday 12th October,
Twenty-eighth Sunday in Ordinary Time   Isaiah 25:6–8

On this mountain the Lord of hosts will make for all peoples a feast of rich food, a feast of well-matured wines, of rich food filled with marrow, of well-matured wines strained clear. And he will destroy on this mountain the shroud that is cast over all peoples, the sheet that is spread over all nations; he will swallow up death for ever. Then the Lord God will wipe away the tears from all faces, and the disgrace of his people he will take away from all the earth.

- The kingdom of heaven is often presented under the image of a great banquet. With Jesus the Kingdom is already here. Could it be that I am slow to accept the gifts that God offers me now?
- Everything that veils and deadens love will be removed in God's time. I pray that I may play my part in removing anything that prevents people becoming fully alive.

Monday 13th October   Luke 11:29–32

When the crowds were increasing, Jesus began to say, "This generation is an evil generation; it asks for a sign, but no sign will be given to it except the sign of Jonah. For just as Jonah became a sign to the people of Nineveh, so the Son of Man will be to this generation. The queen of the South will rise at the judgment with the people of this generation and condemn them, because she came from the ends of the earth to listen to the wisdom of Solomon, and see, something greater than Solomon is here! The people of Nineveh will rise up at the judgment with this generation and condemn it, because they repented at the proclamation of Jonah, and see, something greater than Jonah is here!"

- The queen of the South sought out Solomon for his wisdom, and the people of Nineveh listened attentively to Jonah and repented. Jesus far surpasses Solomon and Jonah, but his hearers are still looking for "signs" instead of listening to what he says.
- Have I enough faith to accept Jesus not only as a great prophet but as the Son of God, and his word as the wisdom of God?

Tuesday 14th October   Luke 11:37–41

While Jesus was speaking, a Pharisee invited him to dine with him; so he went in and took his place at the table. The Pharisee was amazed to see that he did not first wash before dinner. Then the Lord said to him, "Now you Pharisees clean the outside of the cup and of the dish, but inside you are full of greed and wickedness. You fools! Did not the one who made the outside make the inside also? So give for alms those things that are within; and see, everything will be clean for you."

- Jesus is focussed on what is inside a person, in the human heart. The Pharisee, in sharp contrast, is primarily concerned with external observance of rules and regulations, such as the ritual washing before a meal.
- What is my focus?

Wednesday 15th October   Luke 11:42–46

"But woe to you Pharisees! For you tithe mint and rue and herbs of all kinds, and neglect justice and the love of God; it is these you ought to have practiced, without neglecting the others. Woe to you Pharisees! For you love to have the seat of honor in the synagogues and to be greeted with respect in the market-places. Woe to you! For you are like unmarked graves, and people walk over them without realizing it." One of the lawyers answered him, "Teacher, when you say these things, you insult us too." And he said, "Woe also to you lawyers! For you load people with burdens hard to bear, and you yourselves do not lift a finger to ease them."

- Jesus is again highly critical of those who are fixated on external observance and ritual. They neglect the more important aspects of life, such as justice, love of God and neighbour.
- In my own attitudes and values, do I display the mentality of a Pharisee or a Christian?

Thursday 16th October   Luke 11:47–51

Jesus said to the lawyers, "Woe to you! For you build the tombs of the prophets whom your ancestors killed. So you are witnesses and approve of the deeds of your ancestors; for they killed them, and you build their tombs. Therefore also the Wisdom of God said, 'I will send them prophets and apostles, some of whom they will kill and persecute,' so that this generation may be charged with the blood of all the prophets shed since the foundation of the world, from the blood of Abel to the blood of Zechariah, who perished between the altar and the sanctuary. Yes, I tell you, it will be charged against this generation."

- Jesus did not mince words when confronting casuistry and legalism.
- Jesus brings us back from external behavior to the heart. God is no attorney general planning to prove us guilty. He looks into our hearts, and loves us as his children.

Friday 17th October   Luke 12:1, 4–7

Meanwhile, when the crowd gathered by the thousands, so that they trampled on one another, Jesus began to speak first to his disciples, "I tell you, my friends, do not fear those who kill the body, and after that can do nothing more. But I will warn you whom to fear: fear him who, after he has killed, has authority to cast into hell. Yes, I tell you, fear him! Are not five sparrows sold for two pennies? Yet not one of them is forgotten in God's sight. But even the hairs of your head are all counted. Do not be afraid; you are of more value than many sparrows."

- I ask God that I may not live out of fear but out of belief that I am limitlessly valued by God. I pray as a member of that great "crowd" which comes to hear the Word of God, the *Sacred Space* community; may it continue to grow all over the world.
- I contemplate a sparrow and learn from it the care of God for me.

Saturday 18th October,
St Luke, Evangelist   Luke 10:1–9

After this the Lord appointed seventy others and sent them on ahead of him in pairs to every town and place where he himself intended to go. He said to them, "The harvest is plentiful, but the laborers are few; therefore ask the Lord of the harvest to send out laborers into his harvest. Go on your way. See, I am sending you out like lambs into the midst of wolves. Carry no purse, no bag, no sandals; and greet no one on the road. Whatever house you enter, first say, 'Peace to this house!' And if anyone is there who shares in peace, your peace will rest on that person; but if not, it will return to you. Remain in the same house, eating and drinking whatever they provide, for the laborer deserves to be paid. Do not move about from house to house. Whenever you enter a town and its people welcome you, eat what is set before you; cure the sick who are there, and say to them, 'The kingdom of God has come near to you.'"

- Today we celebrate the feast of the gospel writer, Saint Luke. We see in this passage a strong sense of mission.
- I am one of the seventy who are sent out to prepare the way for the Lord. I must witness in my life to Christ Jesus and his message. Do I see this calling not only as a duty but as a great privilege?

Something to think and pray about each day this week:

On God's side

"Do not work for food that cannot last" (John 6:27). What is Jesus pointing to here? He is saying that there is another kind of food and another kind of hunger which bread cannot satisfy. The way of Jesus is deeper, it invites us down to the level of heart and spirit. There is a space in each of us that only God can fill. That deep space is a hunger. During prayer, we let that hunger become conscious. The food that matches this deep hunger is relationship with Jesus in faith. Jesus is offering this relationship. It is as if he is saying to each of us, "Believe, come into the circle of relationship with me. It will satisfy your deepest hunger. You are made for this. It is worth working at."

In true prayer you "cross over to the other side"—not of the Lake of Galilee, but of yourself. You reach down to your authentic self. You go over to God's side. Your journey leads you to Jesus, the bread of life.

Prayer means idleness for God, emptiness before God. Prayer time is time put beyond usefulness to yourself. You bring yourself and your time and your desire to be with God: you come with your availability. The fact that you are not busy but idle or unemployed, suggests that God is the main actor in your prayer: what happens in prayer is God's agenda.

The Presence of God
To be present is to arrive as one is and open up to the other.
At this instant, as I arrive here, God is present waiting for me.
God always arrives before me, desiring to connect with me
even more than my most intimate friend.
I take a moment and greet my loving God.

Freedom
"In these days, God taught me
as a schoolteacher teaches a pupil" (St Ignatius).
I remind myself that there are things God has to teach me yet,
and ask for the grace to hear them and let them change me.

Consciousness
In the presence of my loving Creator,
I look honestly at my feelings over the last day,
the highs, the lows and the level ground.
Can I see where the Lord has been present?

The Word
I take my time to read the Word of God, slowly, a few times,
allowing myself to dwell on anything that strikes me. (Please
turn to your scripture on the following pages. Inspiration
points are there should you need them. When you are ready,
return here to continue.)

Conversation
What feelings are rising in me
as I pray and reflect on God's Word?
I imagine Jesus himself sitting or standing beside me,
and open my heart to him.

Conclusion
Glory be to the Father, and to the Son, and to the Holy Spirit,
As it was in the beginning, is now and ever shall be,
World without end. Amen

Sunday 19th October,
Twenty-ninth Sunday
in Ordinary Time

Matthew 22:15–21

Then the Pharisees went and plotted to entrap him in what he said. So they sent their disciples to him, along with the Herodians, saying, "Teacher, we know that you are sincere, and teach the way of God in accordance with truth, and show deference to no one; for you do not regard people with partiality. Tell us, then, what you think. Is it lawful to pay taxes to the emperor, or not?" But Jesus, aware of their malice, said, "Why are you putting me to the test, you hypocrites? Show me the coin used for the tax." And they brought him a denarius. Then he said to them, "Whose head is this, and whose title?" They answered, "The emperor's." Then he said to them, "Give therefore to the emperor the things that are the emperor's, and to God the things that are God's."

- Jesus remains free and firm in face of the plots against him. I ask for his courage to stand up for what is true and just.
- To be a good citizen and to serve God are not in contradiction, since God works through all human systems and institutions to build the final community of love. God needs me to help build good relationships wherever I find myself.

Monday 20th October　　　　　　　　　**Luke 12:13–21**

Someone in the crowd said to Jesus, "Teacher, tell my brother to divide the family inheritance with me." But he said to him, "Friend, who set me to be a judge or arbitrator over you?" And he said to them, "Take care! Be on your guard against all kinds of greed; for one's life does not consist in the abundance of possessions." Then he told them a parable: "The land of a rich man produced abundantly. And he thought to himself, 'What should I do, for I have no place to store my crops?' Then he said, 'I will do this: I will pull down my barns and build larger ones, and there I will store all my grain and my goods.' And I will say to my soul, 'Soul, you have ample goods laid up for many years; relax, eat, drink, be merry.' But God said to him, 'You fool! This very night your life is being demanded of you. And the things you have prepared, whose will they be?' So it is with those who store up treasures for themselves but are not rich toward God."

- In this parable Jesus attacks greed and egotism. This rich man is living for this world and this life only. He is thinking only of himself, with no awareness of the needs of others, despite his own abundance.
- All the rich man's ambitious planning is in vain because that same night he was to die. Who would inherit his substantial fortune, since he cannot take it with him, though he lived as if he could? I ask Jesus to show me what are the real values and riches in my own life.

Tuesday 21st October   Luke 12:36–38

Jesus said to his disciples, "Be dressed for action and have your lamps lit; be like those who are waiting for their master to return from the wedding banquet, so that they may open the door for him as soon as he comes and knocks. Blessed are those slaves whom the master finds alert when he comes; truly I tell you, he will fasten his belt and have them sit down to eat, and he will come and serve them. If he comes during the middle of the night, or near dawn, and finds them so, blessed are those slaves."

- The role-reversal on the part of the master, who serves those slaves who were awake and alert, says much about God's gracious bounty and generosity.
- In discipleship there is no room for complacency or half-heartedness. The commitment required is total and the reward is equally great. The lighted lamps symbolise the alertness required of us. How is my lamp?

Wednesday 22nd October   Luke 12:39–40

Jesus said to the people, "But know this: if the owner of the house had known at what hour the thief was coming, he would not have let his house be broken into. You also must be ready, for the Son of Man is coming at an unexpected hour."

- Today's gospel continues the message of being awake, alert and ready. Each day is a microcosm of life, and we are called to live it as fully and as meaningfully as possible. "The glory of God is the human person fully alive!" So says Saint Irenaeus.

Thursday 23rd October   Luke 12:49–53

Jesus said to the crowds, "I came to bring fire to the earth, and how I wish it were already kindled! I have a baptism with which to be baptized, and what stress I am under until it is completed! Do you think that I have come to bring peace to the earth? No, I tell you, but rather division! From now on five in one household will be divided, three against two and two against three; they will be divided: father against son and son against father, mother against daughter and daughter against mother, mother-in-law against her daughter-in-law and daughter-in-law against mother-in-law."

- Jesus does not set out to cause conflict, but so radical is his message that it inevitably does cause division in certain situations and relationships. The gospel is a call to becoming "a new creation." It means shedding the skin of a former way of living.
- Does my Christian faith make a real difference to the kind of person I am and to the kind of life I lead?

Friday 24th October   Luke 12:54–59

Jesus also said to the crowds, "When you see a cloud rising in the west, you immediately say, 'It is going to rain'; and so it happens. And when you see the south wind blowing, you say, 'There will be scorching heat'; and it happens. You hypocrites! You know how to interpret the appearance of earth and sky, but why do you not know how to interpret the present time? And why do you not judge for yourselves what is right? Thus, when you go with your accuser before a magistrate, on the way make an effort to settle the case, or you may be dragged before the judge, and the judge hand you over to the officer, and the officer throw you in prison. I tell you, you will never get out until you have paid the very last penny."

- Jesus unmasks the blind spot in the crowds: while they can read the signs of nature, they are failing or refusing to recognize in Jesus one who comes from God.
- Am I as knowledgeable about Jesus and his good news as I am about other aspects of life?

Saturday 25th October   Luke 13:6–9

Then Jesus told this parable: "A man had a fig tree planted in his vineyard; and he came looking for fruit on it and found none. So he said to the gardener, 'See here! For three years I have come looking for fruit on this fig tree, and still I find none. Cut it down! Why should it be wasting the soil?' He replied, 'Sir, let it alone for one more year, until I dig round it and put manure on it. If it bears fruit next year, well and good; but if not, you can cut it down.'"

- We are presented here with two contrasting attitudes. The owner sees only that the barren fig tree is wasting valuable space. But the gardener loves the tree and sees it has potential with proper care and nurturing; he wants to give it another chance.
- The gardener represents God's compassion, and also his activity in my life to make me blossom.

Something to think and pray about each day this week:

The everlasting gift

As November draws near, it is good to reflect on dying and how to face it. Christian faith offers the "sure and certain hope" that Jesus, my life-companion, will be waiting to welcome me home. God's love has sustained me over a lifetime. Now I am entering on what life was always meant to be about—to live through love in God's presence. I will be safe in this love, this welcoming smile. I am eternally "God's beloved." My dying, then, can be an active self-giving: a handing over of myself into loving hands. They are loving hands, for on their palms my very own name is inscribed.

Let me then in good time, while I still have my wits about me, say to God, "Into your hands I commend my spirit." Ask now that Jesus may make of you "an everlasting gift" to the Father.

My dying is not simply a "systems failure." The medical staff may say, "She didn't make it" but God in fact is making me his own. Death means that my preparation is complete. I am now ready for God. So Jesus comes for me as a bridegroom comes for his bride, and guides me through "the dark valley of death" to take me to himself, so that I may be where he is.

The Presence of God

As I sit here, the beating of my heart,
the ebb and flow of my breathing, the movements of my mind
are all signs of God's ongoing creation of me.
I pause for a moment, and become aware
of this presence of God within me.

Freedom

Lord, grant me the grace to be free from the excesses of
this life.
Let me not get caught up with the desire for wealth.
Keep my heart and mind free to love and serve you.

Consciousness

In God's loving presence I unwind the past day,
starting from now and looking back, moment by moment.
I gather in all the goodness and light, in gratitude.
I attend to the shadows and what they say to me,
seeking healing, courage, forgiveness.

The Word

God speaks to each one of us individually. I need to listen to
what he is saying to me. (Please turn to your scripture on the
following pages. Inspiration points are there should you need
them. When you are ready, return here to continue.)

Conversation

What is stirring in me as I pray?
Am I consoled, troubled, left cold?
I imagine Jesus himself standing or sitting at my side,
and share my feelings with him.

Conclusion

Glory be to the Father, and to the Son, and to the Holy Spirit,
As it was in the beginning, is now and ever shall be,
World without end. Amen

Sunday 26th October,
Thirtieth Sunday in Ordinary Time   Matthew 22:34–40

When the Pharisees heard that he had silenced the Sadducees, they gathered together, and one of them, a lawyer, asked him a question to test him. "Teacher, which commandment in the law is the greatest?" He said to him, "'You shall love the Lord your God with all your heart, and with all your soul, and with all your mind.' This is the greatest and first commandment. And a second is like it: 'You shall love your neighbor as yourself.' On these two commandments hang all the law and the prophets."

- Why should I love God totally? Because that is how God loves me. Nothing I do could make God love me more. God's love shines on me like the sun shines on earth.
- Real prayer includes resting gratefully in that love.

Monday 27th October   Luke 13:10–17

Now Jesus was teaching in one of the synagogues on the sabbath. And just then there appeared a woman with a spirit that had crippled her for eighteen years. She was bent over and was quite unable to stand up straight. When Jesus saw her, he called her over and said, "Woman, you are set free from your ailment." When he laid his hands on her, immediately she stood up straight and began praising God. But the leader of the synagogue, indignant because Jesus had cured on the sabbath, kept saying to the crowd, "There are six days on which work ought to be done; come on those days and be cured, and not on the sabbath day." But the Lord answered him and said, "You hypocrites! Does not each of you on the sabbath untie his ox or his donkey from the manger, and lead it away to give it water? And ought not this woman, a daughter of Abraham whom Satan bound for eighteen long years, be set free from this bondage on the sabbath day?" When he said this, all his opponents were put to shame; and the entire crowd was rejoicing at all the wonderful things that he was doing.

- The synagogue leader asserts that the Sabbath is not an appropriate time for God to manifest his compassion and mercy. Jesus, on the other hand, claims that God's actions cannot be dictated to or restricted by humans.
- God's mercy and healing know no limits of time or place, if we but turn to God in a spirit of trust.

Tuesday 28th October,
Ss Simon & Jude, Apostles   Luke 6:12–16

Now during those days he went out to the mountain to pray; and he spent the night in prayer to God. And when day came, he called his disciples and chose twelve of them, whom he also named apostles: Simon, whom he named Peter, and his brother Andrew, and James, and John, and Philip, and Bartholomew, and Matthew, and Thomas, and James son of Alphaeus, and Simon, who was called the Zealot, and Judas son of James, and Judas Iscariot, who became a traitor.

- The call of the disciples is rooted in the call of Jesus, and this call is to change their lives for ever. The disciples are not only to hear the word of God but act on it.
- Jesus will go on to teach the disciples a new way of life, for they cannot be open to the work of God unless they have their ears opened by His word.

Wednesday 29th October   Luke 13:22–30

Jesus went through one town and village after another, teaching as he made his way to Jerusalem. Someone asked him, "Lord, will only a few be saved?" He said to them, "Strive to enter through the narrow door; for many, I tell you, will try to enter and will not be able. When once the owner of the house has got up and shut the door, and you begin to stand outside and to knock at the door, saying, 'Lord, open to us', then in reply he will say to you, 'I do not know where you come from.' Then you will begin to say, 'We ate and drank with you, and you taught in our streets.' But he will say, 'I do not know where you come from; go away from me, all you evildoers!' There will be weeping and gnashing of teeth when you see Abraham and Isaac and Jacob and all the prophets in the kingdom of God, and you yourselves thrown out. Then people will come from east and west, from north and south, and will eat in the kingdom of God. Indeed, some are last who will be first, and some are first who will be last."

- Even though the door to God's kingdom may be narrow, due to the degree of commitment required, it is open and available to everyone.
- Those who "stand outside" are those who refuse to accept the reign of peace and justice, joy and love, which God so graciously and freely offers to everyone.

Thursday 30th October · Luke 13:31–34

At that very hour some Pharisees came and said to him, "Get away from here, for Herod wants to kill you." He said to them, "Go and tell that fox for me, 'Listen, I am casting out demons and performing cures today and tomorrow, and on the third day I finish my work. Yet today, tomorrow, and the next day I must be on my way, because it is impossible for a prophet to be killed outside of Jerusalem.' Jerusalem, Jerusalem, the city that kills the prophets and stones those who are sent to it! How often have I desired to gather your children together as a hen gathers her brood under her wings, and you were not willing!"

- Jesus wants to gather the people in Jerusalem into his love and protection. It is they who refuse, not God who changes his mind.
- It looks as if God is a failure when God's children turn away, like parents feel when their children in some way get lost in their way through the world. But God never gives up on us—God will return and be praised.

Friday 31st October · Luke 14:1–6

On one occasion when Jesus was going to the house of a leader of the Pharisees to eat a meal on the sabbath, they were watching him closely. Just then, in front of him, there was a man who had dropsy. And Jesus asked the lawyers and

Pharisees, "Is it lawful to cure people on the sabbath, or not?" But they were silent. So Jesus took him and healed him, and sent him away. Then he said to them, "If one of you has a child or an ox that has fallen into a well, will you not immediately pull it out on a sabbath day?" And they could not reply to this.

- Another row about the Sabbath! Jesus knows that religious attitudes can harden hearts and people may be ignored.
- The sick are forgotten while we go to pray! In prayer today I remember people close to me whose needs I may, wittingly or unwittingly, ignore.

Saturday 1st November, Feast of All Saints   Matthew 5:1–12

When Jesus saw the crowds, he went up the mountain; and after he sat down, his disciples came to him. Then he began to speak, and taught them, saying: "Blessed are the poor in spirit, for theirs is the kingdom of heaven. Blessed are those who mourn, for they will be comforted. Blessed are the meek, for they will inherit the earth. Blessed are those who hunger and thirst for righteousness, for they will be filled. Blessed are the merciful, for they will receive mercy. Blessed are the pure in heart, for they will see God. Blessed are the peacemakers, for they will be called children of God. Blessed are those who are persecuted for righteousness' sake, for theirs is the kingdom of heaven. Blessed are you when people revile you and persecute you and utter all kinds of evil against you falsely on my account. Rejoice and be glad, for your reward is great in heaven, for in the same way they persecuted the prophets who were before you."

- Imagine you are sitting on the hillside listening to Jesus. Which of the Beatitudes affects you most?
- Jesus, help us to listen to you with our hearts as well as our ears and help us to come alive to your word, to your teaching, to your desire to draw us ever closer to you.

Something to think and pray about each day this week:

Alive to the end

I notice more and more frequently the shadow of mortality which lies across my path. I go to the funerals of younger friends. My doctor treats a skin cancer with the humorous assurance that I'll die "with" it but not "of" it. I am also gathering companions in my body for the last stage of my journey. The skin cancer, the back ache, the high blood pressure—all these are going to stay with me to the end.

What is marvellous is that we last so long nowadays. Glasses, hearing and walking aids, dentures, hip replacements—we would rather not need them, but they make it possible for our real life, the life of heart and mind and soul, to blossom ever further. One over-riding desire I do cherish: as psychologist Winnicott put it, "May I be alive when I die!"

I think of a good friend who has narrowed his horizon to his pains and medication. He is wedded to trivial routines as though life depended on them. He is sadly almost dead, long before he dies. Other friends, happily, are "alive" when they die. They look back on their years with gratitude and some amusement. They are not overburdened about their mistakes or misfortunes, but entrust them to a good God who can make all things well again. These friends are outgoing to the end. I want to be like that. "May I be alive when I die!"

The Presence of God
God is with me, but more, God is within me.
Let me dwell for a moment on God's life-giving presence
in my body, in my mind, in my heart,
as I sit here, right now.

Freedom
I need to rise above the noise;
the noise that interrupts, that separates,
the noise that isolates.
I need to listen to God again.

Consciousness
I remind myself that I am in the presence of the Lord.
I will take refuge in His loving heart.
He is my strength in times of weakness.
He is my comforter in times of sorrow.

The Word
I read the Word of God slowly, a few times over, and I listen
to what God is saying to me. (Please turn to your scripture on
the following pages. Inspiration points are there should you
need them. When you are ready, return here to continue.)

Conversation
Do I notice myself reacting as I pray with the Word of God?
Do I feel challenged, comforted, angry?
Imagining Jesus sitting or standing by me,
I speak out my feelings, as one trusted friend to another.

Conclusion
Glory be to the Father, and to the Son, and to the Holy Spirit,
As it was in the beginning, is now and ever shall be,
World without end. Amen

Sunday 2nd November,
Feast of All Souls   Matthew 11:28–30

At that time Jesus said, "Come to me, all you that are weary and are carrying heavy burdens, and I will give you rest. Take my yoke upon you, and learn from me; for I am gentle and humble in heart, and you will find rest for your souls. For my yoke is easy, and my burden is light."

- Jesus offers us a lifeline, "Come to me," He says. Sounds simple, doesn't it? And yet we find it difficult to believe that reaching out to Him can make a difference.
- Lord, you invite us to take your hand and walk with you through this "valley of tears" how stubborn we can be sometimes. Help us to be open to your whispered invitation and respond with faith and generosity.

Monday 3rd November   Luke 14:12–14

Jesus said also to the one who had invited him, "When you give a luncheon or a dinner, do not invite your friends or your brothers or your relatives or rich neighbors, in case they may invite you in return, and you would be repaid. But when you give a banquet, invite the poor, the crippled, the lame, and the blind. And you will be blessed, because they cannot repay you, for you will be repaid at the resurrection of the righteous."

- Jesus warns us about having ulterior motives in relation to how we act towards one another.
- We must not seek reward for our actions towards others but always do what is best for them and treat them with the respect they deserve without expecting anything in return.

Tuesday 4th November   Luke 14:15–24

One of the dinner guests said to Jesus, "Blessed is anyone who will eat bread in the kingdom of God!" Then Jesus said to him, "Someone gave a great dinner and invited many. At the time for the dinner he sent his slave to say to those who had been invited, 'Come; for everything is ready now.' But they all alike began to make excuses. The first said to him, 'I have bought a piece of land, and I must go out and see it; please accept my apologies.' Another said, 'I have bought five yoke of oxen, and I am going to try them out; please accept my apologies.' Another said, 'I have just been married, and therefore I cannot come.' So the slave returned and reported this to his master. Then the owner of the house became angry and said to his slave, 'Go out at once into the streets and lanes of the town and bring in the poor, the crippled, the blind, and the lame.' And the slave said, 'Sir, what you ordered has been done, and there is still room.' Then the master said to the slave, 'Go out into the roads and lanes, and compel people to come in, so that my house may be filled. For I tell you, none of those who were invited will taste my dinner.'"

- Can you cast your mind back to when you last declined an invitation from Jesus? Do you recall when you were too busy to visit that old friend living alone? Or that neighbor who was ill in hospital? Did you say, "I am too busy right now, I will call later?"
- How easy it is to put off something that puts extra pressure on our busy day.

Wednesday 5th November   Luke 14:25–27

Now large crowds were travelling with him; and he turned and said to them, "Whoever comes to me and does not hate father and mother, wife and children, brothers and sisters, yes, and even life itself, cannot be my disciple. Whoever does not carry the cross and follow me cannot be my disciple."

- Here we are asked to turn from anything or anyone who could hamper our journey to our heavenly home. Before all else our minds and hearts belong to the Lord. We must do all in our power to seek Him first and all else will fall into place.
- Teach us to follow you faithfully O Lord. Prepare our way and help us put our feet on the path that leads to freedom.

Thursday 6th November   Luke 15:1–7

Now all the tax-collectors and sinners were coming near to listen to him. And the Pharisees and the scribes were grumbling and saying, "This fellow welcomes sinners and eats with them." So he told them this parable: "Which one of you, having a hundred sheep and losing one of them, does not leave the ninety-nine in the wilderness and go after the one that is lost until he finds it? When he has found it, he lays it on his shoulders and rejoices. And when he comes home, he calls together his friends and neighbours, saying to them, 'Rejoice with me, for I have found my sheep that was lost.' Just so, I tell you, there will be more joy in heaven over one sinner who repents than over ninety-nine righteous people who need no repentance.

•   Jesus, you welcome all into your warm embrace. When we are lost you come to find us. When we are in despair You come to lift us up. When we feel forsaken, You remind us of your great love for each one of us. Thank you for loving us just as we are.

Friday 7th November   Luke 16:1–8

Then Jesus said to the disciples, "There was a rich man who had a manager, and charges were brought to him that this man was squandering his property. So he summoned him and said to him, 'What is this that I hear about you? Give me an accounting of your management, because you cannot be my manager any longer.' Then the manager said to himself, 'What will I do, now that my master is taking the position away from me? I am not strong enough to dig, and I am ashamed to beg. I have decided what to do so that, when I am dismissed as manager, people may welcome me into their homes.' So, summoning his master's debtors one by one, he asked the first, 'How much do you owe my master?' He answered, 'A hundred jugs of olive oil.' He said to him, 'Take your bill, sit down quickly, and make it fifty.' Then he asked another, 'And how much do you owe?' He replied, 'A hundred containers of wheat.' He said to him, 'Take your bill and make it eighty.' And his master commended the dishonest manager because he had acted shrewdly; for the children of this age are more shrewd in dealing with their own generation than are the children of light."

- Jesus says that we can learn even from dishonest people who are smart! The manager adapts quickly to a crisis.
- When a crisis hits me, do I turn to God and work out what to do, or do I let the crisis ruin my life?

Saturday 8th November   Luke 16:9–12

Jesus said to the disciples, "And I tell you, make friends for yourselves by means of dishonest wealth so that when it is gone, they may welcome you into the eternal homes. Whoever is faithful in a very little is faithful also in much; and whoever is dishonest in a very little is dishonest also in much. If then you have not been faithful with the dishonest wealth, who will entrust to you the true riches? And if you have not been faithful with what belongs to another, who will give you what is your own?"

- Jesus tells us that we cannot serve two masters; we cannot sit on the fence. We must come down on the side of righteousness or be bereft of all that is good.
- If we have possessions, let us use them so as to gain eternal life.

Something to think and pray about each day this week:

Filled to the brim

What does it mean "to be alive when I die?" Do we even guess what Jesus means by "life to the full"? C. S. Lewis says that the gospel pages rustle with a secret—that nothing less than "our divinisation" is the final step for humankind. That means "being alive with nothing less than the limitless life which God enjoys." Can we risk setting our sights on that hope? It will bring us a new freedom: our self-imposed boundaries will fade. Pondering our own potential godliness will give us new respect for everyone else, and that will change our world!

A friend shyly confided that the teacher in the crèche had remarked to his wife: "You've a very exceptional child there!" We went on to talk about a letter written by a wise man to a younger one some 1800 years ago. My friend liked it so much that he shortened it into a letter to his three-year-old son. Neither of us understood it well, but that didn't matter: we knew we were in the presence of blissful mystery. It ran like this:

Dear Patrick

When you are freed from suffering and disease, you will be a companion of God and a co-heir with Christ, for you will have become divine. All that belongs to God, God has promised to give you. You will become like him. He will make you divine for his glory. Congratulations! Your loving Dad.

Presence of God

What is present to me is what has a hold on my becoming.
I reflect on the presence of God always there in love,
amidst the many things that have a hold on me.
I pause and pray that I may let God
affect my becoming in this precise moment.

Freedom

If God were trying to tell me something, would I know?
If God were reassuring me or challenging me, would I notice?
I ask for the grace to be free of my own preoccupations
and open to what God may be saying to me.

Consciousness

Knowing that God loves me unconditionally,
I look honestly over the last day, its events and my feelings.
Do I have something to be grateful for? Then I give thanks.
Is there something I am sorry for? Then I ask forgiveness.

The Word

I take my time to read the Word of God, slowly, a few times,
allowing myself to dwell on anything that strikes me. (Please
turn to your scripture on the following pages. Inspiration
points are there should you need them. When you are ready,
return here to continue.)

Conversation

Remembering that I am still in God's presence,
I imagine Jesus himself standing or sitting beside me,
and say whatever is on my mind, whatever is in my heart,
speaking as one friend to another.

Conclusion

Glory be to the Father, and to the Son, and to the Holy Spirit,
As it was in the beginning, is now and ever shall be,
World without end. Amen

Sunday 9th November,
Dedication of the Lateran Basilica   John 2:13–22

The Passover of the Jews was near, and Jesus went up to Jerusalem. In the temple he found people selling cattle, sheep, and doves, and the money changers seated at their tables. Making a whip of cords, he drove all of them out of the temple, both the sheep and the cattle. He also poured out the coins of the money changers and overturned their tables. He told those who were selling the doves, "Take these things out of here! Stop making my Father's house a marketplace!" His disciples remembered that it was written, "Zeal for your house will consume me." The Jews then said to him, "What sign can you show us for doing this?" Jesus answered them, "Destroy this temple, and in three days I will raise it up." The Jews then said, "This temple has been under construction for forty-six years, and will you raise it up in three days?" But he was speaking of the temple of his body. After he was raised from the dead, his disciples remembered that he had said this; and they believed the scripture and the word that Jesus had spoken.

- Jesus is angry as he sees the lack of respect the people have for His Father's house, the place of prayer, the place of Presence. The people are blind to who Jesus is, and deaf to his message.
- How patient you are with us Lord as we stumble and weave our way through life without the realisation of your silent Presence waiting for us to awaken to your unfailing love.

Monday 10th November   Luke 17:1–6

Jesus said to his disciples, "Occasions for stumbling are bound to come, but woe to anyone by whom they come! It would be better for you if a millstone were hung around your neck and you were thrown into the sea than for you to cause one of these little ones to stumble. Be on your guard! If another disciple sins, you must rebuke the offender, and if there is repentance, you must forgive. And if the same person sins against you seven times a day, and turns back to you seven times and says, 'I repent,' you must forgive." The apostles said to the Lord, "Increase our faith!" The Lord replied, "If you had faith the size of a mustard seed, you could say to this mulberry tree, 'Be uprooted and planted in the sea,' and it would obey you."

- Today, Jesus is warning us to be very careful as to how we influence each other. We must not tempt anyone to act in any way that is against what God may want.
- We are also called to repentance, if someone hurts us or angers us we are asked to forgive them, and we are also asked to seek forgiveness if we are in the wrong.

Tuesday 11th November   Luke 17:7–10

Jesus said to his disciples, "Who among you would say to your slave who has just come in from plowing or tending sheep in the field, 'Come here at once and take your place at the table'? Would you not rather say to him, 'Prepare supper for me, put on your apron and serve me while I eat and drink; later you may eat and drink'? Do you thank the slave for doing what was commanded? So you also, when you have done all that you were ordered to do, say, 'We are worthless slaves; we have done only what we ought to have done!'"

- How many of us, when we do a good deed, look for reward in one way or another? Today we are reminded that in following Jesus' teaching as we live our lives, we do so without any strings attached.
- You have so much to teach us still Lord; we can do nothing without your help. Inspire us Lord to live a life worthy of being called a follower of yours.

Wednesday 12th November   Luke 17:11–19

On the way to Jerusalem Jesus was going through the region between Samaria and Galilee. As he entered a village, ten lepers approached him. Keeping their distance, they called out, saying, "Jesus, Master, have mercy on us!" When he saw them, he said to them, "Go and show yourselves to the priests." And as they went, they were made clean. Then one of them, when he saw that he was healed, turned back, praising God with a loud voice. He prostrated himself at Jesus' feet and thanked him. And he was a Samaritan. Then Jesus asked, "Were not ten made clean? But the other nine, where are they? Was none of them found to return and give praise to God except this foreigner?" Then he said to him, "Get up and go on your way; your faith has made you well."

- When we are in great trouble and distress many of us in desperation turn to prayer. We plead for help, crying out as the lepers did from the depth of our being.
- And Jesus responds to our prayer in a way that is best for us. But we can forget, so often, to say "thank you."

Thursday 13th November   Luke 17:20–25

Once Jesus was asked by the Pharisees when the kingdom of God was coming, and he answered, "The kingdom of God is not coming with things that can be observed; nor will they say, 'Look, here it is!' or 'There it is!' For, in fact, the kingdom of God is among you." Then he said to the disciples, "The days are coming when you will long to see one of the days of the Son of Man, and you will not see it. They will say to you, 'Look there!' or 'Look here!' Do not go, do not set off in pursuit. For as the lightning flashes and lights up the sky from one side to the other, so will the Son of Man be in his day. But first he must endure much suffering and be rejected by this generation."

- Jesus' kingdom is not of this world. It is not an earthly kingdom but a kingdom of the heart where truth and justice, righteousness and peace reigns.
- To live in the kingdom we must hold on to the teaching of Jesus. "Seek ye first the kingdom of God and His righteousness" and all will be well.

Friday 14th November   Luke 17:26–37

Just as it was in the days of Noah, so too it will be in the days of the Son of Man. They were eating and drinking, and marrying and being given in marriage, until the day Noah entered the ark, and the flood came and destroyed all of them.

Likewise, just as it was in the days of Lot: they were eating and drinking, buying and selling, planting and building, but on the day that Lot left Sodom, it rained fire and sulfur from heaven and destroyed all of them—it will be like that on the day that the Son of Man is revealed. On that day, anyone on the housetop who has belongings in the house must not come down to take them away; and likewise anyone in the field must not turn back. Remember Lot's wife. Those who try to make their life secure will lose it, but those who lose their life will keep it. I tell you, on that night there will be two in one bed; one will be taken and the other left. There will be two women grinding meal together; one will be taken and the other left.

- We are not to be tied to anything or anyone to the detriment of forgetting who we are and where we are bound. This earthly life will pass away and so we are not to build our house on the shifting sands of earthly life, but on the rock of God's plan for us.
- Lord, just as you led the Israelites out of Egypt lead us too as we seek to do your will to "love you more dearly and follow you more nearly" all the days of our life.

Saturday 15th November   Luke 18:1–8

Then Jesus told them a parable about their need to pray always and not to lose heart. He said, "In a certain city there was a judge who neither feared God nor had respect for people. In that city there was a widow who kept coming to him and saying, 'Grant me justice against my opponent.' For a while he refused; but later he said to himself, 'Though I have no fear of God and no respect for anyone, yet because this widow keeps bothering me, I will grant her justice, so that she may not wear me out by continually coming.'" And the Lord said, "Listen to what the unjust judge says. And will not God grant justice to his chosen ones who cry to him day and night? Will he delay long in helping them? I tell you, he will quickly grant justice to them. And yet, when the Son of Man comes, will he find faith on earth?"

- We can feel that God has not heard our prayers when they are not answered immediately. We live in a world of instant gratification, instant coffee, instant contact, a touch of a button on our computer and we can be anywhere in the world!

- But Jesus in today's gospel is asking us to be patient, "pray always and do not lose heart." Our prayers will be answered, maybe not in the way we are expecting, but answered in the way that is beneficial to us.

Sacred Space

november 16–22

Something to think and pray about each day this week:

At life's edge

At my age, the question is never far from my conscious mind: "What awaits me when I have shuffled off this mortal coil?" When I pass beyond that uncharted moment which is the act of dying, will I—miracle of miracles—find myself waking up?

Some, who have gone to the edge of what we call "life," tell a consistent story. They sense themselves moving across a bridge towards a bright, beautiful place on the other side. They feel happy, buoyed up by a feeling of joy and anticipation. They feel free of their bodies, and that they are moving at incredible speed towards God, and being bathed in God's love as though it were an avalanche of warm light. In that brightness nothing else matters, neither sin nor misfortune nor worry nor suffering. Their hearts and souls are filled with the presence of God's glory.

Two of my friends have returned from the edge of death with a sense of disappointment, as though they were being dragged back from perfect happiness. Those who have been surprised in this way lose their fear of death. They know that there is limitless love and joy to look forward to, and that their future will be beautiful. As the psalmist prays: "Lord, I shall be filled, when I awake, with the sight of your glory!" (Psalm 73:24).

The Presence of God

At any time of the day or night we can call on Jesus.
He is always waiting, listening for our call.
What a wonderful blessing.
No phone needed, no emails, just a whisper.

Freedom

Lord, grant me the grace to be free from the excesses of
this life.
Let me not get caught up with the desire for wealth.
Keep my heart and mind free to love and serve you.

Consciousness

I exist in a web of relationships—links to nature, people, God.
I trace out these links, giving thanks for the life that flows
through them.
Some links are twisted or broken: I may feel regret, anger,
disappointment.
I pray for the gift of acceptance and forgiveness.

The Word

I take my time to read the Word of God, slowly, a few times,
allowing myself to dwell on anything that strikes me. (Please
turn to your scripture on the following pages. Inspiration
points are there should you need them. When you are ready,
return here to continue.)

Conversation

Remembering that I am still in God's presence,
I imagine Jesus himself standing or sitting beside me,
and say whatever is on my mind, whatever is in my heart,
speaking as one friend to another.

Conclusion

Glory be to the Father, and to the Son, and to the Holy Spirit,
As it was in the beginning, is now and ever shall be,
World without end. Amen

Sunday 16th November,
Thirty-third Sunday
in Ordinary Time

Matthew 25:14–15.19–21

Jesus told his disciples this parable, "For it is as if a man, going on a journey, summoned his slaves and entrusted his property to them; to one he gave five talents, to another two, to another one, to each according to his ability. Then he went away. After a long time the master of those slaves came and settled accounts with them. Then the one who had received the five talents came forward, bringing five more talents, saying, 'Master, you handed over to me five talents; see, I have made five more talents.' His master said to him, 'Well done, good and trustworthy slave; you have been trustworthy in a few things, I will put you in charge of many things; enter into the joy of your master.'"

- I take a few moments with Jesus to review my talents and be grateful for them. Then I ask him if I am using them in ways that respond to the needs of those around me.
- It is a wonderful thing that I should be able to bring joy to God. Jesus set out to please his Father (John 8:29), and my life takes on new colour when I do likewise.

Monday 17th November

Luke 18:35–43

As he approached Jericho, a blind man was sitting by the roadside begging. When he heard a crowd going by, he asked what was happening. They told him, "Jesus of Nazareth is passing by." Then he shouted, "Jesus, Son of David, have mercy on me!" Those who were in front sternly ordered him to be quiet; but he shouted even more loudly, "Son of David, have mercy on me!" Jesus stood still and ordered the man to be brought to him; and when he came near, he asked him, "What do you want me to do for you?" He said, "Lord, let me see again." Jesus said to him, "Receive your sight; your faith has saved you." Immediately he regained his sight and followed him, glorifying God; and all the people, when they saw it, praised God.

- Jesus asks an unusual question: "What do you want me to do for you?" Even though his need was obvious Jesus still wanted him to ask.
- Today, Jesus asks you "what do you want me to do for you." Talk to him today and tell him of your needs.

Tuesday 18th November   Luke 19:1–10

Jesus entered Jericho and was passing through it. A man was there named Zacchaeus; he was a chief tax-collector and was rich. He was trying to see who Jesus was, but on account of the crowd he could not, because he was short in stature. So he ran ahead and climbed a sycamore tree to see him, because he was going to pass that way. When Jesus came to the place, he looked up and said to him, "Zacchaeus, hurry and come down; for I must stay at your house today." So he hurried down and was happy to welcome him. All who saw it began to grumble and said, "He has gone to be the guest of one who is a sinner." Zacchaeus stood there and said to the Lord, "Look, half of my possessions, Lord, I will give to the poor; and if I have defrauded anyone of anything, I will pay back four times as much." Then Jesus said to him, "Today salvation has come to this house, because he too is a son of Abraham. For the Son of Man came to seek out and to save the lost."

- Lord, you met Zacchaeus where he was at, and changed him completely, bringing salvation to his house.
- "Repent" means turn around. Help me to turn my life around and repent of the many faults and failings of my life.

Wednesday 19th November   Luke 19:11–28

As they were listening to this, he went on to tell a parable, because he was near Jerusalem, and because they supposed that the kingdom of God was to appear immediately. So he said, "A nobleman went to a distant country to get royal power for himself and then return. He summoned ten of his slaves, and gave them ten pounds, and said to them, 'Do business with these until I come back.' But the citizens of his country hated him and sent a delegation after him, saying, 'We do not want this man to rule over us.' When he returned, having received royal power, he ordered these slaves, to whom he had given the money, to be summoned so that he might find out what they had gained by trading. The first came forward and said, 'Lord, your pound has made ten more pounds.' He said to him, 'Well done, good slave! Because you have been trustworthy in a very small thing, take charge of ten cities.' Then the second came, saying, 'Lord, your pound has made five pounds.' He said to him, 'And you, rule over five cities.' Then the other came, saying, 'Lord, here is your pound. I wrapped it up in a piece of cloth, for I was afraid of you, because you are a harsh man; you take what you did not deposit, and reap what you did not sow.' He said to him, 'I will judge you by your own words, you wicked slave! You knew, did you, that I was a harsh man, taking what I did not deposit and reaping what I did not sow? Why then did you not put my money into the bank? Then when I returned, I could have collected it with interest.' He said to the bystanders, 'Take the pound from him and give it to the one who has ten pounds.' (And they said to him, 'Lord, he has ten pounds!') 'I tell you, to all those who have, more will be given; but from those who have nothing, even what they have will be taken away. But as for these enemies of mine who did not want me to be king over them—bring them here and slaughter them in my presence.'"

- The nobleman gives what he has to the servants; it's as if his work is to be done now by others.
- The same for Jesus and ourselves now; we are the ones entrusted with the mission and the life of Jesus for today. What gifts and talents can we bring to the service of God here and now?

Thursday 20th November   **Luke 19:41–44**

As Jesus came near and saw the city, he wept over it, saying, "If you, even you, had only recognized on this day the things that make for peace! But now they are hidden from your eyes. Indeed, the days will come upon you, when your enemies will set up ramparts around you and surround you, and hem you in on every side. They will crush you to the ground, you and your children within you, and they will not leave within you one stone upon another; because you did not recognize the time of your visitation from God."

- Jesus weeps over Jerusalem as a mother weeps over her child. Jesus' heart was full. Shortly before this, he had experienced a triumphant entry in Jerusalem.
- Jesus, who was there to help you carry your burdens? Who was there in moments of sadness or loneliness? Yet you are so near to comfort us in the dark moments of our lives. Thank you for your great love for us.

Friday 21st November   Luke 19:45–48

Then Jesus entered the temple and began to drive out those who were selling things there; and he said, "It is written, 'My house shall be a house of prayer'; but you have made it a den of robbers." Every day he was teaching in the temple. The chief priests, the scribes, and the leaders of the people kept looking for a way to kill him; but they did not find anything they could do, for all the people were spellbound by what they heard.

- It is hard to think of Jesus losing his temper, yet when he entered the temple he was angry to see it set up just like a market place. Anger is not a bad thing as some of us might believe; it is what we do with the anger that can cause pain and upset.
- Lord help us to turn to you whenever we feel that we are out of control. In situations that upset and hurt us, Lord, may we call upon you to be with us and help us do the right thing.

Saturday 22nd November   Luke 20:27–40

Some Sadducees, those who say there is no resurrection, came to him and asked him a question, "Teacher, Moses wrote for us that if a man's brother dies, leaving a wife but no children, the man shall marry the widow and raise up children for his brother. Now there were seven brothers; the first married, and died childless; then the second and the third married her, and so in the same way all seven died childless. Finally the woman also died. In the resurrection, therefore, whose wife will the woman be? For the seven had married her." Jesus said to them, "Those who belong to this age marry and are given in marriage; but those who are considered worthy of a place in that age and in the resurrection from the dead neither marry nor are given in marriage. Indeed they cannot die any more, because they are like angels and are children of God, being children of the resurrection. And the fact that the dead are raised Moses himself showed, in the story about the bush, where he speaks of the Lord as the God of Abraham, the God of Isaac, and the God of Jacob. Now he is God not of the dead, but of the living; for to him all of them are alive." Then some of the scribes answered, "Teacher, you have spoken well." For they no longer dared to ask him another question.

- Earthly conditions do not persist in the heavenly world. Jesus tells us that we are children of the resurrection and are neither married nor given in marriage in the heavenly world.

- Jesus, sometimes it is hard to understand your word, help us to give more time to reading and discussing Scripture so that we may develop some insight into your teachings.

Sacred Space

Something to think and pray about each day this week:

Fully encountering God

"Lord, I shall be filled, when I awake, with the sight of your glory." What may it mean for us "to be filled with the sight of God's glory?"

We may believe that when God meets us directly in death we will be totally and happily overwhelmed. We will bow spontaneously in adoration. "Adoration" means "to put your hand to your mouth." We can find ourselves doing this when something extraordinary crosses our path. So it was with Peter when he saw the miraculous catch of fish. So it was with the terrified disciples when Jesus calmed the storm. They discover themselves to be in the presence of Someone totally wonderful. Silence, awe, reverence, tears, gratitude, bowing down—such are some of the images connoted by the word "adoration."

In death, then, we will lose our safe footing through the mind-blowing experience of being encountered by the One we name as "God." Bumping into God will indeed shake us to our inmost recesses, but not in a frightening way. The Greeks devised the term "ecstasy" to point to this experience. "Ecstasy" means "to stand outside oneself." We will be caught up, happily, into something infinitely greater than ourselves, yet we will be ourselves. We will recognize that mysteriously we are now "safe and at home"—enfolded in limitless love, filled with glory.

The Presence of God

I pause for a moment
and reflect on God's life-giving presence
in every part of my body, in everything around me,
in the whole of my life.

Freedom

God is not foreign to my freedom.
Instead the Spirit breathes life into my most intimate desires,
gently nudging me towards all that is good.
I ask for the grace to let myself be enfolded by the Spirit.

Consciousness

I exist in a web of relationships—links to nature, people, God.
I trace out these links, giving thanks for the life that flows
through them.
Some links are twisted or broken: I may feel regret, anger,
disappointment.
I pray for the gift of acceptance and forgiveness.

The Word

God speaks to each one of us individually. I need to listen to
what he is saying to me. (Please turn to your scripture on the
following pages. Inspiration points are there should you need
them. When you are ready, return here to continue.)

Conversation

How has God's Word moved me? Has it left me cold?
Has it consoled me or moved me to act in a new way?
I imagine Jesus standing or sitting beside me,
I turn and share my feelings with him.

Conclusion

Glory be to the Father, and to the Son, and to the Holy Spirit,
As it was in the beginning, is now and ever shall be,
World without end. Amen

Sunday 23rd November,
Feast of Christ the King   Matthew 25:31–46

"When the Son of Man comes in his glory, and all the angels with him, then he will sit on the throne of his glory. All the nations will be gathered before him, and he will separate people one from another as a shepherd separates the sheep from the goats, and he will put the sheep at his right hand and the goats at the left. Then the king will say to those at his right hand, 'Come, you that are blessed by my Father, inherit the kingdom prepared for you from the foundation of the world; for I was hungry and you gave me food, I was thirsty and you gave me something to drink, I was a stranger and you welcomed me, I was naked and you gave me clothing, I was sick and you took care of me, I was in prison and you visited me.' Then the righteous will answer him, 'Lord, when was it that we saw you hungry and gave you food, or thirsty and gave you something to drink? And when was it that we saw you a stranger and welcomed you, or naked and gave you clothing? And when was it that we saw you sick or in prison and visited you?' And the king will answer them, 'Truly I tell you, just as you did it to one of the least of these who are members of my family, you did it to me.' Then he will say to those at his left hand, 'You that are accursed, depart from me into the eternal fire prepared for the devil and his angels; for I was hungry and you gave me no food, I was thirsty and you gave me nothing to drink, I was a stranger and you did not welcome me, naked and you did not give me clothing, sick and in prison and you did not visit me.' Then they also will answer, 'Lord, when was it that we saw you hungry or thirsty or a stranger or naked or sick or in prison, and did not take care of you?' Then he will answer them, 'Truly I tell you, just as you did not do it to one of the least of these, you did not do it to me.' And these will go away into eternal punishment, but the righteous into eternal life."

- This dramatic story calls me to conversion to my sisters and brothers who are in need. With Jesus I look at my life. Do I put myself out for others and share what I can?

- Jesus identifies with the needy. Everyone I meet is a sister or brother for whom Christ died, as St Paul says. I may not be able to do much for others, but I can show them the respect and dignity which they need most of all.

Monday 24th November   Luke 21:1–4

Jesus looked up and saw rich people putting their gifts into the treasury; he also saw a poor widow put in two small copper coins. He said, "Truly I tell you, this poor widow has put in more than all of them; for all of them have contributed out of their abundance, but she out of her poverty has put in all she had to live on."

- In today's reading Jesus reproaches the rich people who give out of their abundance, whilst this poor widow gives everything that she has to live on.
- Lord, help us to be generous and share the many gifts you have bestowed on us. Teach us how to give and not count the cost.

Tuesday 25th November   Luke 21:5–11

When some were speaking about the temple, how it was adorned with beautiful stones and gifts dedicated to God, Jesus said, "As for these things that you see, the days will come when not one stone will be left upon another; all will be thrown down." They asked him, "Teacher, when will this be, and what will be the sign that this is about to take place?" And he said, "Beware that you are not led astray; for many will come in my name and say, 'I am he!' and, 'The time is near!' Do not go after them. When you hear of wars and insurrections, do not be terrified; for these things must take place first, but the end will not follow immediately." Then he said to them, "Nation will rise against nation, and kingdom against kingdom; there will be great earthquakes, and in various places famines and plagues; and there will be dreadful portents and great signs from heaven."

- Jesus warns about following "gurus," so to speak, those who claim to know when the end is coming. It is easy in times of distress or when people are terrified to look for someone to show the way.

- But Jesus is the Way and the Truth and the Life. In the *Sacred Space* community we try to keep our eyes on Jesus only.

Wednesday 26th November   Luke 21:12–19

Jesus said to his disciples, "But before all this occurs, they will arrest you and persecute you; they will hand you over to synagogues and prisons, and you will be brought before kings and governors because of my name. This will give you an opportunity to testify. So make up your minds not to prepare your defense in advance; for I will give you words and a wisdom that none of your opponents will be able to withstand or contradict. You will be betrayed even by parents and brothers, by relatives and friends; and they will put some of you to death. You will be hated by all because of my name. But not a hair of your head will perish. By your endurance you will gain your souls."

- Jesus warns his disciples that their witness to Him would bring about tension and separation from friends and relations, and some of them would even be put to death. But Jesus assures them that their endurance will win their souls.
- Jesus, help us to live in the here and now, to bear witness to you wherever we can. Not to fear but to trust in your loving care for us, and to stand up and be counted as followers of the Way.

Thursday 27th November   Luke 21:20–28

Jesus said to the disciples, "When you see Jerusalem surrounded by armies, then know that its desolation has come near. Then those in Judea must flee to the mountains, and those inside the city must leave it, and those out in the country must not enter it; for these are days of vengeance, as a fulfillment of all that is written. Woe to those who are pregnant and to those who are nursing infants in those days! For there will be great distress on the earth and wrath against this people; they will fall by the edge of the sword and be taken away as captives among all nations; and Jerusalem will be trampled on by the Gentiles, until the times of the Gentiles are fulfilled. There will be signs in the sun, the moon, and the stars, and on the earth distress among nations confused by the roaring of the sea and the waves. People will faint from fear and foreboding of what is coming upon the world, for the powers of the heavens will be shaken. Then they will see 'the Son of Man coming in a cloud' with power and great glory. Now when these things begin to take place, stand up and raise your heads, because your redemption is drawing near."

- Lord, how we need the gift of your peace in our world today. All around us wars are raging and your people are suffering.
- Help us join in the search for peace, help us remember those suffering now and show us Lord how to be of service to them.

Friday 28th November   Luke 21:29–31

Then Jesus told them a parable: "Look at the fig tree and all the trees; as soon as they sprout leaves you can see for yourselves and know that summer is already near. So also, when you see these things taking place, you know that the kingdom of God is near."

- Let me take time off to look at the good signs of the times. We have moved from world wars to relative peace. There is less hunger, disease and infant mortality, better communication and mutual help.
- The kingdom of God has a distance to go, but it is getting nearer.

Saturday 29th November   Luke 21:34–36

Jesus said to his disciples, "Be on guard so that your hearts are not weighed down with dissipation and drunkenness and the worries of this life, and that day catch you unexpectedly, like a trap. For it will come upon all who live on the face of the whole earth. Be alert at all times, praying that you may have the strength to escape all these things that will take place, and to stand before the Son of Man."

- The first Christians had a hard time of it, through persecution, poverty and political turmoil. I ask them to help me when things are hard. I ask Jesus to give me more faith, hope and love, so that I may not get lost in daily distractions.
- "To be alert at all times" means to keep my eyes on Jesus. The *Sacred Space* community tries to do that daily, and so becomes a blessing for a heedless world. Those who pray hold the world together, Pope Benedict XVI said.

Sacred Space Prayer

Dear Lord
The music of our lives is meant to be a symphony
of love.

Endlessly and lovingly you sustain us
and we learn to respond as best we can.

You gaze on us and you smile, and we smile back.

You speak your life-giving Word in our hearts
and refresh us constantly through our daily prayer.

Grant that we, the Sacred Space Community, may
become the 'Good News in the present tense' to a
needy world.